*Agentic AI
in Law & Finance*

AGENTIC AI

in Law & Finance

*Navigating a New Era of
Autonomous Systems*

MICHAEL J. BOMMARITO II

DANIEL M. KATZ

JILLIAN BOMMARITO

FIRST EDITION

2026

This book is part of the **AI for Law and Finance** project. The companion website offers working source code, interactive exercises, and practical tutorials that complement this book's conceptual foundation. If you are reading digitally and want a printed copy, the website also provides links to print-on-demand services at cost.

Online Resources

- Project website: `https://ai4lf.com`
- Source code: `https://github.com/mjbommar/ai-law-finance-book`
- License details: `https://creativecommons.org/licenses/by-sa/4.0/`

First Edition, 2026

ISBN 979-8-9943457-0-2 (paperback)

ISBN 979-8-9943457-1-9 (ebook)

Publisher's Cataloging-in-Publication Data
Names: Bommarito, Michael J., II; Katz, Daniel M.; Bommarito, Jillian, authors.
Title: Agentic AI in law and finance :
    navigating a new era of autonomous systems / Michael J Bommarito II, Daniel M Katz, Jillian Bommarito.
Description: First edition. | Michigan : 2026. | Includes bibliographical references and glossary.
Identifiers: ISBN 979-8-9943457-0-2 (paperback) | ISBN 979-8-9943457-1-9 (ebook)
Subjects: LCSH:
    Artificial intelligence—Law and legislation.
    Artificial intelligence—Finance.
    Intelligent agents (Computer software).
    Machine learning.

Classification: LCC K564.C6 .B66 2026 | DDC 343.09—dc23

Contents

Preface

Why This Book

Everyone is talking about agents. Vendors announce "agentic AI" capabilities, researchers develop "agent benchmarks," and practitioners deploy "AI agents" in production. Yet when you ask what makes something an agent, the answers vary wildly. This ambiguity is not just an academic problem. It creates confusion in vendor evaluations, architectural decisions, and regulatory discussions. In law and finance, where precision matters and mistakes carry consequences, we need clearer thinking.

This book offers that clarity. We synthesize seven decades of scholarship, spanning philosophy and psychology through economics and computer science, into a unified framework for understanding, designing, and governing AI agents. The framework is practical enough for immediate application yet grounded in foundations that will remain relevant as the technology evolves.

A Book Written with Agents

We should acknowledge from the outset: this book about AI agents was written with substantial assistance from AI agents.

Our previous textbook took three years to complete, even with professional support from Cambridge University Press. This book took under three months from conception to completion. The difference is not that we worked harder or faster. The difference is that we worked *with* agents.

Throughout the drafting, editing, and production process, we used Claude Code, Codex CLI, Google Gemini CLI, and OpenCode to assist with research synthesis, bibliographic work, figure generation, LaTeX formatting, and iterative revision. These tools helped us locate and integrate sources, maintain consistent terminology and cross-references, and identify gaps in our arguments.

We do not claim that agents wrote this book. The intellectual framework, the selection and interpretation of sources, the judgments about what matters and why: these remain human contributions. But the production process has been fundamentally transformed. We see this acceleration as direct evidence of the capabilities we analyze in the chapters that follow.

If you find value in this book, you are experiencing what well-governed agentic collaboration can produce. If you find errors, you are experiencing why the governance frameworks in Chapter 3 matter.

Who This Book Is For

We wrote this book for professionals who need to work with AI agents thoughtfully and responsibly:

- **Legal practitioners** evaluating AI tools for research, document review, and client service;
- **Financial professionals** deploying automated systems for analysis, trading, and compliance;
- **Technology leaders** making architectural and vendor selection decisions;
- **Risk and compliance officers** developing governance frameworks for AI adoption;
- **Regulators and policymakers** seeking to understand the systems they oversee; and
- **Researchers** building the next generation of agentic systems.

We assume technical literacy but not specialized expertise. Legal professionals need not be engineers; technologists need not be lawyers. The goal is mutual understanding across disciplines.

A Note on Scope

This book is extracted from a forthcoming textbook, *Artificial Intelligence for Law and Finance*, and revised to stand alone. The full work covers foundational topics such as machine learning, natural language processing, and knowledge representation, alongside domain applications in legal research, contract analysis, regulatory compliance, and financial modeling. These chapters form a self-contained arc: what agents are, how to build them, and how to govern them responsibly.

You will notice that we focus on concepts rather than code. This is intentional. Today's hot framework is tomorrow's legacy system; the model everyone uses this year may be obsolete by the next. We want this material to remain useful whether you are working with LangChain or AutoGen, Python or TypeScript, OpenAI or Anthropic or whatever comes next. The architectural questions, such as how agents perceive, decide, act, and terminate, do not change when you swap out the underlying technology.

For readers who want hands-on implementation, the companion website offers working source code, interactive exercises, and practical tutorials. That material will satisfy the appetite for technical depth while this book provides the conceptual foundation that makes implementation choices intelligible. The source code for the book itself is also available for those who wish to build on this work.

The field evolves rapidly. We have included citations through January 2026 and will update this material as developments warrant.

Online Resources

- Project website: `https://ai4lf.com`
- Source code: `https://github.com/mjbommar/ai-law-finance-book`

Acknowledgments

This work synthesizes insights from decades of scholarship across multiple disciplines. We are grateful to the researchers whose foundational work made this synthesis possible, from Anscombe and Bratman in philosophy, through Bandura in psychology, to Russell, Norvig, and the contemporary LLM agent community in computer science.

Michael J. Bommarito II, Daniel Martin Katz, and Jillian Bommarito
January 2026

How to Read This Book

Chapter Outline

The three chapters follow a logical sequence: *definition* → *design* → *governance*. Read straight through for cumulative understanding, or jump to whichever chapter addresses your immediate need.

Chapter 1: What is an Agent? provides definitional clarity. If you need to cut through marketing hype, evaluate vendor claims, or simply use the term "agent" with precision, start here. The chapter synthesizes perspectives from philosophy, computer science, law, and economics into a unified framework with practical evaluation tools. For a shorter read, Sections 1.1–1.2 deliver the core framework; the remaining sections add historical context and disciplinary depth.

Chapter 2: How to Design an Agent addresses architectural decisions. If you are building, evaluating, or procuring an agentic system, this chapter provides a structured way to think through key design choices, from how work enters the system to how it coordinates with humans and other agents. Each section stands alone, so you can read selectively based on which decisions you face.

Chapter 3: How to Govern an Agent covers risk, compliance, and accountability. If you are responsible for approving agent deployments, this chapter provides frameworks for calibrating oversight to your specific context: what controls to implement, how to structure accountability, and when to escalate. Note that this chapter provides conceptual tools, not legal advice; consult qualified experts for your jurisdiction and sector.

Visual Elements

Colored boxes signal different types of content. Color is functional, not decorative; it indicates how to read what follows.

> **Key Takeaways**
>
> Orange boxes highlight essential points to remember or operationalize.

> **Definitions**
>
> Blue boxes introduce formal definitions and terms of art used throughout.

> **Concrete Examples**
>
> Green boxes provide scenarios and case studies from law and finance.

> **Practice Checklists**
>
> Teal boxes offer checklists and workflows for direct application.

> **Warnings and Risks**
>
> Red boxes flag error modes, compliance risks, and failure cases.

> **Technical Details**
>
> Indigo boxes contain protocol details and implementation mechanics; optional on first reading.

Reference Materials

Glossary. Technical terms with specific meanings in the agent context appear in the glossary at the end. First uses are often marked with **key term formatting**.

References. The bibliography consolidates citations from all three chapters. Parenthetical citations (Russell and Norvig 2020b) indicate background sources; narrative citations like Russell and Norvig (2020b) appear when the author is part of the sentence.

Chapter 1

What is an Agent?

1.1 Introduction

Agent. *Agentic.*

Few terms generate more confusion despite widespread use. While these words appear everywhere, from marketing copy to academic papers, their meanings remain contested and often unclear. Yet despite this definitional chaos, the underlying concepts are deeply intuitive and accessible.

At heart, agents are simply **"doers" with a to-do**. As we unpack this accessible starting point, we will discover more explicit conditions for identification. But this four-word formulation captures something essential: agency requires both goals and the capacity to act toward them.

1.1.1 Motivation and Approach

The proliferation of "agentic AI" makes definitional clarity urgent. Existing work remains fragmented across purpose and discipline: computer scientists cite Russell and Norvig (Russell and Norvig 2020b), philosophers reference Bratman (Bratman 1987), legal scholars consult the Restatement of Agency (American Law Institute 2006), and commercial vendors seem untethered by anything other than sales.

Some of this fragmentation reflects genuinely different perspectives, such as whether we recognize agents by their *internal properties* (mental states, intentions) or *external manifestations* (observable behavior, delegated authority); a spectrum we explore in Section 1.4. While theoretical considerations like these can be useful, it is now most critical that we **establish a practical framework** to guide communication and coordination.

The stakes for getting this right are tangible. By late 2025, courts worldwide had identified over 400 cases involving AI-generated hallucinations in legal filings including fabricated citations, fictitious holdings, and nonexistent cases submitted to tribunals. The ABA's Formal Opinion 512 (July 2024) established that attorneys bear full responsibility for verifying AI-generated content. The opinion noted that leading legal AI systems "hallucinate between 17% and 33% of the time" (American Bar Association Standing Committee on Ethics and Professional Responsibility 2024).

These failures share a common pattern: attorneys treated single-shot text generators as if they were research tools, when those systems lacked the ability to search authoritative databases, iterate to verify citations, or escalate uncertainty. An agentic legal research system (one exhibiting all six operational properties we introduce below) would validate citations through tool access, confirm holdings through iteration, and flag unverifiable sources through escalation. The distinction between genuinely agentic systems and sophisticated chatbots is not academic; it is essential for professional practice, regulatory compliance, and client protection.

For legal and financial applications, these six operational properties are *necessary but not sufficient*. Professional deployment demands additional safeguards such as attribution to authoritative sources, auditable provenance, escalation protocols, and confidentiality controls that augment rather than replace the core framework. Section 1.6 addresses these professional deployment requirements in detail.

Building toward these operational requirements, we organize agency into three levels that correspond to the following questions:

Level 1: What makes *something*, biological or otherwise, an agent?

Level 2: What makes computational systems agentic?

Level 3: How do traditional and AI-powered agentic systems differ?

Answering these progressive questions establishes a nested hierarchy with three levels, as illustrated in Figure 1.1.

1.1.2   Level 1: Minimal Agency

We begin with the conceptual foundation. What is the absolute minimum required for something to qualify as an agent, whether human, organizational, or computational? Level 1 establishes this baseline, applicable across all domains and technologies.

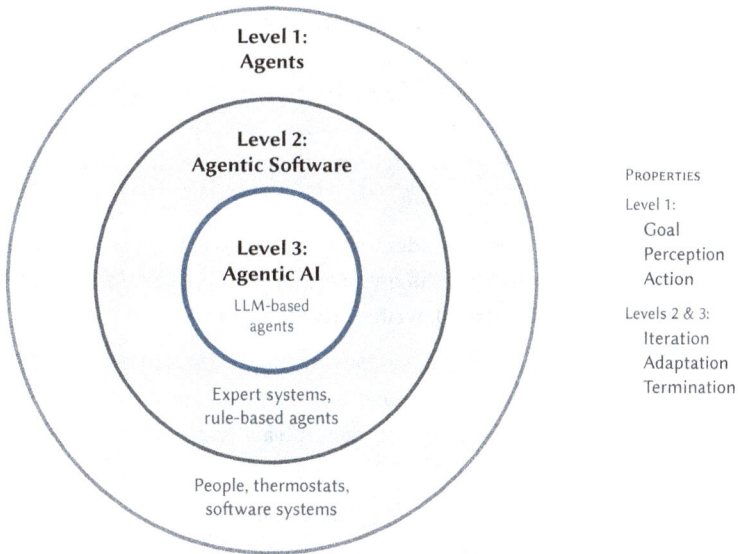

Figure 1.1: The three-level hierarchy of agency. Each level is a subset of the one above it: all agentic AI is agentic software, and all agentic software consists of agents.

Level 1: Agent (Mnemonic: GPA)

An **agent** is any entity that pursues goals through perception and action, with at least minimal discretion over which action to take in response to what it perceives.

Minimal properties:
- **Goal:** Clear objective or performance criterion
- **Perception:** Awareness of environment through sensing
- **Action:** Capability to affect environment

Property Definitions and Falsification Tests:

Goal (G): A clear objective, task specification, or performance criterion that directs behavior. Goals may be simple (maintain temperature) or complex (maximize portfolio returns), provided by external principals or internally generated, fixed or dynamic.

Falsification: If the entity responds identically regardless of desired outcomes, or transforms inputs mechanically without reference to success criteria, it lacks goals. Examples: compilers (execute predetermined transformations), pure lookup tables (no optimization target).

Perception (P): Awareness of environment through sensing capabilities such as sensors, APIs, database access, or document reading. The environment need not be physical; abstract spaces (contract negotiations, market data) qualify. *Legal example:* An agent perceives via EDGAR/Westlaw APIs to read regulatory filings and case law, observes which queries return hits, and uses those observations to refine subsequent searches.

Falsification: If the entity operates identically regardless of environmental state, or cannot observe consequences of its own actions, it lacks perception. Examples: open-loop controllers (no feedback), write-only systems.

Action (A): Capability to affect environment through actuators such as physical forces, variable modifications, tool invocations, API calls, or command execution. Requires minimal discretion: selecting among at least two possible actions contingent on perceptions.

Falsification: If the entity cannot modify its environment, or executes exactly one predetermined sequence regardless of circumstances, it lacks action. The discretion threshold is "≥ 2 policies contingent on perceptions." Examples that fail: pure sensors (read-only), fixed scripts with zero conditional logic, and single-shot transformers that apply one transformation regardless of input. Sophistication alone does not confer agency; a complex translation model still lacks discretion if it cannot choose among alternative actions based on what it observes.

This trinity forms the conceptual bedrock of agency, equally applicable to humans navigating social contexts, organizations pursuing strategic objectives, biological organisms seeking survival, or computational systems executing tasks. While these three characteristics suffice for theoretical classification, practical deployment demands more.

Level 1 Agents in Practice

- **Paralegal**: Goals (comprehensive research), perceives (documents), acts (retrieves and organizes)
- **Thermostat**: Goals (target temperature), perceives (sensor readings), acts (heating/cooling)
- **Organization**: Goals (market position), perceives (competitive dynamics), acts (coordinated initiatives)

Readers from philosophy, psychology, or law may find our inclusion of thermostats jarring. Traditional definitions often require more: philosophers may demand intentional mental states or consciousness; psychologists emphasize self-regulation and reflective awareness; legal scholars define agency through consensual fiduciary relationships; economists presuppose self-interested preference orderings.   A thermostat satisfies none of these richer criteria.

> ### A Note on Definitional Breadth
>
> We adopt a property-based definition deliberately.   Following Dennett (1987)'s intentional stance, we treat agency as a predictive attribution: when it is *useful* to describe an entity as pursuing goals, perceiving its environment, and taking action, we call it an agent.

Rather than adjudicating centuries of debate about what agency "really" requires, we identify the observable properties that consistently appear where entities exhibit goal-directed behavior and that matter for governance. This low definitional floor is not an oversight; it allows the gradient from minimal agents through agentic systems to AI agents to do meaningful analytical work.   The thermostat and the AI legal research assistant are both agents under our framework, but they differ profoundly in autonomy, adaptation, and governance requirements. Those differences, not the shared label, are what matter for professional practice.

These examples span vastly different domains, yet each satisfies the same three-property test. **Distinguishing agents from non-agents reveals equally critical boundaries.** Consider tools we encounter daily that, despite their utility, fail to meet our criteria. A calculator, whether handheld or embedded in a spreadsheet, transforms inputs into outputs but pursues no objectives of its own; it waits passively for instructions.   A legal research database like Westlaw or EDGAR contains vast information and responds to queries, yet it lacks independent goals or the capacity to act on its own initiative. Even a single ChatGPT response, however sophisticated, represents a one-shot generation rather than iterative goal pursuit: the system produces output and stops, without perceiving whether that output succeeded or adapting its approach.

This baseline framework illuminates the essence of agency, yet professional applications demand more. The gap between a simple thermostat cycling toward a temperature target and an AI system conducting legal research spans more than technological sophistication: it requires architectural elements that ensure reliability, adaptability, and accountability. Legal research tools, portfolio management systems, and document review platforms operate in environments where stakes are high and errors costly. These operational realities shape our expanded framework for deployable agentic systems.

1.1.3   Operational Definition: Agentic Systems

While Level 1 establishes what makes something an agent, computational systems in production require three additional properties beyond the minimal three. These six properties together define what we call **agentic systems**: the operational standard that bridges conceptual agency and real-world deployment. Both traditional software (Level 2) and AI-powered implementations (Level 3) can achieve this operational standard, though they differ fundamentally in how they realize each property.

Operational Definition: Agentic System (GPA+IAT)

An **agentic system** is a goal-directed agent that repeatedly perceives and acts in its environment, adapting from observations until clear termination conditions are met (explicit or implicit).

Additional properties beyond Level 1:
- **Iteration**: Repeat perceive-act cycles, not single-shot
- **Adaptation**: Adjust strategy based on feedback/results
- **Termination**: Clear stopping conditions (explicit or implicit)

Together with the three Level 1 properties, agentic systems exhibit six operational properties: Goal, Perception, Action, Iteration, Adaptation, and Termination. For mnemonic convenience, we write this as **GPA + IAT**, representing the foundational three (Goal, Perception, Action) plus the three that distinguish operational systems (Iteration, Adaptation, Termination).

These six properties emerged from decades of agent research as commonly recognized operational requirements for reliable computational deployment. While not formally proven as minimum necessary, they consistently appear across deployed systems in domains from robotics to enterprise software, reflecting lessons from fielding real-world implementations. Section 1.3 traces how each property became recognized as essential through both theoretical development and practical experience.

Additional Property Definitions and Falsification Tests:

Iteration (I): Multiple perceive-act cycles with state preservation across rounds. The entity repeatedly gathers information, takes action, observes results, and continues (not single-shot processing). Crucially, the system must perceive outcomes of prior actions and update subsequent actions accordingly within the same goal pursuit.

Falsification: If the entity processes input once and produces output without maintaining state across cycles, it lacks iteration. Merely repeating the same action without incorporating new observations does not qualify. *Batching vs. iteration:* Batched one-pass pipelines processing multiple items sequentially are not iteration unless the system observes outcomes from earlier items and modifies its approach for later items based on those observations. Examples that fail iteration test: single ChatGPT response (one-shot), batch processors applying identical logic to each item without inter-item learning.

Adaptation (A): Strategy modification based on accumulated observations and feedback within a session or task. The entity adjusts its approach when initial attempts fail, learns which actions succeed, updates its policy based on results.

This definition focuses on *session-level adaptation*: modifying behavior within a single task execution based on immediate feedback. This differs from *cross-session learning*, where a system improves through model retraining across multiple tasks (for example, fine-tuning an LLM on user feedback). For our purposes, within-session adaptation is the operational property that distinguishes agentic systems from static tools. In professional contexts (such as procurement or vendor evaluation), be explicit about which type of learning is in scope.

Falsification: If the entity applies identical logic regardless of outcomes, or cannot modify its approach when initial strategies fail, it lacks adaptation. Fixed rules that never change based on results do not qualify, even if they handle diverse inputs. Examples: basic thermostats (fixed on/off rules), static pattern matchers, rigid workflows that do not adjust to failures.

Termination (T): Clear stopping conditions ensuring bounded operation. Termination may be *implicit* (goal satisfaction, reaching target state, exhausting search space) or *explicit* (resource budgets, time limits, maximum iterations, escalation triggers, confidence thresholds).

Falsification: If the entity has no mechanism for recognizing when to stop, or could cycle indefinitely without bounds, it lacks proper termination. Entities requiring external intervention to halt do not meet this criterion. Examples: infinite loops with no exit condition, systems that run until manually killed.

With all six properties defined, we can identify agentic systems across professional domains:

Agentic Systems in Professional Practice

- **Legal research assistant**: Iterates through queries, adapts based on results, terminates when scope exhausted
- **Contract analysis**: Iterates clause-by-clause, adapts to document type, terminates with risk report
- **Portfolio rebalancing**: Iterates on positions, adapts to market conditions, terminates at target allocation
- **Fraud detection**: Iterates on transactions, adapts thresholds to new patterns, terminates with alerts

The relationship between levels clarifies important boundaries. Every agentic system qualifies as an agent (possessing the minimal three properties), but the reverse does not hold. Many agents lack the operational sophistication of agentic systems. A basic mechanical thermostat illustrates this gap: it has five properties (goal: maintain temperature; perception: sensor readings; action: heating/cooling; iteration: continuous monitoring; termination: implicit when target reached), but lacks adaptation, applying fixed on/off rules without modifying strategy based on outcomes. It responds to temperature changes reactively but does not learn patterns or adjust thresholds. In contrast, a *smart* thermostat qualifies as a full agentic system: it learns occupancy patterns, adjusts heating schedules based on observed behavior, and modifies its strategy when energy costs spike. This distinction between reactive control (basic thermostat) and adaptive learning (smart thermostat) clarifies why minimal agency (Level 1, three properties) differs from operational agentic systems (six properties). Similarly, a human paralegal demonstrates all six properties behaviorally but operates through cognitive processes rather than discrete computational cycles.

This operational framework now raises the implementation question: *How* do computational systems realize these six properties? The answer reveals an architectural distinction. Some systems use traditional programming (rules, algorithms, control logic) to manage planning and orchestration. Others employ AI/ML, particularly large language models, for these functions. We distinguish these as Level 2 (traditional) and Level 3 (AI-powered). Critically, this distinction is architectural, not evaluative: neither approach is inherently superior, and the boundary between them remains fluid and context-dependent.

1.1.4   Level 2: Traditional Agentic Software

Level 2 represents the first computational instantiation of agentic systems. These systems achieve all six operational properties through explicit programming: rules, conditional logic, algorithms, and control flow. What defines Level 2 is runtime behavior: decisions flow through programmed logic paths rather than learned models. Whether a system was coded decades ago or yesterday, if its decision-making follows deterministic rules at runtime, it operates at Level 2.

Level 2: Traditional Agentic Software

Traditional agentic software implements the six operational properties using rules, algorithms, or deterministic logic.

Additional properties beyond agentic systems:
- *No new properties (same 6 as agentic systems)*

Traditional agentic software uses rules, algorithms, or deterministic logic to implement all six properties. Planning and orchestration are explicitly coded through conditional logic, state machines, or control systems. Level 2 systems can be extremely sophisticated: a conflict checking system might employ graph analysis for relationship detection, fuzzy matching for entity resolution, and adaptive threshold tuning, all implemented through traditional programming techniques. The key architectural characteristic is that decision logic is specified by programmers at design time.

To illustrate, a conflicts checking system exemplifies Level 2: it has goals (identify potential conflicts), perception (scans firm databases for client/matter relationships), action (flags matches and escalates to ethics committee), iteration (continuous monitoring as new matters are opened), adaptation (adjusts matching thresholds based on false positive rates), and termination (stops when matter is cleared or rejected). The entity achieves these properties through explicitly programmed logic like rules for relationship detection, graph traversal algorithms for indirect conflicts, and configurable thresholds for fuzzy name matching.

Level 2 systems achieve all six operational properties through traditional software engineering. Their performance depends on design quality, domain expertise, and implementation rigor, not on whether they employ AI/ML techniques. A well-engineered Level 2 system can substantially outperform a poorly designed Level 3 system in reliability, predictability, and effectiveness for its intended domain. Beyond conflicts checking, traditional agentic software appears throughout professional practice:

> ## Traditional Agentic Software Examples
>
> - **Legal**: Conflicts checking with graph traversal and fuzzy matching; docketing systems with deadline tracking
> - **Financial**: Trading compliance monitoring; regulatory threshold alerts; invoice validation workflows

1.1.5   Level 3: AI-Powered Agentic Systems

Level 3 systems use AI/ML, particularly large language models, to manage planning, orchestration, and adaptation. The architectural distinction from Level 2 is straightforward: where Level 2 systems execute explicitly programmed decision logic, Level 3 systems employ neural networks (especially LLMs) or other learned models for these functions. In practice, modern Level 3 systems are typically hybrid: LLMs handle high-level planning and natural language interaction, while traditional code manages structured operations like database queries or API calls. This is what most practitioners mean by "AI agents."

> ## Level 3: AI-Powered Agentic Systems
>
> AI-powered agentic systems implement the six operational properties through strategic integration of artificial intelligence, typically neural network models such as large language models (LLMs) and vision-language models (VLMs), with traditional computational components.
>
> **Additional properties beyond agentic systems:**
> - *No new properties (same 6 as agentic systems)*

The architectural choice to use AI/ML for planning and orchestration has practical implications. LLMs enable natural language interfaces so users can specify goals conversationally rather than through structured formats. These neural network models handle pattern recognition tasks that would require extensive rule engineering. Yet this approach trades some predictability for flexibility: LLM outputs can vary across runs, and behavior may be harder to audit than explicit rule chains. The boundary between Level 2 and Level 3 can blur: is a system using gradient boosting for fraud detection Level 2 or Level 3? Today's practical dividing line focuses on whether LLMs manage high-level planning and orchestration.

Take an AI contract risk analyzer as a Level 3 exemplar. It possesses all six operational properties: goals (identifies and assesses contract risks), perception (reads contract text and clause context), action (flags problematic provisions, generates risk assessments), iteration (reviews document section by section), adaptation (adjusts risk scoring based on clause combinations and jurisdiction), and termination (stops when complete review is done or high-severity risk triggers immediate escalation). The LLM manages high-level planning such as deciding which clauses merit detailed analysis, how to interpret ambiguous language, and when to flag issues versus when to request human review, while traditional code handles document parsing, clause extraction, jurisdiction lookup, and risk score calculation. This hybrid architecture is typical of Level 3 systems: AI handles interpretation and strategic decisions, traditional programming handles structured data operations. Beyond contract analysis, AI-powered agentic systems are emerging across professional domains:

> **AI-Powered Agentic System Examples**
>
> - **Legal**: AI research assistants (iterative case law search); contract risk analyzers (clause interpretation); document review (adaptive classification)
> - **Financial**: AI trading assistants (market analysis); portfolio advisors (natural language recommendations); risk assessment (pattern recognition)

Table 1.1 maps the progression from minimal agency (three properties) through agentic systems (six properties) to implementation paradigms (traditional vs. AI).

Property	Level 1 Agent	Level 2 Traditional	Level 3 AI
Goal	●	●	●
Perception	●	●	●
Action	●	●	●
Iteration	○	●	●
Adaptation	○	●	●
Termination	○	●	●
AI-Powered	○	○	●

Table 1.1: Property requirements by level. Filled = required; empty = optional.

While Levels 2 and 3 share identical property requirements, they differ fundamentally in *how* each property is implemented. Table 1.2 contrasts implementation approaches.

1.1.6 Key Distinctions

Having traced the progression from minimal agency (three properties) through agentic systems (six properties) to implementation paradigms (traditional vs. AI),

Property	Level 2 (Traditional)	Level 3 (AI)
Goal	Config files, explicit targets	Natural language instructions
Perception	APIs, SQL, regex	LLM understanding, semantic search
Action	Function calls, API invocations	LLM tool orchestration
Iteration	Control loops, state machines	LLM reasoning loop
Adaptation	Rule tuning, A/B tests	Chain-of-thought, in-context learning
Termination	Max iterations, timeouts	LLM goal satisfaction check
Planning	Decision trees, rule engines	LLM-generated plans
Logs	Structured audit trails	Reasoning traces

Table 1.2: Implementation contrast: Level 2 vs Level 3.

we can now synthesize what this hierarchy reveals. Level 1 establishes conceptual qualification, the operational definition adds production-readiness requirements, and Levels 2 and 3 distinguish implementation paradigms. This structure clarifies three critical distinctions that cut through definitional confusion:

The critical distinction lies between *properties* and *implementation*. The major jump in capability occurs between Level 1 (three properties) and agentic systems (six properties). Levels 2 and 3, by contrast, have *identical property requirements*, differing only in how those properties are implemented: through explicit rules and logic (Level 2) or through AI/ML models (Level 3).

This hierarchy permits precise terminology. An **"agent"** (noun) refers to anything that exhibits Level 1's three minimal properties. The adjective **"agentic"** describes systems meeting all six operational properties at the system level; we may also use it descriptively at the feature or behavior level (e.g., "agentic behavior" or "agentic properties"), but reserve "agentic system" for six-of-six conformance. Finally, an **"AI agent"** is an agentic system specifically powered by AI/ML capabilities (Level 3).

These definitions allow clear exclusions. Compilers and databases lack goals entirely, failing even Level 1's minimal requirements. A single chatbot response, however sophisticated, lacks iteration and therefore does not qualify as an operational agentic system. Traditional ML classifiers (image recognizers, spam filters, sentiment analyzers) lack both iteration and autonomous goals, processing inputs without pursuing objectives across perceive-act cycles. Rule-based expert systems present a more nuanced case: they can be fully agentic (meeting all six operational properties) but are not AI-powered, placing them at Level 2 rather than Level 3.

This framework provides scaffolding for the historical and theoretical analysis that follows. Section 1.2 provides a practical decision rubric for immediate application. The remaining sections trace where these definitions came from and why they take this particular form, building toward the professional implications explored in Section 1.7.

1.2   How to Recognize an Agent

With the three-level hierarchy and complete definition established in Section 1.1, you now have the conceptual foundation.   But recognizing agents in practice requires operational tools.   We now turn to practical approaches: a detailed evaluation rubric, concrete examples comparing agents to non-agents, and guidance for navigating common misconceptions.

1.2.1   Six-Question Rubric

These six questions operationalize the definition from Section 1.1. The first three establish Level 1 agency; the remaining three add operational properties.

Q1. Does it have goals?

Look for objectives or performance criteria that direct behavior.

Falsification: If it responds identically regardless of desired outcomes, it lacks goals.

In legal contexts, goals include finding relevant precedents or identifying liability clauses.   In finance, goals include maximizing risk-adjusted returns or detecting fraudulent transactions.

Q2. Does it perceive?

Check for environmental awareness through sensors, APIs, or document access. Can it observe results of its own actions?

Falsification: If it operates identically regardless of environmental state, it lacks perception.

Legal systems perceive by reading case law databases or parsing contract text. Financial systems perceive by monitoring market data feeds or accessing regulatory filings.

Q3. Does it act?

Verify capability to affect its environment with at least minimal discretion (two+ actions contingent on perceptions).

Falsification: If it cannot modify its environment or executes exactly one fixed sequence, it lacks action.

Legal actions include generating briefs, flagging risks, or filing reports. Financial actions include executing trades, adjusting positions, or invoking analysis tools.

Q4. Does it iterate?

Confirm multiple perceive-act cycles with state preservation. Does it loop: act → observe → act again?

Falsification: If it processes input once without maintaining state across cycles, it lacks iteration.

Iteration appears in legal research that refines queries based on results, or portfolio management that adjusts positions based on market moves.

Q5. Does it adapt?

Check whether strategy modifies based on observations and feedback. Does it adjust when initial attempts fail?

Falsification: If it applies identical logic regardless of outcomes, it lacks adaptation.

Adaptation includes adjusting search terms when queries return no results, or modifying risk thresholds based on false positive rates.

Q6. Does it terminate?

Verify clear stopping conditions: implicit (goal satisfaction) or explicit (time limits, confidence thresholds, escalation triggers).

Falsification: If it could cycle indefinitely without bounds, it lacks termination.

Termination examples: stop when finding relevant precedent, escalate when confidence is low, halt after maximum API calls, or terminate when portfolio reaches target allocation.

If Q1–Q3 are yes, the entity qualifies as an agent. If all six are yes, it qualifies as an agentic system.

Note on Professional Governance: The six questions above establish whether something is an agent. As noted in Section 1.1, professional deployment in high-stakes domains requires additional governance safeguards beyond the six properties, such as attribution, explanation, escalation, and confidentiality. Section 1.6 details these requirements; Chapter 3 covers implementation.

1.2.2   Common Misconceptions

Understanding what agents are requires equally understanding what they are *not*. Five common misconceptions lead to over-attribution of agency.

Misconception: Single-shot responses are agentic systems. A single response from a language model is not an agentic system, even if sophisticated. Without iteration and adaptation, it is a one-time transformation. A basic API call that sends a prompt and receives a completion demonstrates this limitation, lacking iteration, adaptation to results, and a perception-action loop. The same system could be agentic if it iteratively refined queries based on results, but a single exchange lacks the required properties.

Recent developments blur some boundaries. Reasoning models with extended "thinking" can resemble deliberation; hosted API providers may embed agentic capabilities (web search, code execution) behind a single call, making one response involve hidden iteration. Yet absent such scaffolding, no single inference run integrates perception and action through iteration. Reasoning over internal states, no matter how rich a world model the system has learned, is not the same as perceiving external environments, taking real actions, and adapting based on observed outcomes.

Misconception: Automation alone creates agentic systems. Automation does not imply agency. A data extraction script that automatically runs nightly has goals (extract data) and acts (writes to database), but lacks perception, adaptation, and iteration. It executes a fixed sequence on a schedule. It is a scheduled task, not an agentic system. The automation trigger does not create the perception-action loop or adaptive behavior that define agentic systems.

Misconception: Tool use alone creates agency. Calling external tools does not automatically make an entity agentic. The critical question is whether the entity iterates on tool results, adapting its strategy based on what it observes. A script that queries an API once is not an agent; it lacks iteration and adaptation. A research system that queries the API, evaluates relevance, and decides what to search next based on results may qualify, depending on whether it completes the perception-action-adaptation cycle.

Misconception: Complexity creates agency. Complex entities are not necessarily agents. A document processing pipeline performs sophisticated transformations such as optical character recognition, entity extraction, and format conversion, but follows a fixed sequence without goals, perception of results, or adaptation. Complexity measures sophistication, not agency. Conversely, simple entities can be agents. A basic thermostat has goals (maintain temperature), perceives (reads sensor), acts (turns heat on/off), iterates (continuous monitoring), and terminates (implicit when target reached), though it lacks adaptation through its fixed on/off rules. Simplicity and agency are orthogonal dimensions.

Misconception: AI-powered systems are inherently agentic. Using AI or machine learning does not make something an agent. A neural network that classifies documents in a single forward pass (input to output) is not an agent, regardless of model sophistication. It lacks iteration, adaptation, and the perception-action loop. An AI entity that iteratively reviews content, flags issues, refines assessments based on observed patterns, and adapts its classification strategy across multiple cycles can be an agentic system. The AI component enables flexible reasoning, but agency requires the architectural properties, not merely the presence of neural networks.

1.2.3 Examples: Agents vs Non-Agents

Table 1.3 orders entities along the spectrum of agency, from non-agents through AI-powered agents. Each tier illustrates increasing qualification based on the six core properties. Detailed explanations follow.

Not Agents. These entities lack the minimal properties (goals, perception, action). The **form validation script** checks inputs against rules in a single pass: it has no independent goals beyond validation, no perception of results, and no adaptation.

Agents with Incomplete Agentic System Properties. These entities qualify as agents (they exceed the three-property minimum for Level 1 agency) but lack one or two of the six operational properties required for full agentic systems. **Rule-based pattern detection** has a goal (flag patterns), perceives incoming data, acts (blocks or alerts), and iterates continuously with each input. Still, it typically does not adapt its detection strategy within a session, applying fixed rules instead. **Content suggestion systems** similarly have a goal (suggest relevant content), perceive context, act (display suggestions), and iterate with each interaction. Yet they use

System	Agent?	Properties
Not Agents		
Form validation	No	One-pass; no goals/adaptation
Partial (Missing 1–2 Properties)		
Single research query	Partial	G+P+A only; no iteration
Pattern detection	Partial	Iterates but no adaptation
Content suggestions	Partial	Fixed learning approach
Full: Traditional		
Smart thermostat	Yes	All six; learns patterns
Portfolio rebalancer	Yes	Monitors, adapts, terminates
Full: AI-Powered		
Document review	Yes	Iterative, adaptive learning
AI research assistant	Yes	Tool loop with refinement

Table 1.3: Spectrum of agency by qualification level.

a fixed learning strategy rather than adapting their suggestions based on user acceptance patterns within a session.

Full Agents: Traditional. Thermostats illustrate the boundary case. Basic mechanical thermostats have five clear properties: goal (maintain temperature), perception (sensor readings), action (heat on/off), iteration (continuous monitoring), and implicit termination (stops heating at target temperature). Nevertheless, they lack true adaptation, applying fixed rules without adjusting strategy based on results. **Smart thermostats** qualify as full agentic systems: they learn occupancy patterns, adjust heating schedules based on observed behavior, and implement explicit termination logic like time windows, energy budgets, or away modes. The contrast illustrates how reactive control (basic thermostats) differs from adaptive learning (smart thermostats). **Portfolio rebalancing systems** demonstrate explicit termination through multiple stopping conditions: goal achievement (balanced portfolio), temporal constraints (market close), or resource limits (maximum trades per session). They monitor market data and portfolio drift, generate trade orders, adapt to volatility within predefined parameters, and stop when any termination condition is met.

Full Agents: AI-Powered. Document review systems use machine learning to iteratively classify documents based on relevance criteria. Unlike rule-based entities, they improve their categorization as they process more examples, adapting their classification strategy based on observed patterns. **AI research assistants**

demonstrate the most sophisticated agency: they maintain goals (answer questions), observe search results from multiple sources, query iteratively, refine search strategies when initial approaches fail, and escalate to human oversight when encountering contradictory information or reaching confidence limits. This represents the convergence of all six properties enhanced by AI's flexible reasoning capabilities.

1.2.4   When to Call Something an Agent

Our taxonomy (Section 1.1) distinguishes "agent" (three minimal properties) from "agentic system" (six operational properties). Table 1.4 provides guidance.

Count	Term	Notes
3	agent	G+P+A baseline
6	agentic system	Production-ready
6	agentic AI	AI-powered variant
4–5	"agent with..."	Specify missing properties
1–2	(avoid "agent")	Use "tool," "classifier"

Table 1.4: Terminology by property count.

Precision requirements vary by context. Regulatory filings and academic papers demand explicit enumeration of properties and clear distinction between agent and agentic system. Informal discussions permit looser usage like "agent" for entities meeting the three-property baseline, with specific properties noted when relevant. Marketing claims should specify which properties are present rather than using "agentic AI" without substantiation.

When in doubt, use the six-question rubric (subsection 1.2.1). It provides clear, answerable criteria that cut through ambiguity.

> **Key Takeaways**
>
> **At this point you can:**
>
> - Define agents and agentic systems using the six-property framework
> - Recognize agents using the six-question rubric
> - Distinguish agents from sophisticated non-agents
> - Evaluate marketing claims about "agentic AI"

With these practical tools in hand, the remaining sections provide context rather than prerequisites. Readers focused on immediate application can proceed directly to Chapter 2 or Chapter 3. Those seeking deeper grounding will find value in what follows: Section 1.3 traces how these concepts evolved, Section 1.4 examines how different fields approach agency, Section 1.5 introduces analytical dimensions for comparing systems, and Section 1.6 synthesizes requirements for professional deployment.

1.3 Historical Foundations

Our historical journey traces the evolution of agent definitions across seven decades. The concept of **agency** has evolved dramatically since the mid-20th century, shaped by philosophical inquiry, economic theory, legal doctrine, and technological capability. Tracing agent definitions chronologically reveals how each level of the hierarchy from Section 1.1 emerged historically: philosophical and legal foundations addressed general agency (Level 1), the computer science revolution instantiated these concepts in software (Level 2), and the LLM era added flexible reasoning powered by AI (Level 3). Figure 1.2 provides a visual overview of key milestones.

> **On Etymology**
>
> The semantic complexity surrounding "agent" traces back to the word's origins. The Latin root *agō*, from which *agent* derives, had multiple meanings in classical Latin. With numerous distinct senses in Lewis & Short's classical dictionary, ranging from "driving cattle" to "pleading a case," contemporary definitional debates echo longstanding ambiguity (Lewis and Short 1879).

1.3.1 Origin and Evolution of Agency Law

Agency law, which governs relationships where one party acts on behalf of another, has roots tracing back to ancient civilizations. In Roman law, the concept emerged through institutions like the "mandatum," a gratuitous contract allowing one person to manage affairs for another without compensation, and the "procurator," who handled legal matters on behalf of a principal.

This framework influenced early European legal systems, particularly during the Middle Ages, when mercantile practices in Italy and England began formalizing agency in commercial transactions. Further evolution took place during the Industrial Revolution in the 18th and 19th centuries, as expanding commerce necessitated clearer rules for delegation and liability.

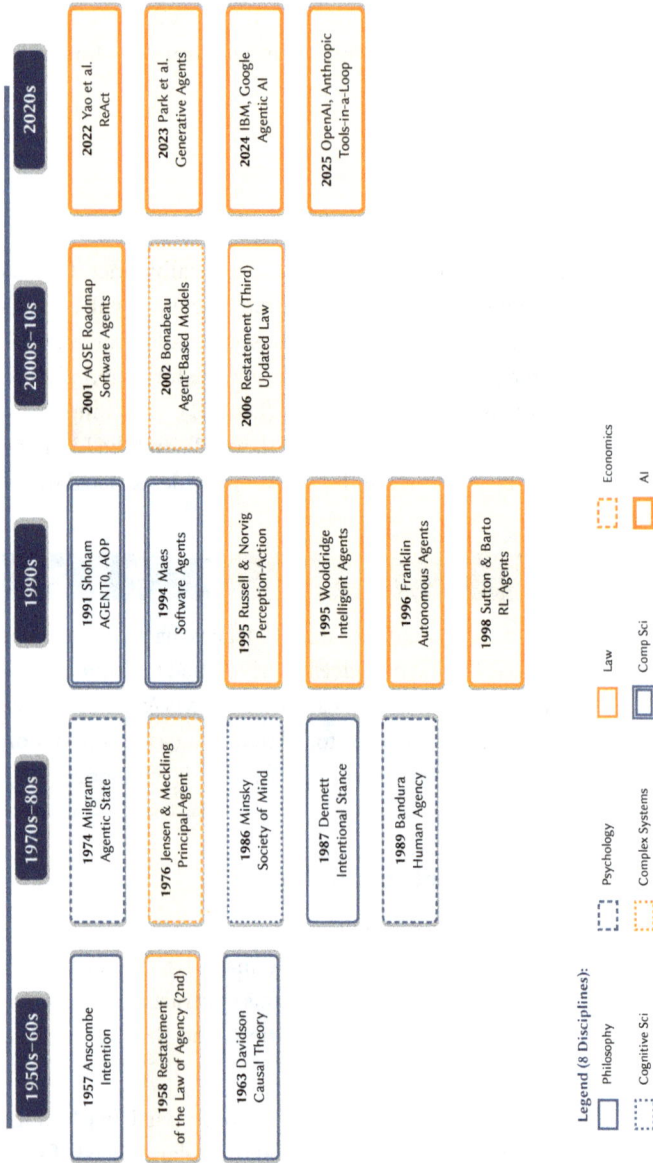

Evolution of Agent Definitions (1957–2025)

1950s–60s	1970s–80s	1990s	2000s–10s	2020s
1957 Anscombe Intention	1974 Milgram Agentic State	1991 Shoham AGENT0, AOP	2001 AOSE Roadmap Software Agents	2022 Yao et al. ReAct
1958 Restatement of the Law of Agency (2nd)	1976 Jensen & Meckling Principal-Agent	1994 Maes Software Agents	2002 Bonabeau Agent-Based Models	2023 Park et al. Generative Agents
1963 Davidson Causal Theory	1986 Minsky Society of Mind	1995 Russell & Norvig Perception-Action	2006 Restatement (Third) Updated Law	2024 IBM, Google Agentic AI
	1987 Dennett Intentional Stance	1995 Wooldridge Intelligent Agents		2025 OpenAI, Anthropic Tools-in-a-Loop
	1989 Bandura Human Agency	1996 Franklin Autonomous Agents		
		1998 Sutton & Barto RL Agents		

Legend (8 Disciplines):

Philosophy | Psychology | Law | Economics
Cognitive Sci | Complex Systems | Comp Sci | AI

Figure 1.2: Timeline of key milestones in agent definitions across eight disciplines (1957–2025), tracing the evolution from philosophical foundations through computational revolution to modern LLM-based convergence. Blue tones denote theoretical disciplines; orange denotes applied domains. Border patterns distinguish individual fields.

More recently, various editions of the Restatement of Agency have been published by the American Law Institute. These foundational treatises have codified and clarified the common law principles governing the creation, scope, and termination of agency relationships between principals and agents.

1.3.2 Modern Philosophical and Legal Foundations (1957 to 1969)

The postwar period witnessed foundational philosophical work on action theory alongside the maturation of legal doctrine concerning agency relationships. These developments occurred independently yet addressed complementary questions: philosophy examined how intention relates to action and how we attribute actions to agents, while law formalized the conditions under which one party acts on behalf of another.

1957: Intention

G.E.M. Anscombe's *Intention* established that actions are **intentional** "under a description" and known through practical knowledge (Anscombe 1957). This introduced the idea that intention plays a basic explanatory role: we understand actions by understanding the reasons under which agents perform them.

1958: Legal Agency

The *Restatement (Second) of Agency* defined **agency relationship**: a principal manifests assent that an agent shall act on the principal's behalf and subject to control (American Law Institute 1958). This emphasizes delegation, fiduciary relation, and control, concepts relevant when discussing AI systems acting on behalf of humans.

1963: Causal Theory. Donald Davidson's "Actions, Reasons, and Causes" defended the **causal theory of action**, arguing that intentional actions are explained by an agent's primary reason (a belief-desire pair) that causally produces the action (Davidson 1963). This framework connected mental states to observable behavior.

These works laid complementary foundations for agency. Philosophy offered frameworks for intention and the causal structure of action, while law formalized delegation and control in principal-agent relationships. Together, they set up core tensions that would animate later debates: the relationship between mental states and observable behavior, the balance between autonomy and control in delegated relationships, and the explanatory role of reasons versus causes. When researchers began implementing computational agents in subsequent decades, they inherited both the conceptual resources and these unresolved tensions; questions that remain live today when we ask whether AI systems truly have intentions or merely simulate goal-directed behavior.

1.3.3   Economic and Social Theory (1970 to 1989)

The 1970s and 1980s witnessed agency concepts migrating from philosophy and law into the social sciences. Economics, sociology, and psychology each adapted the core ideas to their disciplinary concerns, generating new frameworks for understanding human behavior in organizations, social structures, and economic relationships. This period produced a remarkably diverse set of perspectives on agency, from Milgram's minimalist "agentic state" where individuals function as mere instruments, to Bandura's rich conception of human agency with intentionality, forethought, and self-regulation.

1974: The Agentic State. Stanley Milgram's *Obedience to Authority* introduced the "**agentic state**," where individuals see themselves as instruments carrying out another's wishes (Milgram 1974). This anchors one end of the autonomy spectrum: agents as pure delegates without independent judgment.

1976: Principal-Agent Economics

Building upon earlier work by Ronald Coase (Coase 1937), Jensen and Meckling's "Theory of the Firm" formalized the **principal-agent relationship**, defining it as a contract where principals engage agents with delegated decision-making authority (Jensen and Meckling 1976). This established vocabulary of agency costs, information asymmetry, and incentive alignment.

1984: Structuration Theory. Anthony Giddens framed agency as the capacity to make a difference and intervene in the world (Giddens 1984).

1986: Society of Mind. Marvin Minsky's *Society of Mind* popularized the idea of mind as a society of simple "agents" whose interactions generate intelligence, introducing the **multi-agent system** metaphor (Minsky 1986).

1987: Planning Theory (BDI)

Michael Bratman's *Intention, Plans, and Practical Reason* developed a planning theory emphasizing partial plans structuring practical reasoning (Bratman 1987). This introduced the Belief-Desire-Intention (BDI) framework that became foundational for intelligent agent architectures.

1987: The Intentional Stance. Daniel Dennett's *The Intentional Stance* argued we can treat entities as agents when attributing beliefs and desires yields reliable predictions, providing a pragmatic criterion for agency (Dennett 1987).

1989: Human Agency. Albert Bandura synthesized psychological research, defining human agency through intentionality, forethought, self-regulation, and self-reflectiveness: properties increasingly sought in artificial systems (Bandura 1989).

These seven works collectively established a spectrum of autonomy that would prove essential for understanding computational agents. At one extreme, Milgram's agentic state described humans functioning as mere instruments executing another's directives (agents as pure delegates without independent judgment). At the other extreme, Bandura enumerated the rich capacities of human agency: forming intentions, planning ahead, monitoring and regulating behavior, and reflecting on one's own efficacy. Between these poles, each discipline tackled different facets of the agency problem. Economics formalized principal-agent relationships as contracts with delegated decision-making but misaligned incentives, focusing on control mechanisms and information asymmetries. Sociology examined how agents act independently within structural constraints. Cognitive science explored how minds might emerge from societies of simpler agents. Philosophy developed practical frameworks for planning, prediction, and attributing mental states.

This diversity reflected genuine differences in disciplinary focus, but the frameworks proved complementary rather than contradictory. When researchers began implementing computational agents in the 1990s, they inherited this rich conceptual toolkit and translated it into software architectures. Bratman's BDI framework became the dominant architecture for intelligent agents. Dennett's intentional stance provided a pragmatic criterion for when to treat systems as agents, namely when doing so yields reliable predictions. Bandura's enumeration of human agency properties became a checklist for evaluating artificial systems. The spectrum from minimal delegation to full autonomy helped designers understand where their systems fell and what capabilities they still needed to develop.

1.3.4 The Computer Science Revolution (1990 to 1999)

The 1990s transformed agency from philosophical concept to computational reality. Previous decades had provided rich conceptual frameworks such as intention, planning, autonomy, and perception-action cycles, but these primarily described human or abstract theoretical entities. The convergence of distributed systems research, AI advances, and the explosive growth of the internet created conditions for a decisive shift: researchers began implementing agents directly in software, creating systems designed from the ground up as autonomous entities rather than traditional programs.

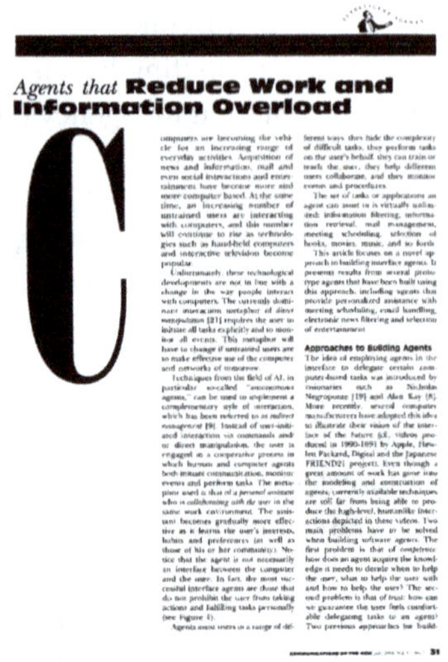

Agents that **Reduce Work and Information Overload**

Computers are becoming the vehicle for an increasing range of everyday activities. Acquisition of news and information, mail and even social interactions and entertainment have become more and more computer based. At the same time, an increasing number of untrained users are interacting with computers, and this number will continue to rise as technologies such as hand-held computers and interactive television become popular.

Unfortunately, these technological developments are not in line with a change in the way people interact with computers. The currently dominant interaction metaphor of *direct manipulation* [21] requires the user to initiate all tasks explicitly and to monitor all events. This metaphor will have to change if untrained users are to make effective use of the computers and networks of tomorrow.

Techniques from the field of AI, in particular so-called "autonomous agents," can be used to implement a complementary style of interaction, which has been referred to as *indirect management* [9]. Instead of user-initiated interaction via commands and/or direct manipulation, the user is engaged in a cooperative process in which human and computer agents both initiate communication, monitor events and perform tasks. The metaphor used is that of a *personal assistant* who is *collaborating with the user* in the same work environment. The assistant becomes gradually more effective as it learns the user's interests, habits and preferences (as well as those of his or her community). Notice that the agent is not necessarily an interface between the computer and the user. In fact, the most successful interface agents are those that do not prohibit the user from taking actions and fulfilling tasks personally (see Figure 1).

Agents assist users in a range of different ways: they hide the complexity of difficult tasks, they perform tasks on the user's behalf, they can train or teach the user, they help different users collaborate, and they monitor events and procedures.

The set of tasks or applications an agent can assist in is virtually unlimited: information filtering, information retrieval, mail management, meeting scheduling, selection of books, movies, music, and so forth.

This article focuses on a novel approach to building interface agents. It presents results from several prototype agents that have been built using this approach, including agents that provide personalized assistance with meeting scheduling, email handling, electronic news filtering and selection of entertainment.

Approaches to Building Agents

The idea of employing agents in the interface to delegate certain computer-based tasks was introduced by visionaries such as Nicholas Negroponte [19] and Alan Kay [8]. More recently, several computer manufacturers have adopted this idea to illustrate their vision of the interface of the future (cf. videos produced in 1990-1991 by Apple, Hewlett Packard, Digital and the Japanese FRIEND21 project). Even though a great amount of work has gone into the modeling and construction of agents, currently available techniques are still far from being able to produce the high-level, humanlike interactions depicted in these videos. Two main problems have to be solved when building software agents. The first problem is that of *competence*: how does an agent acquire the knowledge it needs to decide when to help the user, what to help the user with and how to help the user? The second problem is that of *trust*: how can we guarantee the user feels comfortable delegating tasks to an agent? Two previous approaches for build-

31

Figure 1.3: **Maes (1994): A prescient vision.** The opening of Maes's seminal CACM article outlined agents that learn user preferences, provide personalized assistance, and shift interaction from "direct manipulation" to collaborative delegation; patterns that resurface three decades later in modern LLM-based agentic systems.

This transition posed fundamental translation challenges. How should beliefs and intentions be represented computationally? What distinguishes an autonomous agent from a reactive program? When do interactions among simple agents produce emergent intelligence? The decade's answers emerged through diverse implementations, each formalizing different aspects of the prior decades' conceptual toolkit. By decade's end, agent-oriented computing had established itself as a distinct paradigm with its own methods, architectures, and standards.

1991 to 1993: Agent-Oriented Programming. Yoav Shoham's AGENT0 and "Agent-Oriented Programming" implemented agents as computational entities characterized in mentalistic terms (beliefs, commitments, obligations) (Shoham 1993). This established **agent-oriented programming** as distinct from object-oriented programming and was closely related to the BDI (Belief-Desire-Intention) architecture.

1994: Learning Interface Agents. Pattie Maes pioneered **learning interface agents**, adaptive software assistants that reduce work and information overload by learning user preferences through observation, feedback, and collaborative filtering (Maes 1994). Her work on systems like Ringo (music recommendations) showed personalization through learning, introducing adaptation as a core agentic capability (Shardanand and Maes 1995).

Three major 1995 publications crystallized distinct approaches to defining computational agents, each addressing the translation challenge from a different angle:

1995: Intelligent Agents. Wooldridge & Jennings defined **intelligent agents** as exhibiting autonomy, reactivity, proactivity, and social ability (Wooldridge and Jennings 1995).

1995: Perception-Action Agents

Russell & Norvig's *Artificial Intelligence: A Modern Approach* defined an **agent** as anything that perceives its environment through sensors and acts through actuators (Russell and Norvig 1995). This perception-action framework became the standard model in AI education and practice.

1995: Complex Adaptive Systems. Holland defined **complex adaptive system agents** exhibiting local interactions under simple rules that produce emergent behavior (Holland 1995).

The remaining years extended these frameworks into specialized domains and established enduring computational paradigms:

1996: Autonomous Agents. Franklin and Graesser distinguished **autonomous agents** as entities situated within an environment that sense and act over time in pursuit of their own agendas (Franklin and Graesser 1997) (ATAL'96; published 1997 in LNCS).

1996: Agent-Based Modeling. Epstein and Axtell's *Growing Artificial Societies* established agent-based modeling (ABM), defining agents as autonomous heterogeneous individuals whose local interactions produce emergent macro patterns (Epstein and Axtell 1996).

1998: Reinforcement Learning

Sutton and Barto's *Reinforcement Learning* defined agents maximizing cumulative reward through environmental interaction, establishing the **RL framework** (Sutton and Barto 1998). This framework would prove foundational for deep RL breakthroughs two decades later.

1999: Multi-Agent Systems. Textbooks by Jacques Ferber and Gerhard Weiss consolidated **multi-agent systems (MAS)**, defining agents as autonomous problem-solving entities that cooperate, compete, and negotiate to achieve individual and collective goals (Weiss 1999; Ferber 1999).

The decade's diverse frameworks addressed these challenges from complementary angles. On representing beliefs computationally, Shoham's agent-oriented programming offered mentalistic implementations (beliefs, commitments, obligations). Concerning observable properties distinguishing agents from programs, Wooldridge and Jennings enumerated autonomy, reactivity, proactivity, and social ability. On functional architecture, Russell and Norvig established the perception-action cycle. For learning and adaptation, Maes demonstrated how agents could improve through observation and feedback. And on emergence, Holland and the ABM community showed how simple local rules generate collective intelligence. These were not competing theories but different levels of description including internal architectures, observable properties, functional patterns, adaptive mechanisms, and emergent phenomena.

Two computational paradigms proved particularly durable. Agent-based modeling demonstrated how to generate social phenomena from individual interactions, bridging agent theory and social science applications. Reinforcement learning formalized agents as reward maximizers learning through environmental feedback, a framework that would scale far beyond the decade's initial demonstrations. By 1999, multi-agent systems had matured into a distinct field with established conferences, textbooks, and architectural patterns. These 1990s frameworks (mental states, observable properties, perception-action cycles, learning mechanisms, and emergence) would shape agent definitions for the next two decades, until large language models introduced qualitatively new capabilities.

1.3.5   Consolidation and Formalization (Late 1990s to 2019)

The early 21st century marked a period of consolidation rather than conceptual revolution. Following the 1990s explosion of agent definitions and implementations, the field matured through educational resources that trained new generations of researchers, reference works that synthesized accumulated knowledge, and successful demonstrations that validated the frameworks at scale. The dot-com boom and bust, the rise of Web 2.0, mobile computing, and eventually the deep learning revolution all occurred during this period, yet they produced remarkably few new definitional frameworks for agency itself.

Two early definitional contributions framed the era's concerns. Kauffman raised fundamental questions about the relationship between physical and virtual agency, proposing thermodynamic criteria that most software agents clearly failed to meet. Jennings, Sycara, and Wooldridge formalized agent-oriented software engineering, translating the 1990s research insights into practical development methodologies. Beyond these, the period's major developments were consolidative: Wooldridge's *Introduction to MultiAgent Systems* and Epstein's *Generative Social Science* codified best practices, legal updates like the Restatement (Third) of Agency maintained doctrinal continuity, and reference works like the Stanford Encyclopedia entries provided authoritative syntheses.

The period's most dramatic developments came from demonstrations of existing frameworks at unprecedented scale. Deep reinforcement learning combined neural networks with the RL framework established by Sutton and Barto in 1998, achieving superhuman performance first in Atari games and then notably with AlphaGo's victories over world champions. These successes validated that the 1990s conceptual frameworks could scale to complex domains without requiring fundamental redefinition. By 2019, the field had mature definitions, established pedagogical resources, and powerful demonstrations, but also growing awareness that large language models might catalyze the next definitional shift.

2000: Physical Agency. Stuart Kauffman's *Investigations* proposed thermodynamic criteria: natural autonomous agents must reproduce and perform thermodynamic work cycles, highlighting tensions between embodied and virtual agency (Kauffman 2000).

1998: Defining Agents. A research roadmap by Jennings, Sycara, and Wooldridge synthesized community consensus: an agent is "an encapsulated computer system that is situated in some environment, and that is capable of flexible, autonomous action in that environment in order to meet its design objectives" (Jennings et al. 1998; Wooldridge and Jennings 1995). As a historical definition from computer science, they used "system" to mean a computational entity. This definition grounded agent-oriented software engineering (AOSE) work throughout the 2000s.

2006: Restatement (Third) of Agency. The *Restatement (Third) of Agency* updated legal doctrine while retaining core concepts of fiduciary duty and delegated authority (American Law Institute 2006).

2013–2015: Deep Reinforcement Learning

Deep RL combined neural networks with established RL frameworks, achieving superhuman performance in complex domains. DeepMind's DQN mastered Atari games from raw pixels (Mnih et al. 2015), and AlphaGo defeated world champions at Go (Silver et al. 2016), demonstrating that learned agents could exceed human capabilities in domains previously considered intractable.

The period's consolidation reflected the 1990s frameworks' success; they fit the technological capabilities available. Wooldridge's *Introduction to MultiAgent Systems* and Bonabeau's agent-based modeling syntheses trained new generations of practitioners (Wooldridge 2009; Bonabeau 2002). Epstein's *Generative Social Science* articulated ABM's explanatory program: explaining phenomena through simple rule-based actors whose local interactions generate macro patterns (Epstein 2006). Stanford Encyclopedia entries on "Agency" and "Action" provided philosophical syntheses (Schlosser 2019; Wilson and Shpall 2022). By 2020, Russell and Norvig's 4th edition of AIMA had refined agent definitions incorporating ML progress (Russell and Norvig 2020b).

Kauffman's thermodynamic criteria highlighted ongoing tension between physical and virtual agency, a question that remains contentious as purely software-based LLM agents proliferate. Jennings and colleagues' software engineering formalization helped practitioners but did not redefine agency itself. Deep RL validated existing frameworks at unprecedented scale: agents learning through environmental interaction could achieve superhuman performance, confirming Sutton and Barto's 1998 framework rather than replacing it. The stage was set, however, for disruption. Large language models' capacity for flexible reasoning, few-shot learning, and natural language understanding would soon enable agent architectures qualitatively different from the hand-coded systems of previous decades.

1.3.6   The LLM Era (2020 to 2025)

Large language models brought capabilities that catalyzed a new wave of agent definitions. GPT-3's release in 2020 demonstrated few-shot learning and flexible reasoning at scale. ChatGPT's public launch in 2022 made conversational AI mainstream. But the definitional shift came not from language modeling itself, but from discovering that LLMs could orchestrate tool use, maintain working memory, and iteratively refine approaches to achieve complex goals. This combination (flexible reasoning plus tool use) enabled agent architectures qualitatively different from previous decades' hand-coded systems.

The key insight emerged in 2022: LLMs could implement the classical perception-action cycle not through programmer-specified rules but through learned parameters. The ReAct pattern (Reasoning and Acting) demonstrated LLMs interleaving chain-of-thought reasoning with tool use, iteratively planning, acting, and observing until goals were achieved. This simple pattern proved general, spurring implementations across research labs and commercial frameworks. Unlike previous decades' diversity of agent architectures, the LLM era quickly converged on a dominant pattern: an LLM iteratively calling tools, observing results, updating state, and choosing next actions.

This architectural convergence reflects several factors: the flexibility of LLMs as general-purpose reasoners, the natural fit between language models and tool APIs, and the economic incentives driving rapid commercialization. Where 1990s agent definitions emerged from academic research programs over a decade, LLM agent definitions coalesced in months through practitioner experimentation and commercial deployment. The speed of convergence is unprecedented, though whether this pattern will prove as durable as the 1990s frameworks remains to be seen.

2022: The LLM-as-Agent Pattern

Yao et al.'s "ReAct: Synergizing Reasoning and Acting in Language Models" showed that LLMs can interleave chain-of-thought reasoning with tool use, iteratively planning, acting, and observing to achieve goals (Yao et al. 2022). This catalyzed the "**LLM-as-agent**" pattern in contemporary practice. As Simon Willison concisely puts it: "an LLM agent runs tools in a loop to achieve a goal" (Willison 2025).

Commercial frameworks adopted this pattern. LangChain defines agents as entities that use LLMs to iteratively call tools until a stop condition is met (LangChain Documentation 2024). OpenAI's Agents SDK similarly describes agents as LLMs configured with instructions and tools, operating in loops where the LLM decides which tools to call based on iterative feedback (OpenAI 2024). This convergence across academic research and commercial frameworks reflects rapid standardization around a single architectural pattern.

2023: Generative Agents

Park et al.'s "Generative Agents" showcased LLM-powered agents simulating believable human behaviors over long horizons via memory, planning, and reflection (Park et al. 2023). This demonstrated that LLM-based agents could sustain coherent behavior over extended time horizons through architectural extensions: memory streams, reflection mechanisms, and dynamic planning modules.

2023: The Rise of LLM Agents. Xi et al.'s survey "The Rise and Potential of Large Language Model Based Agents" documented the emerging architectural consensus: entities using LLMs to iteratively call tools, observe results, and adapt until goals are achieved (Xi et al. 2023).

2024 to 2025: Commercial Frameworks. LangChain defines agents as entities using LLMs to iteratively call tools until a stop condition is met (LangChain Documentation 2024). OpenAI's Agents SDK describes agents as LLMs configured with instructions and tools, operating in loops where the LLM decides which tools to call based on iterative feedback (OpenAI 2024). This convergence represents an emerging architectural consensus across research and commercial frameworks.

Figure 1: Generative agents are believable simulacra of human behavior for interactive applications. In this work, we demonstrate generative agents by populating a sandbox environment, reminiscent of The Sims, with twenty-five agents. Users can observe and intervene as agents plan their days, share news, form relationships, and coordinate group activities.

Figure 1.4: Park et al. (2023): Generative agents in Smallville. Twenty-five LLM-powered agents inhabit a sandbox environment, each with memories, routines, and social relationships. The architecture extends an LLM with memory streams, reflection mechanisms, and dynamic planning. From a single seed notion (one agent wanting to throw a Valentine's Day party) agents autonomously spread invitations, formed acquaintances, and coordinated attendance, demonstrating coherent behavior over extended horizons. Source: Park et al. (2023), Figure 1.

The LLM era's definitional landscape differs from previous periods. Rather than multiple competing frameworks addressing different facets of agency, the field quickly converged on architectural patterns exploiting LLMs' flexible reasoning. ReAct established the tool-orchestration template in 2022, and within months implementations proliferated across academia and industry. Park's generative agents demonstrated a complementary pattern (memory, reflection, and planning enabling sustained believable behavior in social simulations) while commercial frameworks embedded tool orchestration as default infrastructure.

What is genuinely new remains debated. Skeptics note that the perception-action cycle, goal-directed behavior, and tool use all appeared in 1990s definitions; the

LLM era implements these through learned parameters rather than programmer-specified logic. Proponents argue that flexible reasoning over natural language representations enables qualitatively different agentic capabilities. A plausible resolution is that LLMs shifted where decision-making knowledge resides (from code to weights) without fundamentally changing the functional architecture of agency. Regardless, the speed of convergence (from research demonstration to industry standard in under three years) marks the LLM era as distinctive in the seven-decade history of agent definitions.

1.3.7 Historical Patterns

Five patterns emerge across seven decades:

Broadening entity frames. Early definitions focused on humans or human–AI relationships. By the 1990s, purely computational agents became common. The LLM era introduced hybrid framings: humans provided goals, AI systems executed multi-step tasks.

Increasing autonomy. Definitions evolved from delegated proxies (1958) to perception-action systems (1995) to tool orchestrators (2025). The locus of decision-making shifted progressively toward the agent, reflecting evolving expectations of autonomy.

From mental states to observable behavior. Philosophical definitions emphasized intention and reasoning. Computer science implemented these as mentalistic constructs. Contemporary definitions focus on observable capabilities like tool use, iterative problem solving, and task completion.

"Tools-in-a-loop" convergence. The AI engineering community has converged toward iterative tool orchestration patterns, documented in practitioner accounts (Willison 2025) and academic surveys (Xi et al. 2023). This reflects technological maturity (LLMs capable of reliable tool use), research foundations (ReAct and related frameworks), and market pressures (customers evaluating empirical capabilities). While not yet a formal standard, this architectural pattern dominates contemporary implementations.

From hand-coded to learned behavior. Early agents used explicit rules and plans. Deep RL then showed agents could learn behaviors through environmental interaction. LLMs shifted the architectural locus of planning and orchestration from programmer-specified logic to learned parameters, changing where decision-making knowledge resides rather than the fundamental agentic capabilities.

These patterns help explain why contemporary definitions vary: they reflect different points in this evolutionary trajectory and different disciplinary emphases.

The next section examines how different disciplines approached agency, revealing persistent tensions and complementary insights.

1.4   Disciplinary Perspectives

While Section 1.3 traced chronological evolution, this section examines how different disciplines approach agency from distinct theoretical foundations. Each field emphasizes different facets of agency, revealing complementary insights and persistent tensions.

1.4.1   Philosophy: Intentionality and Reasons

Philosophy's distinctive contribution centers on **intentional descriptions**, responsibility for actions, and predictive stances. Anscombe (1957) established that actions are intentional "under a description." The same physical movement can be intentional under one description ("signing a contract") but not another ("smudging ink"). This insight matters for AI agents: when we attribute intentions to entities, we are choosing explanatory frameworks, not discovering intrinsic properties.

Bratman (1987)'s planning theory and Dennett (1987)'s **intentional stance** provide complementary perspectives: agents act according to their plans and commitments (Bratman) or can be treated as rational goal-pursuers regardless of internal mechanism (Dennett). Philosophy emphasizes *reasons* for action over mechanical causation, focusing on responsibility for actions and conceptual foundations rather than implementation.

1.4.2   Psychology: Self-Regulation and Control

Psychology approaches agency through **self-regulation**, **perceived control**, and contextual variability. Bakan's agency-communion spectrum characterizes fundamental modes of human existence, while Milgram (1974)'s agentic state describes conditions under which people suppress personal judgment and defer to authority. Bandura (1989)'s social cognitive theory emphasizes human agency as exercised through intentionality, forethought, self-reactiveness, and self-reflectiveness.

Psychology's distinctive insight: agency is not merely a property of isolated actions but a stable characteristic of cognitive entities capable of self-regulation. Crucially, agency exists on a spectrum and can be diminished by context (Milgram 1974) or enhanced through **self-efficacy** beliefs. For AI systems, this highlights how humans *perceive* AI agency, affecting trust and delegation decisions.

1.4.3 Law: Delegation and Fiduciary Duty

Legal doctrine understands agency through **delegated authority, fiduciary duties**, and **institutional contexts**. The Restatement of Agency defines the relationship as arising when a principal manifests assent that an agent shall act on the principal's behalf and subject to the principal's control. Key elements include: (1) relational structure requiring a principal-agent pair, (2) delegated authority derived from the principal, (3) fiduciary obligations of loyalty and care, and (4) liability attribution within scope of authority.

Law's distinctive approach focuses on external authority structures and legally enforceable duties rather than internal intentions or motivations. Legal frameworks embed agency in formal mechanisms such as contracts, corporate charters, and powers of attorney that create, bound, and terminate authority relationships. For AI systems, this raises immediate questions: Can an AI be an agent in the legal sense? Who serves as principal? As illustrated in Section 1.1, misunderstanding these relationships can have serious consequences when entities lack mechanisms for fulfilling fiduciary duties.

1.4.4 Economics: Incentives and Information Asymmetry

Economic analysis frames agency through **utility alignment**, **information asymmetry**, and **organizational design**. Jensen and Meckling (1976)'s principal-agent model identifies the core problem: principals and agents have divergent preferences and asymmetric information. Agents may pursue self-interest at principals' expense (**moral hazard**), or principals may struggle to assess agent quality ex ante (**adverse selection**).

Economics' distinctive approach emphasizes cost-benefit analysis and divergence of preferences rather than rights or duties. The focus is pragmatic: given that perfect alignment is impossible, how do we minimize **agency costs** through compensation structures, performance metrics, and oversight mechanisms? For AI systems, economic frameworks highlight alignment challenges: How do we design "reward functions" that elicit desired behavior? What monitoring mechanisms detect when AI agents pursue proxy metrics rather than true objectives?

1.4.5 Cognitive Science: Mental Architecture and Plans

Cognitive science approaches agency through **modular mental societies, plan-based control**, and **representational structures**. Minsky (1986)'s Society of Mind framed intelligence as emerging from interactions among simple processes without central control. Bratman (1987)'s planning theory emphasized that intentions are elements of partial plans structuring practical reasoning over time. The **BDI**

(**Belief-Desire-Intention**) architecture implements this: agents maintain beliefs about the world, desires representing goals, and intentions as committed plans.

Cognitive science's distinctive insight treats agency as a lens on *mental architecture*, not just overt action, focusing on information processing, symbolic manipulation, and hierarchical plan structures. The framework readily generalizes from human to machine minds via abstraction. For AI systems, cognitive science provides architectural blueprints. The BDI framework has directly influenced agent programming languages, and concepts like partial plans and means-end reasoning transfer naturally to computational implementations.

1.4.6   Complex Systems: Emergence and Local Rules

Complex systems science characterizes agency through **local rules generating global effects**, **adaptation**, and **environmental coupling**. Holland (1995)'s complex adaptive systems, Epstein and Axtell (1996)'s agent-based models, and Kauffman (2000)'s autonomous agents emphasize that interesting behavior emerges from interactions among rule-following entities. Individual agents need not be sophisticated; simple local rules, diversity, and environmental feedback suffice to produce **emergent macro patterns**.

Complex systems' distinctive insight treats agents as embedded in adaptive networks rather than as isolated actors. Behaviors co-evolve through selection pressures, learning, and resource flows. For AI systems, this perspective highlights how collections of simple agents exhibit sophisticated collective behavior (multi-agent systems, swarm robotics), but also warns against over-attributing agency to individual components when behavior primarily reflects system-level dynamics.

1.4.7   Computer Science: Protocols and Mentalistic Abstractions

Computer science, particularly agent-oriented software engineering, frames agency through **mentalistic programming abstractions**, **interaction protocols**, and **organizational modeling**. Shoham (1993)'s agent-oriented programming introduced beliefs, commitments, and choices as first-class programming constructs. Unlike object-oriented programming (encapsulation and message-passing), agent-oriented programming treats components as having mental states and engaging in speech acts. FIPA agent communication languages formalized performatives (inform, request, propose) modeled on human **speech acts**.

Computer science's distinctive approach uses mentalistic vocabulary as an *engineering tool* rather than philosophical claim. Attributing beliefs to software entities improves code clarity and reasoning about distributed systems, whether or not agents "really" have beliefs. For AI systems, computer science provides the middleware such as communication standards, coordination mechanisms, and organizational structures that enable multi-agent systems to function. Agents negotiate rather than merely receiving method calls.

1.4.8 Cross-Disciplinary Synthesis

Table 1.5 summarizes key differences across disciplines.

Discipline	Autonomy			Entity Focus		
	Low	Med	High	Human	Hybrid	Machine
Responsibility-oriented (normative)						
Philosophy	●	○	○	●	○	○
Psychology	○	●	○	●	○	○
Law	●	○	○	○	●	○
Economics	○	●	○	○	●	○
Capability-oriented (descriptive)						
Cognitive Science	○	●	○	●	○	○
Complex Systems	○	○	●	○	●	●
Computer Science	○	○	●	○	●	●
AI	○	○	●	○	○	●

Table 1.5: Cross-disciplinary agency perspectives. Filled = primary focus; empty = not emphasized.

Several patterns emerge:

- **Autonomy gradient**: Disciplines focusing on human-AI relationships (law, economics) assume lower autonomy, while those focused on machine capabilities (AI, complex systems) assume higher autonomy

- **Entity frames**: Philosophy, psychology, and cognitive science start with humans; law and economics examine hybrid relationships; complex systems, computer science, and AI embrace machine entities

- **Mechanism diversity**: Each discipline emphasizes different causal mechanisms (intentions, self-regulation, incentives, plans, rules, protocols, actions)

- **Normative vs descriptive**: Philosophy and law are more normative (concerned with responsibility and duty), while AI and complex systems are more descriptive (concerned with observable behavior)

Understanding agentic AI in professional contexts requires synthesis across these disciplines. Philosophy provides conceptual foundations for attributing agency;

psychology illuminates how humans perceive and interact with AI agents. Law establishes liability frameworks and professional responsibilities; economics offers tools for analyzing alignment problems. Cognitive science suggests architectural patterns; complex systems warns about emergent behavior in multi-agent contexts. Computer science provides implementation protocols; AI defines practical capabilities and evaluation criteria.

The next section extracts analytical dimensions that cut across these disciplinary perspectives.

1.5   Analytical Dimensions

While different disciplines approach agency from distinct theoretical foundations (Section 1.4), certain analytical dimensions cut across disciplinary boundaries. Here we identify four key dimensions that structure variation in how agency is understood: **autonomy, entity frames, goal dynamics,** and **persistence**.

1.5.1   Autonomy Spectrum

Perhaps the most fundamental dimension along which agent definitions vary is **autonomy spectrum**: the degree to which an agent can set its own agenda, select tactics, and own accountability for outcomes.

Three plain-language questions help position any definition on the autonomy spectrum:

> **Who sets the goal?**
>
> Does the agent accept goals from an external principal, or does it generate its own objectives? Delegated proxies follow instructions; self-directed entities set their own agendas.

> **Who decides the next step?**
>
> Does the agent execute predefined plans step-by-step, or does it choose actions autonomously? Delegated proxies follow explicit instructions. Contract-bound delegates choose methods (how) but not objectives (what). Perception-action planners select both tactics and timing independently.

> ### Who carries responsibility if things go wrong?
>
> Does accountability remain with the principal, or does the agent own outcomes? Low-autonomy agents are instruments; high-autonomy agents bear responsibility for their choices.

Definitions range from delegated proxies at one extreme to self-directed entities at the other.

Delegated Proxies (Low Autonomy). The Restatement (Second) of Agency (1958) exemplifies this end: agents execute their principal's instructions within bounded authority. Goals, evaluation criteria, and ultimate responsibility remain with the principal. Milgram (1974)'s "agentic state" captures the psychological correlate, where individuals see themselves as mere instruments of authority, disclaiming personal responsibility.

Contract-Bound Delegates (Low-Moderate Autonomy). Jensen and Meckling (1976)'s principal-agent model grants agents tactical discretion within incentive contracts but evaluates them solely on principals' payoffs. Agents choose means but not ends, operating under monitoring and compensation schemes designed to align behavior.

Self-Regulating Actors (Moderate Autonomy). Bandura (1989)'s human agency emphasizes that individuals set sub-goals, monitor progress, and self-adjust within social structures. Maes (1994)'s software agents learn user preferences and initiate actions based on high-level intent rather than step-by-step commands.

Perception-Action Planners (Moderate-High Autonomy). Russell and Norvig (1995)'s AI agents sense environments and select actions via performance-driven policies without waiting for commands. Franklin and Graesser (1997)'s autonomous agents pursue their own agendas over time, acting to influence future perceptions.

Learning Loop Owners (High Autonomy). Sutton and Barto (1998)'s reinforcement learning agents experiment with actions and update policies from reward signals without human step-by-step guidance. The agent owns the exploration-exploitation trade-off.

Tool Orchestrators (Very High). Modern tool-use APIs (2025) choose when and how to invoke tools, integrating outputs into their reasoning loops. Contemporary LLM frameworks provide one implementation approach for this architectural pattern, "independently accomplish[ing] tasks on behalf of users," planning, sequencing, and completing multi-step workflows before reporting back.

Table 1.6 summarizes this progression.

Position	Source	Description
Delegated proxy	American Law Institute (2006)	Follows instructions
Obedience	Milgram (1974)	Defers to authority
Contract-bound	Jensen and Meckling (1976)	Bounded tactics
Self-regulating	Bandura (1989)	Self-monitors
Adaptive assistant	Maes (1994)	Learns, initiates
Perception-action	Russell and Norvig (1995)	Sense-act loop
Agenda-setting	Franklin and Graesser (1997)	Independent agenda
Learning loop	Sutton and Barto (1998)	Reward learning
Tool orchestrator	Yao et al. (2022)	Selects tools
Independent finisher	Xi et al. (2023)	End-to-end execution

Table 1.6: Autonomy spectrum: from delegated proxies to self-directed entities.

This dimension correlates with but differs from technological capability. Rule-based expert systems can exhibit moderate autonomy (goal-directed loops), while capable neural networks, including LLMs, operating in single-shot mode exhibit none. Autonomy is architectural, not merely a function of model sophistication.

Autonomy and Governance: The autonomy level directly determines governance requirements. Low-autonomy agents (delegated proxies, contract-bound delegates) operate under tight principal control with lighter oversight burdens: the principal validates each step or constrains choices through explicit contracts. High-autonomy agents (tool orchestrators, independent finishers) make consequential decisions with minimal intervention, demanding mandatory precommit limits (resource budgets, scope boundaries), explicit escalation triggers (confidence thresholds, high-stakes decisions), and robust audit trails. *Governance principle:* Oversight rigor must scale with autonomy level. An agent that independently orchestrates tools and completes multi-step tasks requires explicit termination mechanisms, human-in-the-loop checkpoints for irreversible actions, and clear accountability mapping. These safeguards are unnecessary for agents executing predefined scripts under direct supervision.

1.5.2   Entity Frames

Agent definitions often talk past each other because they quietly assume different kinds of **entities**. We identify three clusters:

Human-Centered. These definitions privilege individual humans and their cognition or morality. Anscombe (1957)'s intentional action explores agency as practical knowledge held by persons. Milgram (1974)'s agentic state examines how people respond to authority. Bandura (1989)'s human agency emphasizes internal cognitive machinery such as intentionality, forethought, self-reactiveness, and self-reflectiveness. The hallmark questions: *What intentions animate the person? How is responsibility assigned?*

Institutional/Hybrid. These definitions situate agency in socio-technical collectives, such as humans embedded in contracts, firms, or organizational structures. The Restatement of Agency (1958) defines the principal-agent pair, not isolated individuals. Jensen and Meckling (1976)'s economic model examines "manager-with-contract" as the effective actor. Epstein and Axtell (1996)'s agent-based models simulate rule-following individuals shaped by local interactions. The hallmark questions: *What structure channels decisions? How are incentives and authority shared?*

Machine-Centered. These definitions assign agency to computational entities managing perception/action loops. Russell and Norvig (1995)'s AI agents perceive through sensors and act via actuators. Franklin and Graesser (1997)'s autonomous agents are persistent systems pursuing agendas. Contemporary LLM frameworks (2025) are explicitly software coordinating tools. The hallmark questions: *How does the entity sense, plan, and act? What loop keeps it going?*

Table 1.7 summarizes representative examples. Importantly, these frames are not mutually exclusive. Contemporary "agentic AI" often involves hybrid entities: AI systems acting on behalf of human principals, with goals supplied by humans but tactics chosen by machines. The legal and ethical challenges arise precisely at these boundaries.

1.5.3 Goal Dynamics

Definitions also vary in how they understand the **relationship between agents and goals**. We identify three stances:

Goal Acceptance. The agent receives a mandate and optimizes for it without debate. The Restatement of Agency (1958) requires agents to follow principal objectives; divergence invites breach. Sutton and Barto (1998)'s RL agent maximizes a fixed reward function supplied externally. Contemporary LLM frameworks (2025) "independently accomplish tasks on behalf of users," but user goals remain the north star. Success equals compliance or reward maximization.

Frame	Source	Description
Human	Anscombe (1957)	Human minds, intentions
	Milgram (1974)	
	Bandura (1989)	
Institutional	American Law Institute (2006)	Organizations, authority structures
	Jensen and Meckling (1976)	
	Epstein and Axtell (1996)	
Machine	Russell and Norvig (1995)	Computational entities, loops
	Franklin and Graesser (1997)	
	Xi et al. (2023)	

Table 1.7: Entity frames: human minds, institutional relationships, or computational entities. *Accessibility:* Categorization table with 3 columns (Frame, Source, Description) and 3 rows representing three fundamental approaches. Row 1: Human frame (philosophy/psychology) emphasizes human minds and intentions. Row 2: Institutional frame (law/economics) emphasizes organizations and authority structures. Row 3: Machine frame (computer science/AI) emphasizes computational entities and loops. Multiple scholars cited per frame showing discipline-spanning taxonomy.

Goal Adaptation. The agent refines, reprioritizes, or balances goals within constraints. Maes (1994)'s software agents learn user preferences and decide when to intervene, reprioritizing information flows. Russell and Norvig (1995)'s agents balance performance measures, trading off actions based on context. Modern tool-use APIs (2025) interpret instructions, break them down, and choose which tools serve user intent. The agent has discretion in interpretation and tactics.

Goal Negotiation. The agent co-determines objectives with others, often through communication. Weiss (1999)'s multi-agent systems coordinate, cooperate, and negotiate when goals conflict. Jennings et al. (1998)'s AOSE roadmap treats agents as social entities that negotiate commitments and allocate tasks. Multi-agent frameworks (2025) enable multi-agent applications where agents message each other to propose plans, critique, and converge collaboratively.

Table 1.8 summarizes this dimension.

This dimension has direct implications for legal accountability. If an AI agent merely accepts goals, responsibility flows clearly to whoever set them. If it adapts goals through interpretation, questions arise about faithful execution. If it negotiates goals with other agents or humans, traditional principal-agent frameworks may not apply cleanly.

Stance	Source	Description
Acceptance	American Law Institute (2006)	Follows supplied objectives
	Sutton and Barto (1998)	
	Xi et al. (2023)	
Adaptation	Maes (1994)	Refines goals, chooses tactics
	Russell and Norvig (1995)	
	Yao et al. (2022)	
Negotiation	Weiss (1999)	Co-determines objectives
	Jennings et al. (1998)	

Table 1.8: Goal dynamics: from acceptance through adaptation to negotiation. *Accessibility:* Progressive stance table with 3 columns (Stance, Source, Description) and 3 rows showing increasing autonomy in goal-setting. Row 1: Acceptance stance (follows supplied objectives without modification). Row 2: Adaptation stance (refines goals and chooses tactics within constraints). Row 3: Negotiation stance (co-determines objectives through communication). Progression has direct implications for legal accountability.

1.5.4 Persistence and Embodiment

Two additional dimensions merit brief mention:

Temporal Persistence. Franklin and Graesser (1997) distinguish programs from agents partly on **persistence**; agents maintain state and pursue objectives over extended periods. This contrasts with reactive systems that respond to inputs without memory. Modern LLM agents incorporate conversation history and tool-use results, creating persistence within sessions. As discussed in Section 1.1, single-shot LLM usage lacks the persistent goal pursuit that characterizes agentic systems.

Embodiment. Kauffman (2000)'s autonomous agents require physical **embodiment** capable of performing thermodynamic work cycles. This biological grounding contrasts sharply with purely virtual agents. Robotics and embodied AI represent one implementation; cloud-based LLM agents represent another. Whether virtual agents merit the term "agent" in the fullest sense remains philosophically contentious, though pragmatically settled in favor of inclusion.

1.5.5 Implications for Agentic AI

These four dimensions (autonomy, entity frames, goal dynamics, persistence) provide organizing principles for evaluating contemporary systems. When someone claims an entity is "agentic," four questions create a shared, falsifiable basis for evaluation.

Question 1: Autonomy

How much **discretion** does the entity have in selecting **goals** and **tactics**, and where does **accountability** reside when outcomes go wrong? Describe the locus of **control** and any **constraints** (contracts, prompts, policies).

Question 2: Entity

What kind of **entity** are we evaluating: a pure **machine** entity, a **human–AI** team, or an **institution**al arrangement? Clarifying the entity prevents conflating a tool with the broader organization that wields it.

Question 3: Goals

Does the entity merely accept **goals**, **adapt** them through interpretation, or **negotiate** them with other agents or humans? State how **goals** are set, refined, and **verified** in practice.

Question 4: Persistence

Does the entity maintain **state** and pursue **objectives** across multiple steps or sessions, or does it operate in **single-shot** mode? Specify how **memory**, **logs**, or **context windows** support continuity.

These questions cut across the marketing hype and disciplinary jargon, providing a shared vocabulary for more precise discourse. The next section synthesizes these insights into a working definition grounded in theoretical foundations.

1.6 Synthesis

Having traced the historical evolution (Section 1.3), examined disciplinary perspectives (Section 1.4), and identified analytical dimensions (Section 1.5), we now synthesize these insights into a coherent analytical framework. This framework provides both the theoretical foundation for understanding agency and practical tools for evaluating real-world systems.

1.6.1   Cross-Cutting Patterns

Our analysis across disciplines reveals four fundamental patterns that consistently appear when scholars and practitioners identify agency. These patterns transcend individual fields, providing a shared foundation for recognizing agentic behavior regardless of whether we are examining human decision-makers, organizational structures, or computational entities.

> **Pattern 1: Goal-Directedness**
>
> Agents pursue objectives (whether called intentions, rewards, mandates, or incentives) exhibiting behavior oriented toward outcomes rather than merely reacting to stimuli.

> **Pattern 2: Perception–Action Coupling**
>
> Agents operate through iterative cycles of sensing and acting. Entities that transform inputs once without iteration, such as compilers and single-shot classifiers, lack this essential coupling.

> **Pattern 3: Selective Autonomy**
>
> Agents exercise discretion in their choices. Entities executing fixed scripts without decision-making capacity do not qualify.

> **Pattern 4: Termination**
>
> Agents must recognize when to stop, either through explicit controls or implicit goal satisfaction. Entities running indefinitely without stopping conditions lack goal-oriented closure. Section 2.8 provides detailed implementation guidance for termination conditions.

1.6.2   Precise Definitions

The four patterns above provide intuition. Now we make them precise. A rigorous framework lets us make testable claims: given any system, we can determine whether it qualifies as an agent, an agentic system, or an AI agent and defend that determination.

This property-based approach is a deliberate choice. As noted in Section 1.1, our framework trades alignment with any single discipline's historical conception of agency for something more practically useful: falsifiable tests grounded in observable properties. Readers may translate our claims into their preferred vocabulary (intentional systems, autonomous actors, goal-directed mechanisms) while preserving the operational distinctions that matter for design and governance.

The Six Properties. Our framework rests on six observable properties. The first three establish minimal agency; the additional three distinguish fully operational agentic systems:

- **Goal**: a clear objective or performance criterion that directs behavior
- **Perception**: the capability to sense and gather information from the environment
- **Action**: the capability to affect or change the environment
- **Iteration**: operating across multiple steps while preserving state between cycles
- **Adaptation**: modifying strategy based on accumulated observations and feedback
- **Termination**: recognizing when to stop, through explicit controls or goal satisfaction

The mnemonic **GPA + IAT** captures this structure: Goals, Perception, and Action form the minimal foundation; Iteration, Adaptation, and Termination complete the operational requirements. Autonomy (explored in Section 1.5) describes *how* these properties are exercised rather than serving as a separate core property.

Three Categories of Entities

- **Agent** (minimal): Has goals, perception, and action. Includes humans, organizations, animals, and computational systems.
- **Agentic System** (operational): Has all six properties. Ready for deployment; operates through cycles, learns from feedback, knows when to stop.
- **AI Agent**: An agentic system implemented using AI/ML technologies.

These categories form a strict hierarchy: every AI agent is an agentic system, and every agentic system is an agent, but the reverse does not hold. A single-shot image classifier qualifies as an agent (goals, perception, action) but lacks iteration, adaptation, and termination, so it fails as an agentic system. Individual features can be "agentic" without the whole system qualifying.

Termination in Detail. Termination deserves special attention because runaway processes pose real risks in professional contexts. An entity can satisfy the termination requirement through either of two mechanisms, or both:

 Explicit termination involves programmed hard limits: resource budgets, time-out constraints, and escalation triggers. **Implicit termination** occurs naturally when goals are satisfied, no further actions are available, or task episodes end. Professional deployments combine both. A legal research agent terminates implicitly upon finding precedent while respecting explicit resource limits. Section 2.8 examines five categories of termination conditions (success, resource budgets, confidence thresholds, error conditions, and escalation triggers), while Section 2.9 addresses when agents should pause and request human input rather than terminating outright.

1.6.3   Foundations in Context

Our formal framework draws from multiple theoretical traditions, each contributing essential insights about how agents operate. Understanding these foundations helps practitioners from different backgrounds connect our framework to established concepts in their fields.

Plan-Based Control. Plan-based control emphasizes how agents decompose goals into actionable steps. This approach, central to cognitive science and AI planning systems, treats agency as means-end reasoning that connects what we want to achieve with how to achieve it. In legal practice, we see this pattern in structured workflows like due diligence, where complex objectives decompose into systematic review tasks. Modern AI agents employ similar hierarchical planning when breaking down user requests into sequences of tool calls and sub-tasks.

Reactive Control. Not all intelligent behavior requires elaborate planning. The reactive control paradigm demonstrates that simple perception-action rules can produce sophisticated behavior when properly designed. This insight, pioneered in robotics by researchers like Rodney Brooks, shows that agents can be effective without maintaining complex world models. In fast-changing environments or when sensing is reliable, responsive behavior often outperforms deliberative planning. Contemporary LLM agents balance both approaches, maintaining high-level plans while reacting dynamically to unexpected outputs or errors.

BDI Models. The **Belief-Desire-Intention** (BDI) framework provides a structured account of agent mental states. Agents maintain beliefs about their environment, desires about preferred outcomes, and intentions representing committed plans. This model, influential in agent-oriented programming, explains how agents form and revise commitments as new information arrives. Legal agents exemplify this pattern: maintaining beliefs about applicable law, desires to serve client interests, and intentions manifested as filed documents or negotiation positions.

Reinforcement Learning. The **reinforcement learning** paradigm formalizes how agents learn from experience. Through cycles of action, observation, and reward, agents discover which behaviors achieve their goals. This framework clarifies why iterative interaction outperforms single-shot processing: each cycle provides information that improves future decisions. Modern AI agents increasingly incorporate reinforcement learning, whether through fine-tuning on human feedback or real-time adaptation during task execution.

Intentional Stance. Following philosopher Daniel Dennett's influential work (Dennett 1987), the **intentional stance** treats agency as a pragmatic attribution rather than metaphysical fact. We describe systems as having beliefs, desires, and intentions when such descriptions improve our ability to predict and control their behavior. This perspective liberates us from endless debates about whether AI systems "really" have goals or merely simulate goal-directed behavior. What matters is whether treating them as agents yields practical benefits.

These foundations directly inform how we build and evaluate agentic systems. Together, they ground the six-property framework in established theory while keeping it practically usable across disciplines from law to computer science.

> **From Theory to Practice**
>
> - **Planning** supports goal decomposition and task orchestration
> - **Reactive control** validates simple, robust responses to changing environments
> - **BDI models** supply architectures for managing commitments and updating beliefs
> - **Reinforcement learning** explains improvement through experience and feedback
> - **Intentional stance** guides when to treat systems as agents for prediction and control

1.6.4   Boundary Cases and Clarifications

Testing our framework against boundary cases reveals both its strengths and the subtleties of applying formal definitions to real-world systems. These edge cases illuminate practical fault lines: where practitioners disagree about agency and where our framework proves most valuable.

Thermostats and the Agency Spectrum. A basic mechanical thermostat demonstrates the spectrum from minimal agency to full agentic systems. It has five of six properties: goal (maintain temperature), perception (sensor readings), action (heating/cooling), iteration (continuous monitoring), and termination (implicit when target reached). Yet it lacks adaptation, applying fixed on/off rules without modifying strategy based on outcomes. This distinguishes reactive control from adaptive learning. Smart thermostats, by contrast, qualify as full agentic systems: they learn occupancy patterns, adjust schedules based on observed behavior, and implement explicit termination logic. This progression illustrates why minimal agency (Level 1) sets a deliberately low bar, while agentic systems (all six properties) require operational sophistication suitable for professional deployment.

Multi-Agent Collectives and Emergent Behavior. When multiple agents interact, the collective can exhibit properties no single agent possesses. A trading floor, legal team, or swarm of autonomous vehicles may demonstrate emergent behaviors that challenge our individual-focused definitions. Legal systems have long grappled with this through doctrines distinguishing corporate from individual liability. Our framework accommodates both perspectives: we can analyze individual agents within the system or treat the collective itself as an agent with emergent goals and capabilities. The choice depends on analytical purpose. Attribution questions favor individual analysis, while coordination and emergent behavior favor collective treatment.

Virtual versus Embodied Agents. Software agents need not have physical bodies to qualify as agents. Consider a contract analysis system operating entirely in cloud infrastructure; it satisfies all six properties without any physical embodiment. While robotics researchers sometimes insist on embodiment as essential to agency, our framework follows the broader AI tradition of recognizing virtual agents as fully legitimate instances. The perception-action loop operates equally well whether the environment is physical (sensor readings, motor commands) or virtual (API queries, database updates). Professional legal and financial applications predominantly involve virtual agents, making this inclusive stance practically necessary.

Single-Shot LLM Interactions. A single ChatGPT response, however sophisticated, typically lacks the iteration property required for agentic systems. It processes input once and generates output without maintaining state across multiple perception-action cycles. The system does not observe results, adjust strategy, and continue pursuing goals; it completes and stops. For the purposes of this framework, we treat such single-shot LLM calls as non-iterative, even if they internally perform multiple reasoning steps, because they do not observe and react to *external* feedback within a perception-action loop.

Tool Use versus Tool-Using Agents. Simply using tools does not make an entity agentic. A script that calls an API once is not an agent; it lacks the iteration and adaptation that characterize agentic systems. What matters is purposeful, iterative tool use directed toward goals. **Simply calling an API once does *not* make a system an agent; the difference lies in goal-directed, iterative tool use with adaptation.** An LLM that repeatedly queries databases, processes results, and decides which tool to invoke next based on accumulated information exhibits agency. The distinction lies in the goal-directed iteration, not the mere presence of tool use. Advanced agentic systems extend this further by creating new tools, including writing Python scripts to expand their capabilities or composing prompts that define specialized sub-agents (Anthropic 2025b). This recursive capability, where agents manage the design and implementation of their own tools, represents a meta-level of agency beyond mere tool invocation.

Continuous Control and Implicit Termination. Entities engaged in continuous control, like systems maintaining server uptime or monitoring market conditions, might seem to violate our termination requirement. In practice, these entities typically operate in bounded episodes with implicit termination conditions: achieving steady state, exhausting available actions, or reaching time limits. Even "always-on" entities have mechanisms for recognizing when to stop particular behaviors, satisfying our termination criterion. A market monitoring system may run continuously, but individual monitoring tasks terminate when specific conditions trigger alerts or when trading sessions close. The distinction between the persistent entity and its bounded tasks resolves the apparent contradiction.

1.6.5   Professional Deployment

Understanding what makes an entity agentic is only the first step. In regulated domains like law and finance, deploying AI agents demands robust governance frameworks that ensure compliance, maintain professional standards, and protect sensitive information. The stakes are high: errors can trigger regulatory sanctions, breach fiduciary duties, or compromise client confidentiality.

> **Governance Cannot Be Retrofitted**
>
> Systems designed without audit logging cannot produce compliance reports when regulators arrive. Those lacking approval gates cannot enforce human oversight after deployment. Build governance in from the start.

Professional deployment demands that we move beyond theoretical properties to operational safeguards. Each of the six properties creates both opportunities and risks that must be managed through careful design and governance controls. Chapter 2 addresses the *how*, designing agents with governance-aware architecture, while Chapter 3 addresses the *what*: the five-layer regulatory framework and organizational accountability structures that deployed agents must satisfy.

Attribution and Auditability. Every factual claim must be traceable to its source, including case law, regulatory filings, market data, or expert analysis. Modern AI agents should maintain citation chains that satisfy legal brief or investment memorandum standards. Beyond citations, log major reasoning steps, tool invocations, and decision points in forms that preserve privilege while facilitating review. Section 2.11.1 details the logging architecture that makes this possible; Section 3.4.2 specifies what governance frameworks demand.

Bounded Operation. Without explicit termination conditions, agentic systems lack the property that distinguishes controlled systems from runaway processes. Enforce computational budgets, time constraints, and maximum iteration counts. In financial contexts, limit market data queries; in legal contexts, cap document review cycles. Section 2.8 provides implementation guidance for five categories of termination conditions; Section 2.8.4 addresses guardrails that detect and interrupt unproductive loops.

Escalation Pathways. Clear triggers, such as low confidence, high-stakes decisions, or detected conflicts, should route matters to human review. A contract review agent might escalate unusual liability provisions; a trading agent might pause before executing orders that exceed authorization thresholds. Escalation represents professionalism, not failure: recognizing when you need help is exactly what we expect from junior professionals. Section 2.9 examines when agents should escalate; Section 3.4.4 addresses human-in-the-loop patterns.

Confidentiality Controls. Attorney-client privilege, insider trading restrictions, and client confidentiality duties are non-delegable professional obligations. Governance systems must operationalize them through technical controls (ethical walls between matters, role-based access, and redaction rules) rather than relying on agent "judgment." Section 2.11.4 addresses least-privilege enforcement, and Section 3.3.3 maps the professional responsibility rules governing legal and financial practice.

Accountability Mapping. Establish clear responsibility lines before deployment: Who configured the agent? Who reviewed its outputs? Who authorized deployment? These questions must have answers before processing the first client matter.

Section 3.5 presents organizational governance models and examines how liability flows when agents cause harm.

> **From Framework to Practice**
>
> This chapter establishes *what* agents are. The chapters that follow address *how* to build them (Chapter 2) and *how* to govern them (Chapter 3). The six properties and governance controls introduced here reappear throughout: as design requirements, as audit checkpoints, and as the foundation for regulatory compliance.

1.6.6   Common Questions About Agency

Our framework inevitably raises questions about edge cases and apparent contradictions. Here we address the most common concerns that arise when applying these definitions to real-world systems.

Is iteration just repeated action? Iteration means more than simply repeating the same action multiple times. True iteration involves maintaining state across perception-action cycles, enabling the entity to learn from previous attempts and adjust its approach. An entity that simply retries the same failing action indefinitely is not iterating in our sense; it is stuck in a loop. Iteration requires the ability to incorporate feedback, correct errors, and make progress toward goals through successive refinements. A system that queries the same API endpoint repeatedly with identical parameters is not iterating; one that refines its query based on previous results is. This connection between iteration, memory, and adaptation is fundamental: Section 2.6 examines how agents maintain state across cycles, while Section 2.6.6 addresses how memory enables behavioral change based on experience. Single-shot entities, no matter how sophisticated, do not qualify as agentic systems under our framework because they lack this capacity to learn and adjust.

Do continuous tasks violate the termination requirement? Entities performing continuous tasks like monitoring or maintenance might seem to run forever, apparently violating our termination requirement. However, these entities still satisfy the termination property through implicit or explicit mechanisms. Implicit termination occurs when the entity reaches a steady state or exhausts available actions. Explicit termination happens through resource budgets, time limits, or escalation triggers. Even an entity that monitors markets continuously operates in bounded episodes (trading sessions, reporting periods, or maintenance windows). The key is that the entity has clear conditions under which it will cease its current behavior pattern, even if it later resumes. The termination requirement ensures predictable resource consumption and prevents runaway processes, not that entities can never restart.

If thermostats count as agents, have we trivialized the concept? Recognizing basic thermostats as minimal agents does not trivialize agency; it establishes a meaningful floor. Many entities fail even this basic test: databases lack goals, compilers lack perception-action loops, and lookup tables lack any form of action. More importantly, while basic thermostats have five operational properties (lacking adaptation), they demonstrate precisely why we distinguish minimal agency (Level 1: three properties) from agentic systems (six properties). The distinction between a basic thermostat and an AI legal research assistant is not whether they are agents, but the degree of autonomy, adaptation capability, sophistication, and responsibility they possess. Our framework acknowledges the thermostat's basic agency while reserving "agentic system" status for entities with all six properties (like smart thermostats that learn patterns), and "AI agent" designation for those using AI/ML for implementation. The gradient from simple to sophisticated agents reflects operational reality.

Is "AI agent" just marketing hype? In our framework, "AI agent" has a precise, falsifiable meaning: an agentic system that uses AI or machine learning (particularly large language models) for planning and orchestration. This excludes single-shot chat completions, no matter how impressive, because they lack iteration. It excludes traditional rule-based systems, even if they meet all six properties, because they do not use AI for implementation. It also excludes simple ML classifiers that lack goal-directedness and autonomous action. When vendors claim their product is an "AI agent," we can test this claim against our six properties and the AI implementation requirement. This transforms marketing language into testable assertions about system architecture and capabilities. The framework provides accountability; vendors must demonstrate iteration, adaptation, and termination mechanisms, not just AI-powered text generation.

1.7   Conclusion

This chapter established the conceptual foundations for understanding agency. You now have a three-level hierarchy distinguishing agents (goals, perception, action) from agentic systems (adding iteration, adaptation, termination) from AI agents (implementing these properties with machine learning). You have a six-question rubric for evaluating vendor claims and four analytical dimensions explaining why disciplines define agency differently.

1.7.1   Why These Foundations Matter

The distinction between marketing labels and architectural reality has direct professional consequences. These foundations enable **clearer evaluation**: when vendors claim "AI agents," you can demand evidence of iteration, adaptation, and termination, not just conversational ability. They enable **better coordination**: scholars and practitioners can specify which properties their systems exhibit rather than relying on ambiguous labels. They enable **informed regulation**: policies can target measurable capabilities rather than product categories that shift with each press release. And they enable **accountability**: procurement shifts from marketing promises to verified capabilities when you can test claims against the six-property framework.

The stakes are particularly high in professional domains like law and finance, where autonomous action by AI systems raises questions of liability, professional responsibility, and public safety. Without shared definitions linking architectural properties to operational requirements, we cannot write enforceable contracts, establish professional standards, or hold entities accountable when things go wrong.

1.7.2   What Comes Next

With conceptual foundations established, the practical questions become urgent: How do you actually build an agentic system? And once built, how do you govern it responsibly?

Chapter 2 addresses the first question through ten design decisions every agentic system must resolve. How does the agent get activated? How does it understand what you want? How does it gather information and take action? How does it remember across sessions? How does it plan multi-step tasks? How does it know when to stop, and when to ask for help? How do multiple agents coordinate? And critically, how do you design systems that *can* be governed? Each question maps directly to the six properties introduced here: triggers and intent extraction implement goals; perception tools implement sensing; action controls implement environmental effects; memory systems enable iteration and adaptation; termination conditions and escalation pathways complete the operational requirements.

Chapter 3 addresses the second question by mapping the regulatory landscape onto the governance controls that deployed agents must satisfy. Where Chapter 2 establishes how to build governance-aware architecture, Chapter 3 establishes what that architecture must accomplish: risk assessment, human oversight, audit logging, explainability, vendor management, and incident response. The chapter examines how to calibrate controls to autonomy levels, assign organizational accountability, and navigate liability when agents cause harm.

Together, these three chapters form a complete arc: understanding what agents are, designing them well, and governing them responsibly.

1.7.3   Further Learning

For practitioners seeking deeper engagement with these foundations:

- **American Law Institute (2006), Restatement (Third) of Agency.**   The authoritative legal framework for agency relationships, fiduciary duties, and attribution—essential for liability analysis and professional responsibility questions.

- **Jensen and Meckling (1976), Theory of the Firm.**   Principal-agent economics explaining information asymmetry, incentive alignment, and monitoring costs; directly applicable to governance design.

- **Wooldridge (2009), An Introduction to MultiAgent Systems.**   Coordination, negotiation, and communication between agents; practical guidance for enterprise deployments involving multiple specialized agents.

- **Xi et al. (2023), The Rise and Potential of Large Language Model Based Agents.**   Contemporary survey connecting classical agent concepts to current LLM-based implementations.

Chapter 2

How to Design an Agent

2.1 Introduction

The previous chapter introduced the GPA+IAT framework: a way to recognize agentic systems through Goals, Perception, Action, Iteration, Adaptation, and Termination. Now we turn to the practical: how do you design one?

The answer starts with a simple observation: agentic systems are meant to do real work, whether augmenting human professionals, automating routine workflows, or even replacing entire organizational functions. Whatever the ambition, the system must handle the same work those humans and organizations currently perform. A contract lifecycle management agent must do what a legal operations team does; a portfolio monitoring agent must "act like" an analyst; a due diligence agent must perform the same tasks as junior associates reviewing acquisition targets. This means an agentic system requires the same structural capabilities as a professional team: receiving and understanding work, coordinating action, and operating under governance controls.

Notably, these structural capabilities don't depend on implementation choices. Building agents inevitably requires choosing between Python and C#, between GPT and Claude, between libraries like LangChain or custom implementations, but the design decisions that matter transcend these details. Many commercial providers and open source libraries obscure the key architectural questions, and you will learn best by building your own conceptual foundation before adopting any particular vendor's framework.

> ### Agents are not magic; they are architecture
>
> Behind each architectural question lies a design decision with real tradeoffs. Capabilities that make agents useful require concrete choices about how systems should work, and those choices determine not just what the system can do but how reliably it performs, how it fails, and what controls remain available when things go wrong.

This chapter organizes those architectural decisions into ten questions: the kind you should be asking whether you're building, evaluating, deploying, or governing an agentic system.

2.1.1   Ten Questions

Designing an agent means answering these ten questions. The capabilities an agent needs are not determined by the technology; they are determined by the work. And work has structure that any system, human or artificial, must accommodate.

Examine how a law firm operates. Work arrives through defined channels: a client calls, court filings appear on the docket, or an originating attorney refers a matter to a specialist. That work typically arrives as instructions that need clarification, and associates quickly learn to read between the lines, developing heuristics for what partners actually want rather than what they literally said.

Research demands access to the right databases (Westlaw, Lexis, PACER, internal matter management systems) and thoughtful search strategies. Actions like filing motions or sending client letters have real consequences and require appropriate authorization and privilege review. Institutional knowledge accumulates in case files, precedent databases, and practice group work product repositories.

Complex matters break down into workstreams with dependencies: discovery must complete before summary judgment motions, corporate due diligence must finish before closing, compliance audits must conclude before regulatory filings. Each work product has clear completion criteria and quality standards.

Associates know when to escalate to partners: when legal issues exceed their experience, when client relationship implications arise, or when matter budgets risk overruns. Teams coordinate across practice groups, with corporate attorneys working alongside litigators on acquisition disputes, or securities lawyers collaborating with compliance specialists on disclosure obligations.

Throughout, ethics rules and professional responsibility standards keep the whole operation within bounds: conflicts checks before engagement, confidentiality protections during representation, and privilege safeguards in every communication.

A discretionary portfolio management team follows the same pattern. Market data and research flow through defined feeds, and analysts must interpret investment committee mandates that leave room for judgment. Research requires access to financial databases, company filings, and market intelligence. Trades have real-world consequences that demand compliance checks before execution. Position history and investment theses persist across quarters, informing future decisions. Portfolio construction breaks down into sector allocation, security selection, and risk management, each with its own completion criteria. Analysts escalate to portfolio managers when positions approach limits, teams coordinate across asset classes, and regulatory controls ensure fiduciary compliance throughout.

These structural parallels are not coincidental. Law firms and investment teams are both *cognitive work systems*: organizations that process information, make decisions, and take consequential actions under uncertainty (Hollnagel and Woods 2005; Hollan et al. 2000). Agentic systems are cognitive work systems too (Wang et al. 2024a; Rao and Georgeff 1995), which means they face the same architectural challenges and require the same structural capabilities.

This mapping has practical implications. When you evaluate a contract review agent, you can ask the same questions you would ask about a junior associate: How does it know which clauses require partner review? How does it maintain client confidentiality across concurrent matters? When you design governance for a regulatory compliance monitoring agent, you can draw on the same frameworks that govern compliance departments: approval workflows, audit trails, exception handling procedures. When you communicate with technical teams building a litigation support agent or a portfolio optimization agent, you can use organizational language they will understand: escalation paths, authorization levels, quality control checkpoints.

Table 2.1 lists these ten questions in the order an agent encounters them during execution.

Each section addresses one question through organizational analogies, architectural concepts, domain-specific considerations for law and finance, and governance implications. You can read sequentially for cumulative understanding, jump directly to whichever question matters most, or skip to the end for synthesis.

Lastly, remember that, like other human processes or software systems, agents require governance. Chapter 3 addresses compliance frameworks and controls in detail.

Table 2.1: Architectural questions for agentic systems

Section	Architectural Question
Triggers	How does the agent know when it has work to do?
Intent	How does the agent understand what is being asked?
Perception	How does the agent find things out?
Action	How does the agent make things happen?
Memory	How does the agent remember things?
Planning	How does the agent break a big job into steps?
Termination	How does the agent know when it is done?
Escalation	How does the agent know when to ask for help?
Delegation	How does the agent work with other agents?
Governance by Design	How do we design systems that can be governed?

2.2   Triggers

How does an agent know when it has work to do? Take a day in the life of an average attorney. How does work reach their desk? Typically, a client calls with a question, a court docket updates with a new filing, a calendar reminds them of an upcoming motion, or a junior associate knocks on their door with a question that exceeds their expertise. Agentic systems operate in the same way. Building on Chapter 1's GPA+IAT framework, no matter how sophisticated a system's perception and action capabilities, it remains idle until work "arrives"; the architectural question is how these triggers and channels are defined and designed.

> ### Triggers
>
> **Triggers** are the events that start agent execution. In practice, a trigger might be a docket alert, a price crossing a threshold, a calendar deadline coming due, or an internal "I can't proceed safely" signal from the agent itself. Without a trigger, even a highly capable system sits idle.

The distinction between triggers and channels matters for system design. A trigger is the *what*: the event that demands attention. A channel is the *how*: the pathway through which that event reaches the agent. The same trigger, such as an approaching deadline, might arrive through different channels depending on context. It could come from a calendar system, an email reminder, or a human prompt asking "what's due this week?" Understanding this separation helps you design systems that can receive work from multiple sources while maintaining consistent processing logic.

Triggers also create the audit trail that governance depends on. Every action an agent takes traces back to the trigger that initiated it, and when a regulator asks why the system flagged a transaction, or when a court demands production of the agent's reasoning, you need to show what event started the chain of analysis. Systems that cannot trace actions back to triggers cannot be meaningfully audited, and in highly regulated fields like law and finance, what cannot be audited likely should not be deployed. We formalize this requirement as part of the logging architecture in Section 2.11.1.

Channels

Channels are how triggers reach the agent. In professional practice, four channels cover almost all work intake:

External feeds: The world pushes work to you (court filings, market data, regulatory updates).

Human prompts: People request work directly (chat, email, collaboration platforms).

Scheduled jobs: Time itself triggers execution (deadlines, periodic checks, end-of-day).

Escalation events: Internal signals that ask for human help (budget exhaustion, low confidence).

Each channel type serves a different operational need. External feeds enable reactive monitoring, allowing the system to respond to events as they occur in the world. Human prompts enable interactive collaboration, letting professionals direct the system's attention as needs arise. Scheduled jobs enable proactive workflows, ensuring that routine tasks happen reliably without requiring someone to remember to initiate them. And escalation events close the loop on human oversight by ensuring the system asks for help when it reaches its limits, a topic we explore in depth in Section 2.9.

The underlying point is simple but easy to overlook: before an agentic system can reason or act, it must first notice that work exists. Channels are the sensory apparatus of the system, the means by which it becomes aware of its environment and the tasks waiting to be accomplished. A lawyer cannot respond to a redlined contract they never received, and an agent cannot act on a trigger it never observed.

Triggers and channels are architectural concerns: questions about how work reaches the system, how events are routed, and how actions are logged for audit. But architecture alone does not determine whether an agentic system succeeds in practice. Professionals must actually use the system, and that raises a different set of questions: through what interaction modality do users engage? Is the experience synchronous or asynchronous? Does the system push information or wait to be asked? These are user experience questions, and they center on the concept of *surfaces.*

Compare the litigator who explores docket alerts through an interactive research session, refining queries as understanding develops, versus one who receives a daily summary email, versus one who gets a polished memo only when something requires attention. The underlying trigger is identical. The channel is the same. What differs is the surface, and surface design is the province of UX professionals, not system architects.

We address surfaces in this section because they complete the picture of the human-agent interface. Triggers, channels, and surfaces together determine whether an agentic system fits naturally into professional workflows or feels like an awkward intrusion. System architects must understand surfaces to design appropriate triggers and channels; UX designers must understand triggers and channels to design effective surfaces. The disciplines are distinct but interdependent. After examining how work arrives through each channel type, we turn to how users experience the system through different surfaces (Section 2.2.5).

2.2.1   External Feeds

External feeds deliver events from systems outside the agentic system's direct control. The external system pushes notifications when events occur, much like receiving service of process instead of checking the courthouse daily to see if you have been sued.

Legal and Regulatory Feeds: Court docket systems and e-filing platforms notify you when documents are filed in cases you monitor. An agentic system can retrieve the filing, analyze it, and respond by flagging motions for review, updating timelines, or drafting response memos. SEC filing systems enable similar monitoring for corporate disclosures. Citator services alert you when relevant cases are cited or overruled.

Financial Market Feeds: Portfolio agents subscribe to price alerts from providers like Bloomberg and Reuters. When thresholds are crossed, the agent evaluates whether rebalancing is warranted and either executes within pre-approved limits or escalates. News feeds deliver earnings, analyst ratings, and headlines for materiality assessment.

> ### Speed vs. Reasoning
>
> Market data arrives in milliseconds; LLM reasoning takes seconds to minutes. Agentic systems are unsuited for high-frequency trading but well suited for strategic decisions and compliance. The pattern: fast deterministic systems capture data and detect thresholds; the agent processes only after alerts fire.

Reliability Matters: Integration architecture affects governance. Some approaches prioritize speed but may miss events; others guarantee delivery with complete logs but add latency. For regulated applications, prefer the latter: every event recorded, processed in order, and auditable. Ask vendors: does your integration guarantee delivery, or can events be lost?

2.2.2   Human Prompts as Events

Human prompts feel different from external feeds because they are interactive. You type something and expect a response. But at the architectural level, a human prompt is just another event type: the user generates an event, the system receives it through a channel, processes it, and responds. Treating prompts this way simplifies design, because all events flow through the same routing and prioritization logic instead of demanding separate handling for interactive versus background work.

Chat interfaces offer the most direct channel for human interaction, and they are where most professionals first encounter agentic systems. A litigation associate researching a motion to dismiss might type "Find Ninth Circuit cases on personal jurisdiction over foreign corporations with U.S. subsidiaries," review the results, and then refine the query: "Focus on cases after 2018 where the court found jurisdiction." On the finance side, a credit analyst evaluating a loan application might ask "Compare this borrower's debt-to-EBITDA ratio against our portfolio average for manufacturing companies," review the comparison, and follow up with "Show me how it trends over the last three years." What makes chat powerful is exactly this kind of iterative refinement. Each message is simply another event, processed through the same loop as everything else, just with tighter expectations for response time.

But that expectation for quick responses creates real design constraints. When you are waiting for an answer, every second of silence feels like something has gone wrong. Systems built for interactive use need to acknowledge requests immediately, show progress as work unfolds, and deliver results incrementally when possible. This might mean streaming partial responses as they are generated, displaying indicators that show which databases the system is searching, or breaking complex research into visible steps. Without this feedback, a blank screen followed by a complete response thirty seconds later leaves you wondering whether the system is working, stuck, or crashed.

Email routing lets agentic systems handle work that arrives through channels people already use. A general counsel might forward a compliance question from a business unit to a monitored inbox, and the system extracts the question, searches relevant guidance, and drafts a response for review. A portfolio manager might forward a client inquiry about sector exposure to a research assistant inbox, receiving back a summary with current allocations and recent changes. The challenge with email is that the requests tend to be unstructured, often buried in forwarded threads with multiple topics and tangential context that the system must parse to find the actual question.

Collaboration platforms like Slack and Teams let agentic systems appear as team members in the workflow. A deal team negotiating an acquisition can @mention the system in their working channel to check whether a proposed indemnification cap falls within market norms, without anyone switching applications or breaking the flow of discussion. An investment committee preparing for a meeting can request a quick portfolio risk summary in their coordination channel. Users can also invoke specific capabilities through commands like `/research "material adverse change clauses"`. The convenience comes with a security consideration: collaboration platforms log all messages, and channels often include people with different access levels, so systems need to be careful about what information they surface and where.

Voice interfaces are best suited for quick lookups when typing is impractical: checking a position size while walking between meetings, confirming a filing deadline while reviewing documents, or getting a quick summary of overnight market moves during a commute. The tradeoffs are significant, though. Transcription errors can mangle legal and financial terminology, and without a keyboard, verifying identity becomes harder. For anything beyond simple information retrieval, voice interfaces should require explicit confirmation before the system takes action.

These synchronous channels share a common advantage: if the system misunderstands your request, you can clarify immediately. Asynchronous channels like email and background automation do not offer that safety net. When you send a request and walk away, you will not discover a misunderstood instruction until you return to find the wrong output. This is why intent understanding (Section 2.3) and perception design (Section 2.4) matter even more for asynchronous workflows. The system must figure out what you actually want from a single message, gather the right information without guidance, and deliver results that match your expectations on the first attempt. And because no one is watching, asynchronous systems need robust logging and notification so that operators can understand what happened after the fact.

2.2.3   Scheduled Jobs

Unlike the channels we have discussed so far, some work does not wait for an external event or a human request. End-of-day reconciliation, monthly compliance reporting, quarterly reviews, and annual filings all happen on a calendar. For these recurring tasks, time itself becomes the trigger, and the system must initiate work without anyone asking.

Calendar-driven deadlines govern much of legal and financial practice. Litigators live by deadlines: answer the complaint within 21 days, file motions 30 days before hearings, respond to discovery within 30 days. Missing one can mean default judgment or sanctions.

An agentic system can monitor litigation calendars, calculate deadlines while accounting for court holidays and local rules, and escalate as deadlines approach if work remains incomplete. A more sophisticated system might go further, retrieving the complaint a week before the answer is due, extracting the claims, generating a draft answer with standard defenses, and presenting it for attorney review with time to spare.

Financial professionals face analogous deadline pressure: quarterly SEC filings, annual audits, covenant compliance certificates due to lenders, and tax submissions that carry real penalties for delay. The same scheduled-trigger architecture that reminds a litigator about an approaching discovery deadline can remind a fund administrator about an investor reporting obligation.

Periodic compliance checks run on a schedule even when nothing externally triggers a review. At an asset manager, the investment compliance team's system operates every night, checking each portfolio against its investment policy statement, looking for positions that exceed concentration limits, securities that fall outside permitted categories, or exposures that have drifted beyond acceptable ranges. Violations get flagged for review before markets open. Law firms face a parallel challenge with conflicts of interest. A conflicts system can retrieve new docket entries and engagement letters each day, extract party names, and check them against the firm's conflicts database. If the same company name appears on both sides of a matter, the system escalates immediately rather than waiting for someone to notice. These scheduled checks enable continuous monitoring that would be impractical to perform manually across thousands of client accounts or active matters.

End-of-day and end-of-period workflows are critical in both industries. In finance, end-of-day processing is a well-established ritual: when markets close, systems retrieve final prices, mark positions to market, reconcile trades against counterparty confirmations, calculate profit and loss, and generate the risk reports that will be waiting on desks the next morning. If any step fails or produces unexpected results, the system escalates rather than distributing incomplete data. Law firms have their own periodic workflows, though they tend to run on longer cycles. At month-end, a billing system might remind attorneys to enter unbilled time, generate draft invoices based on matter budgets and fee arrangements, and flag anomalies for partner review before bills go to clients. Quarterly, a matter management system might review open matters for staleness and prompt responsible attorneys to update status or close inactive files. The triggers are different, but the architectural pattern is the same: time fires the event, the system performs its work, and humans receive the output or the escalation.

2.2.4   Escalation Events

The previous three channel types bring work into the system from outside: external feeds push events, humans make requests, and scheduled jobs fire on the clock. Escalation events are different. They originate inside the system itself, when an agent reaches a limit and cannot proceed autonomously. The system generates an event signaling that it needs human intervention, transferring control to a decision-maker at precisely the moment when human judgment matters most.

Four types of escalation triggers appear most frequently in practice.

Budget exhaustion occurs when the system approaches resource limits it has been given. These might be token consumption caps, iteration counts, time limits, or cost thresholds. Imagine a due diligence agent working through a data room with thousands of documents. If it burns through its budget analyzing the first hundred contracts without reaching the financial statements, it needs to stop and ask: should I continue with more resources, or should a human reprioritize what I review first? Without this kind of budget-aware escalation, the system either stops arbitrarily or runs up costs without limit.

Low confidence triggers escalation when uncertainty is too high for autonomous action. A research agent might find conflicting authority on a legal question, with a recent circuit court decision that appears to contradict older Supreme Court precedent. Rather than picking one and hoping for the best, the system should surface the conflict and let an attorney decide how to handle it. Similarly, a credit analysis agent encountering a borrower with an unusual corporate structure might recognize that its standard analysis framework does not apply cleanly and escalate for human review rather than forcing the square peg into a round hole.

Approval requirements force escalation for actions that require explicit human authorization regardless of the system's confidence. Some actions are simply too consequential to delegate fully, even when the system is certain it knows the right answer. Filing court documents, sending communications to clients or counterparties, executing trades above a certain size, or making public disclosures all warrant human sign-off. The system may draft the motion, compose the email, or prepare the trade ticket, but a human must authorize the action itself.

Errors and anomalies require human intervention when something unexpected happens. Tools fail, data sources become unavailable, or results do not make sense. A due diligence agent that finds revenue figures in a company's 10-K that do not match the numbers in its earnings press release should not proceed with potentially inconsistent data. A portfolio monitoring agent that cannot reach the pricing service should escalate rather than working with stale prices. These situations require human judgment to determine whether to wait, retry, use alternative sources, or proceed with acknowledged limitations.

We return to escalation design in depth in Section 2.9, including how to calibrate when systems should ask for help versus proceed autonomously, and how to design escalation interfaces that give humans the context they need to make good decisions quickly. The organizational structures that support escalation (such as tiered response models, accountability pathways, and governance reporting) are addressed in Chapter 3.

2.2.5   Surfaces

Triggers and channels are architectural concepts; they answer questions about event routing, message delivery, and system integration. **Surfaces** are user experience concepts; they answer questions about interaction modality, workflow integration, and interface design.

> **Interaction Surfaces**
>
> An **interaction surface** is the user experience modality through which humans engage with an agentic system. Surfaces vary along four dimensions: synchronicity (when results arrive), initiative (who starts the conversation), embodiment (whether the system is visible), and output format (what the system produces).

We include surfaces in this architectural chapter because surface choice constrains architectural decisions: a system designed for conversational interaction needs different trigger handling than one designed for background automation. Architects and UX designers must communicate; when a UX designer specifies that users need real-time research dialogue, the architect must understand what that implies for channel selection and response latency.

Conversational surfaces deserve special attention because they sit at the intersection of architecture and UX. When a litigator types a research question into a chat window, the interface serves two roles simultaneously: it is the pathway through which the human prompt trigger arrives (an architectural function) and the interaction modality through which the user engages with responses (a UX function). This dual role is unique to conversational surfaces. Automation and document surfaces do not receive triggers; they only deliver outputs.

Surface choice matters because it shapes workflow integration. An agentic system with identical capabilities will succeed or fail based partly on whether its surface matches how professionals actually work. Usability researcher Jakob Nielsen argues that generative AI represents the first new user interface paradigm in sixty years, marking a shift from *command-based interaction*, where you tell the computer what to do, to *intent-based outcome specification*, where you tell the computer what you want (Nielsen 2023). But intent-based systems still require interfaces, and those interfaces (the surfaces through which users engage) determine whether the system feels natural or intrusive.

Synchronicity determines when results arrive. Synchronous interactions deliver results while the user waits, as with chat interfaces where you ask a question and watch the response stream in. This suits exploratory work where you refine direction based on what you see. Asynchronous interactions deliver results later through notifications or reports, as with document generation where you specify requirements, do other work, and return when the draft is ready. This suits production tasks where waiting would waste billable time.

Initiative captures who starts the conversation. In pull models, the system waits for the user to initiate. A research assistant that answers questions when asked operates this way, giving the user control over when and whether to engage. In push models, the system reaches out when something needs attention. A docket monitor that alerts you to new filings operates this way, deciding when to interrupt based on relevance and urgency.

Embodiment refers to whether the system is visible in the workflow. Visible systems appear as explicit participants, like a chat avatar or copilot sidebar that makes the agentic system's presence clear. Users know they are interacting with AI and can direct it consciously. Invisible systems operate as infrastructure, like a compliance screening system that flags suspicious transactions in the background. Users experience the outputs without seeing the system that produced them.

Output format determines what the system produces. Conversation turns suit iterative exploration where direction emerges through dialogue, producing chat transcripts from research queries, brainstorming, and strategy discussions. Structured documents suit formal deliverables with defined formats, producing research memos, due diligence reports, and contract summaries ready for distribution. Actions in the world suit automation workflows, where filing a document, sending an alert, or executing a trade produces effects rather than text.

Three primary surfaces dominate current deployments, each suited to different task types and user contexts.

Conversational surfaces present the agentic system as an interactive dialogue partner, best suited for exploratory tasks where users refine direction through iteration, including researching unfamiliar areas, exploring scenarios, and thinking through strategy. The interaction is synchronous and user-initiated. Limitations include the "articulation barrier" (users must express intent in natural language) and lack of visual **affordances** (no menus to browse or buttons to discover capabilities).

Automation surfaces present the agentic system as invisible infrastructure that monitors, analyzes, and acts in the background. Users receive outputs only when something relevant happens. Examples include portfolio surveillance that alerts when positions breach limits, docket monitoring that flags new filings in active matters, and compliance systems that screen transactions against sanctions lists. The interaction is asynchronous and system-initiated.

Automation surfaces suit *monitoring tasks* where continuous human attention is impractical. A compliance officer cannot manually review every transaction, and a litigator cannot check every docket daily. The agentic system handles the routine cases, surfacing only exceptions that require human judgment. The user experience is defined by what *does not* happen, since no alert means no problem.

Document surfaces present the agentic system as a drafting assistant that produces structured work products such as research memos, due diligence reports, deposition summaries, and client presentations. The user specifies requirements, the system produces a document, and the user reviews, edits, and distributes. The interaction is asynchronous because the system works while the user does other things, but it remains user-initiated.

Document surfaces suit *production tasks* with defined deliverables. The associate needs a memo for the partner's review, and the analyst needs a report for the investment committee. The output format matters here because you need a polished document that can be filed, sent to clients, or presented to regulators, not a chat transcript.

> ### Matching Surfaces to Tasks
>
> Surface selection is a design decision, not a technical constraint. Match the surface to how users actually work, not to what the technology makes easiest.

When choosing how users will interact with an agentic system, match the surface to the task type:

- **Exploratory tasks** like research questions, strategy discussions, and ad hoc analysis work best through **chat surfaces** that support iterative refinement.
- **Monitoring tasks** like docket surveillance, compliance screening, and portfolio alerts work best through **automation surfaces** that operate in the background.
- **Production tasks** like research memos, due diligence reports, and regulatory filings work best through **document surfaces** that generate formal deliverables.

Many deployments combine all three surfaces. A litigation support system might offer chat for research, automation for alerts, and document generation for motion drafts. The underlying reasoning capabilities remain constant; only the interaction modality changes.

> ### Surface Mismatches Waste Effort
>
> Forcing chat onto monitoring tasks demands attention no one can sustain. Forcing documents onto exploratory tasks prevents the iteration that produces good results. Match the surface to the work, not the other way around.

The interplay between triggers, channels, and surfaces creates the complete human-agent interface. Table 2.2 illustrates how the same trigger arriving through the same channel can manifest through different surfaces depending on workflow context.

Emerging surfaces include embedded copilots (agentic capabilities integrated into existing applications via sidebars or inline suggestions), ambient interfaces (voice-based interaction, though currently limited by transcription errors in professional contexts), and agentic APIs (machine-to-machine orchestration where the "user" is another system; see Section 2.10).

Surface design draws on decades of human-computer interaction research. What architects need to understand is that surface selection has architectural consequences: conversational surfaces require low-latency response paths, automation surfaces require robust background processing, and document surfaces require generation pipelines. UX designers choose surfaces based on user needs; architects build the infrastructure those surfaces require.

Trigger	Channel	Surface
New court filing	External feed	Automation
New court filing	External feed	Chat
New court filing	External feed	Document
Price threshold crossed	External feed	Automation
Price threshold crossed	External feed	Chat
Price threshold crossed	External feed	Document
Research question	Human prompt	Chat
Report request	Human prompt	Document

Table 2.2: How triggers, channels, and surfaces combine in practice. The same trigger arriving through the same channel can manifest through different surfaces: automation for background monitoring, chat for interactive research, or document generation for formal deliverables.

2.2.6   Evaluation

When evaluating trigger systems, assess five criteria: *coverage* (all relevant event sources), *latency* (acceptable delay for the use case), *reliability* (failure handling and fallbacks), *priority* (distinguishing urgent from routine), and *auditability* (complete trigger logs).

> ## Trigger System Checklist
>
> ☐ **Coverage:** All relevant event sources (feeds, prompts, schedules, escalations) are connected with no gaps
> ☐ **Reliability:** Each channel has documented failure handling, fallbacks, and guaranteed delivery for audit-critical events
> ☐ **Priority:** System can distinguish urgent triggers from routine ones and route them appropriately
> ☐ **Auditability:** Every action traces back to its triggering event with complete logs showing what, when, and through which channel

We have examined the human-agent interface from two disciplinary perspectives. From an architectural standpoint, *triggers* are the events that initiate work, and *channels* are the pathways through which those triggers reach the agent. From a user experience standpoint, *surfaces* are the interaction modalities through which users engage with the agent's capabilities. Architects design trigger routing and channel infrastructure; UX designers choose surfaces that match how professionals actually work. The disciplines address different questions but must align for a system to succeed.

Together, triggers, channels, and surfaces determine how an agentic system fits into professional workflows. A well-designed trigger system ensures no relevant event goes unnoticed. Appropriate channel selection balances latency against reliability. Thoughtful surface choices match interaction modality to task type. And all three must support the audit trails that governance requires, with every action traceable to the trigger that initiated it, through the channel that delivered it, via the surface through which it was experienced.

But triggering is only the beginning. Once an event arrives, the agentic system must:

- **Understand intent**: What is being asked?
- **Perceive information**: What does the system need to know?
- **Take action**: What should the system do?
- **Remember context**: What should persist across sessions?
- **Plan execution**: How should work be decomposed?
- **Recognize completion**: When is the task done?
- **Escalate appropriately**: When should humans intervene?

To see how these questions connect, trace a single event through the system. An external feed delivers a court filing notification, and the system routes it based on matter type and urgency. Depending on the configured surface, a litigator might receive a chat prompt inviting interactive research, a background alert waiting in their queue, or a generated memo summarizing the filing's implications. Whatever the surface, the system retrieves case context from memory, downloads the filed document, analyzes its content, and either proceeds autonomously or escalates for human judgment. Each step in this chain (from trigger to channel to surface to action) represents an architectural decision with consequences for what the system can accomplish and how reliably it performs.

With work arriving through triggers and channels, and users engaging through surfaces, the next question becomes: how does the agentic system understand what is actually being asked? Section 2.3 takes up this problem of intent.

2.3   Intent

How does an agent understand what's being asked? When a partner walks into your office and says "get me up to speed on the Acme acquisition," your first job is understanding what that actually means. You must determine whether this is a quick status check or a request for deep analysis, whether you should answer a specific question or identify all issues, and whether this is urgent work for today's call or background work for next week's meeting. The words you hear are the **instruction**; the underlying purpose that those words point toward is the **intent**.

Every professional develops this skill over time: reading the assignment memo, clarifying ambiguous instructions, and understanding not just what was said but what was meant. Junior associates tend to over-clarify, whereas senior associates internalize firm norms and client expectations and infer appropriately. The best professionals know when to ask and when to proceed.

Agentic systems face the same challenge. The user provides an instruction in natural language, which is inherently ambiguous and sometimes contradictory. Despite this, the agent must extract the user's intent to determine what goal is being pursued, what constraints apply, and what success looks like. This illustrates the second fundamental question: *How does an agent understand what's being asked?*

Four concepts structure this process: instruction, intent, goal, and task. Understanding how they relate, and where gaps arise, is essential for building and governing agentic systems.

Instruction

An **instruction** is the words the user provides: the raw input that starts the process.

"Review this credit agreement for risks."
"Rebalance to reduce tech exposure."
"Get me up to speed on the Acme acquisition."

Instructions are where work begins, but they are rarely complete specifications. The word "risks" raises immediate questions: risks to whom? The lender or borrower? Material risks or all risks? Legal risks, financial risks, or both? "Reduce tech exposure" leaves open the target level, the mechanism (sales, hedges, or both), and tax and timing constraints. "Get me up to speed" specifies neither depth, urgency, nor deliverable format. Instructions are clear enough to start; they are not clear enough to finish.

Pre-LLM systems handled instructions through rigid steps: matching exact words, filling forms, simple if-then checklists. These systems worked for narrow domains with controlled vocabularies but broke on natural language variation. "Find cases on personal jurisdiction" and "What's the law on where you can sue someone?" express similar meanings but look nothing alike to a keyword matcher.

Intent

Intent is the underlying purpose, constraints, and success criteria behind an instruction. Intent captures the human meaning (what the user actually wants, not just what they said). Where an instruction might be "review this credit agreement," the intent might be "identify material risks to the lender by tomorrow for the partner's client call."

This framing assumes the user has clear intent that merely needs to be extracted. Often, they do not. A general counsel asking for "a quick overview of the regulatory landscape" may not understand the domain well enough to know what a useful overview would contain or how comprehensive it needs to be. A partner requesting "a one-page memo on the indemnification issues" may be asking for something impossible if the issues genuinely require five pages to explain competently. A portfolio manager who wants "maximum returns with minimal risk" is expressing a preference, not a coherent goal.

Users operate under their own constraints (time pressure, cognitive load, incomplete domain knowledge) that shape requests in ways that may conflict with the realities of the underlying work. Intent inference must contend not only with unclear expression but with intent that is itself incomplete, conflicted, or impossible to satisfy.

The gap between instruction and intent has always existed; what has changed is our ability to bridge that gap with technological systems. Early AI research on dialogue established that understanding utterances requires inferring the speaker's underlying plans and goals (Allen and Perrault 1980). Large language models dramatically improved intent inference from natural language, particularly after techniques like reinforcement learning from human feedback (RLHF) explicitly optimized models to follow user intent (Ouyang et al. 2022). Where rule-based systems required exact matches, LLMs handle variation, implicit context, and domain-specific jargon. Modern LLMs excel at handling noisy input (misspellings, shorthand, tangential information), resolving references using conversational context, inferring domain-specific meaning, and detecting implicit constraints that professionals take for granted.

Despite these capabilities, intent understanding remains imperfect. As conversations extend, LLMs may lose track of earlier context or constraints. When clarification is needed, LLMs sometimes proceed with a default interpretation rather than asking, resulting in a "helpful but wrong" failure: the agent does *something* reasonable rather than confirming it understood correctly. Professionals also communicate through implication. Phrases like "This needs to be right" signal high stakes, while "When you get a chance" signals low urgency. These signals may not be explicitly parsed by current models.

Goal

A **goal** is the machine-readable specification that intent points toward: the structured outcome that would satisfy the request. As Chapter 1 established, the GPA+IAT framework describes how an agent pursues goals through perception and action. Where intent is "identify material risks to the lender by tomorrow," the goal is "produce a lender-risk memo that meets firm policy and is ready for partner review."

Goals provide the target for planning and the criterion for termination. An agent that understands the goal can determine whether its work is complete: does this memo identify the material risks? Does it meet firm standards? Is it ready for the partner? Without a clear goal, the agent cannot know when to stop. This is the "runaway associate" problem of endless research without a deliverable.

Task

A **task** is the concrete unit of work the agent executes to advance a goal. A single goal typically decomposes into multiple tasks. For the lender-risk memo, tasks might include extracting financial covenants, comparing covenant terms to market standards, identifying collateral coverage gaps, flagging cross-default provisions, and drafting the summary memo.

Tasks are where planning meets execution. Section 2.7 addresses how agents decompose goals into task sequences; Section 2.8 addresses how agents recognize when tasks and goals are complete. Both capabilities depend on clear intent: ambiguous goals yield uncertain plans and unreliable termination criteria.

The flow from instruction to task is: **Instruction** › **Intent** → **Goal** → **Tasks**. Inferring intent bridges the gap between what users say and what they mean. Goals give agents targets to aim for. Tasks give agents concrete work to execute. Failures at any stage propagate forward: misunderstood instructions yield wrong intent; wrong intent yields wrong goals; wrong goals yield wasted tasks.

2.3.1   Bridging the Gap

Traditional enterprise systems classified work using explicit **routing rules**: fixed logic that checked message details and forwarded them to the right handler. A court filing tagged `matter_id=12345` goes straight to litigation monitoring; a portfolio company's SEC filing routes to compliance review. This pattern dominated middleware architecture for decades: message queues, **enterprise service buses (ESBs)**, and workflow engines functioned like a mailroom sorting notices to the right department.

LLM-based agentic systems replace explicit routing logic with semantic reasoning. Instead of maintaining explicit rules for every event type, the model *understands* what kind of work this is. "Review this credit agreement" and "Check this loan doc for problems" express similar intents despite different words; the LLM recognizes both as document review tasks without explicit rules mapping each phrase to a handler.

This architectural shift creates two primary tensions in system design.

The first tension is between flexibility and predictability. Rule-based routing is deterministic: the same input always produces the same classification. LLM-based classification relies on likelihoods and may shift slightly with model updates, prompt phrasing, or context. For regulated applications, this requires additional governance through logging classifications, monitoring for drift, and maintaining override rules for critical categories.

The second tension involves explicit versus implicit knowledge. Routing rules encode domain knowledge explicitly in code, requiring developers to anticipate every category and write rules to match. LLM classification absorbs domain knowledge implicitly through training, recognizing that legal research and case analysis are related without explicit rules. But implicit knowledge is harder to audit because there is no specific rule to inspect, and it may reflect training biases.

Production systems often combine both. Simple, high-volume, time-sensitive tasks use deterministic rules, so a margin call always routes to the trading desk. Complex, ambiguous, or novel requests use LLM reasoning. The rule-based layer handles predictable cases efficiently while the LLM layer handles everything else.

For architects evaluating agentic systems: where must classification be deterministic (regulatory requirements, latency/speed constraints, auditability)? Where does flexibility justify the overhead of LLM reasoning? The answer shapes system design.

Intent Inference Is Not Mind Reading

LLMs infer *probable* intent from language patterns; they do not read minds. Design for clarification, not guessing.

Inference fails when instructions are genuinely ambiguous, when the user's intent differs from typical patterns, when critical context exists outside the conversation (prior meetings, firm norms), or when the user themselves is unclear about what they want. The aim is an agent that surfaces uncertainty and asks, not one that pretends certainty regarding intent.

2.3.2   Goal Extraction from Natural Language

Once the agent receives an instruction, it must extract structured goals that can guide execution. This extraction transforms natural language into actionable specifications through two main processes: intent classification and constraint recognition.

The first step, intent classification, translates the instruction into task types that determine workflow. This step converts raw words into candidate tasks that can advance the underlying goal:

- **Information retrieval**: "What's the current NAV (Net Asset Value)?" "Find the latest 10-K"
- **Research and analysis**: "Research whether we can pierce the corporate veil (hold shareholders liable)"
- **Document review**: "Review the acquisition agreement for change-of-control provisions"
- **Document generation**: "Draft an engagement letter for the Smith matter"
- **Calculation**: "Calculate the IRR (Internal Rate of Return) assuming a 5-year hold"
- **Monitoring**: "Alert me if tech exposure exceeds 30%"

Different task types invoke different tools, planning patterns, and success criteria. A research task requires search and synthesis; a calculation task requires structured computation; a monitoring task requires continuous observation.

Beyond classification, the agent must also recognize entities and constraints. Entity recognition identifies what the task concerns: matters, clients, securities, parties, documents, and jurisdictions. When someone says "Review the Smith acquisition agreement," the agent must recognize a reference to a specific document; "Research Delaware fiduciary duties" references a jurisdiction that shapes which law applies.

Constraint recognition identifies what bounds apply to execution. Temporal constraints include deadlines, as-of dates, and time windows. "By Friday" sets a deadline; "as of year-end 2024" sets a reference date; "over the past quarter" defines a window for analysis. Resource constraints set budget and effort limits, with phrases like "Spend no more than 2 hours" or "focus on Articles 3 and 4" bounding scope. Format constraints specify how deliverables should appear: "Summarize in one page" constrains length, "prepare a memo for the file" specifies format, and "I need something to show the client" signals an external audience requiring different tone and detail.

Two additional constraint types often remain unstated. Audience and privilege constraints determine who will see the output and what confidentiality must be preserved. Risk and compliance constraints set limits that professionals internalize but rarely articulate: a compliance review implicitly requires flagging violations, and a client communication implicitly requires privilege protection.

Once extracted, these components can be organized into structured goal representations that guide execution. These representations resemble short assignment memos that the planning system can act on (Section 2.7) and the termination system can measure against (Section 2.8).

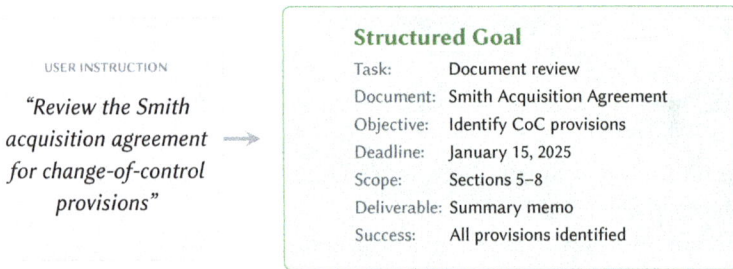

USER INSTRUCTION

"Review the Smith acquisition agreement for change-of-control provisions"

Structured Goal

Task: Document review
Document: Smith Acquisition Agreement
Objective: Identify CoC provisions
Deadline: January 15, 2025
Scope: Sections 5–8
Deliverable: Summary memo
Success: All provisions identified

Figure 2.1: Goal extraction transforms natural language instructions into structured specifications that guide agent execution and define success criteria.

2.3.3   Ambiguity Detection and Clarification

Not all instructions can be unambiguously interpreted. The agent must detect ambiguity and decide whether to clarify or proceed. The decision depends on two factors: ambiguity severity and action stakes.

When both stakes and ambiguity are low, the agent should proceed with its best interpretation. If someone asks "What's Apple's market cap?" and there is slight uncertainty about whether they mean Apple Inc. or Apple Hospitality REIT, the dominant interpretation is obvious and the cost of being wrong is low since correction is easy. When stakes remain low but ambiguity is high, a brief clarification prevents wasted effort. If someone asks "Research the statute of limitations" without specifying the claim type, a quick question saves hours of potentially misdirected work.

When stakes are high but ambiguity is low, the agent should confirm before acting. If the instruction is clear but consequential, such as "File this motion," confirmation prevents irreversible errors even when the agent is confident it understood correctly. When both stakes and ambiguity are high, thorough clarification is essential. If someone says "Handle the regulatory response" for a complex matter, extended clarification is appropriate before taking any action.

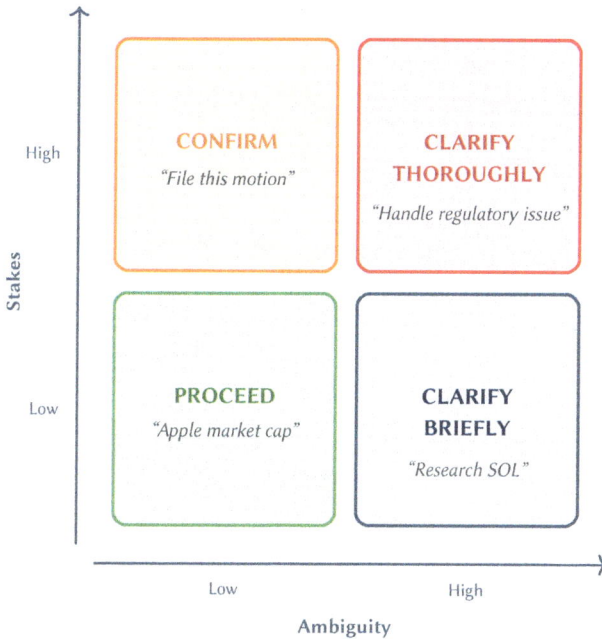

Figure 2.2: Decision matrix for when agents should clarify intent.   Stakes measure consequence of error; ambiguity measures interpretation confidence.

Effective clarification has four characteristics. It is specific, asking "Which jurisdiction's statute of limitations: Delaware or New York?" rather than "Can you clarify?" It is contextual, referencing what the agent already understands: "I understand you want me to review the credit agreement. Should I focus on lender protections, borrower obligations, or both?" It is actionable, offering options rather than open-ended questions: "Should I (a) provide a comprehensive review of all provisions, (b) focus on the financial covenants, or (c) flag only provisions that differ from our standard template?" And it is bounded, limiting clarification rounds. If the agent needs extensive clarification, it may be the wrong tool for the task, or the user may need to think through requirements before delegating.

Poor: "Can you clarify?"

Better: "Should I assess lender risks, borrower risks, or both?"

Best: "You asked to reduce tech exposure. Should I (a) sell tech to 25% target, (b) hedge with options, or (c) add non-tech positions? Which deadline matters: this week or month-end reporting?"

Research has documented that LLMs sometimes select a default interpretation instead of asking for clarification, even when ambiguity is significant (Zhang et al.

2024; Wang et al. 2024b). This "proceed without asking" behavior creates real risk: the agent interprets "review the contract" as a surface-level summary when the user expected deep issue-spotting, delivering work product that is technically responsive but wrong.

Several strategies can mitigate this tendency: prompt engineering that emphasizes clarification for ambiguous requests, confidence thresholds that trigger clarification below a certainty level, user training to provide detailed initial instructions, and checkpoint reviews before significant work begins. From a governance perspective, teams should monitor for cases where the agent proceeded confidently but delivered unexpected results. These cases may indicate calibration problems in ambiguity detection.

Ambiguity detection assumes the user has clear intent that was merely expressed unclearly. Sometimes the problem runs deeper.

> ### When Intent Itself Is Unclear or Conflicted
>
> **Domain expertise gaps**: The user may not understand the subject well enough to specify what they need. "Give me the key issues" presumes the user knows what issues exist and which matter most, knowledge they may be asking the agent to provide.
>
> **Conflicted constraints**: The user may want contradictory things. A one-page memo on a complex acquisition may be impossible without sacrificing the accuracy or completeness that makes the memo useful.
>
> **Unexamined tradeoffs**: The user may not have considered tradeoffs they would care about if surfaced, such as speed versus thoroughness, cost versus quality, or brevity versus nuance.

When an agent detects these deeper problems, it should surface the conflict instead of silently resolving it: "You asked for a one-page summary, but covering the indemnification, representations, and covenant issues adequately would demand three to four pages. Would you prefer (a) a one-page overview that flags issues without detailed analysis, (b) a longer memo with full analysis, or (c) detailed treatment of just one area?" This is harder than detecting ambiguous expression because it needs recognizing when the user's own mental model is incomplete or conflicted, and surfacing that recognition without appearing to second-guess or condescend.

2.3.4 Constraint Identification

Beyond explicit instructions, agents must identify constraints that bound acceptable execution. These constraints fall into several categories that often interact.

Temporal constraints include deadlines and time windows. Some are explicit, like "by Friday." Others are implicit, such as court filing deadlines calculated from procedural rules. Still others are contextual: "before the board meeting" requires knowing when the meeting is scheduled. Resource constraints set budget and effort limits. Token budgets limit API costs; time budgets limit calendar impact; scope constraints focus effort on high-value areas.

Scope constraints define what is in and out of bounds. "Focus on Articles 3 and 4" excludes other articles; "just the Delaware analysis" excludes other jurisdictions. Format and style constraints specify how deliverables should appear: memo versus email versus presentation, formal versus casual tone, internal versus client-facing audience. Risk and compliance constraints specify what must be avoided: privilege protection, conflicts of interest, regulatory restrictions, and confidentiality obligations. These constraints often apply implicitly based on context.

Professionals operate under many constraints they rarely state explicitly. When a partner says "research Section 10(b) liability," implicit constraints include:

- Use authoritative sources (binding precedent, not blog posts)
- Focus on the relevant jurisdiction (probably the circuit where the case is filed)
- Assume current law (not historical analysis unless specified)
- Protect privilege (don't disclose strategy in external searches)
- Operate within budget norms (don't spend 40 hours on a 2-hour task)

Agents must infer these constraints from context, domain knowledge, and organizational norms. Memory systems (Section 2.6) are essential here: they preserve firm-specific expectations across tasks, user profiles accumulate individual preferences, and matter context provides case-specific constraints that sharpen future intent interpretations.

2.3.5   Validation and Domain Examples

Before executing, agents should validate their understanding of intent. Several patterns support this validation.

Reflection and summarization involve the agent pausing (much like an associate double-checking their notes) to restate its understanding before proceeding, giving the user an opportunity to correct misunderstandings before work begins. **Chunked validation**, like partner check-ins after each memo section, breaks complex tasks into phases rather than validating all at once. After completing research, the agent summarizes findings and confirms direction before drafting. After drafting, it confirms the approach before finalizing. Each checkpoint prevents error propagation.

Confidence signaling calls for the agent to indicate how confident it is in its own understanding. When confidence is high, the agent can proceed with light oversight; when confidence is low, the right move is to pause and ask for clarification instead of pressing ahead. Clear confidence signaling helps users decide how much review is needed and whether to treat the output as a draft, a starting point, or a near-final product.

To illustrate, observe how intent extraction and validation work together for a legal task. Given the instruction "Review this credit agreement for risks," the agent classifies this as a document review task and detects that "risks" is ambiguous (risks to whom? what types?). Context gathering reveals this is a lender-side engagement for a senior secured facility. The agent infers implicit constraints (focus on lender risks, prioritize material issues, assume current market terms as baseline) and clarifies: "I'll review from the lender's perspective, focusing on credit risk, collateral coverage, and covenant adequacy. Should I also flag documentation risks (drafting issues, missing provisions) or focus only on substantive credit terms?"

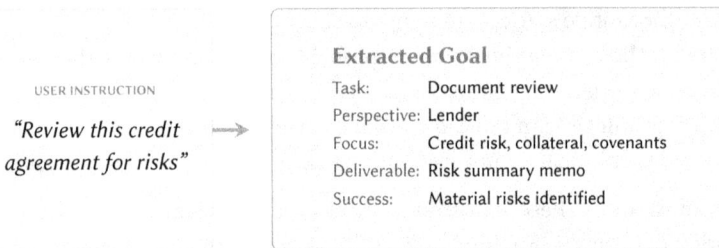

USER INSTRUCTION

"Review this credit
agreement for risks"   ⟶

Extracted Goal

Task:	Document review
Perspective:	Lender
Focus:	Credit risk, collateral, covenants
Deliverable:	Risk summary memo
Success:	Material risks identified

Figure 2.3: Goal extraction for a credit agreement review, showing how ambiguous instructions are refined through context gathering into structured specifications.

The agent validates: "I'll prepare a memo identifying material risks to the lender, comparing key terms to market standards, and recommending negotiation points. I'll have a draft for your review by tomorrow afternoon."

The same pattern applies to financial tasks. Given the instruction "Rebalance to reduce tech exposure," the agent classifies this as a portfolio action task and immediately detects multiple ambiguities: how much reduction? through what mechanism? with what constraints? Context gathering reveals current tech exposure at 35% against a 25% target. Through clarification dialogue, the agent confirms the user wants to reach target through sales while minimizing tax impact, preferring loss harvesting (selling assets at a loss to offset gains) and long-term gains over short-term.

Portfolio Assistant

Rebalance to reduce tech exposure

Current tech exposure is 35%. What's your target?
Should I reduce through sales or reallocation? Any
tax considerations?

EXTRACTED GOAL
Task: Rebalancing
Target: 25% tech
Method: Sales
Constraints: Tax-optimized
Approval: Required

Get to 25% through sales. Minimize taxes;
use loss harvesting.

I'll prepare a plan to reduce tech from 35% to 25%
via sales, optimized for tax efficiency. I'll need your
approval before executing.

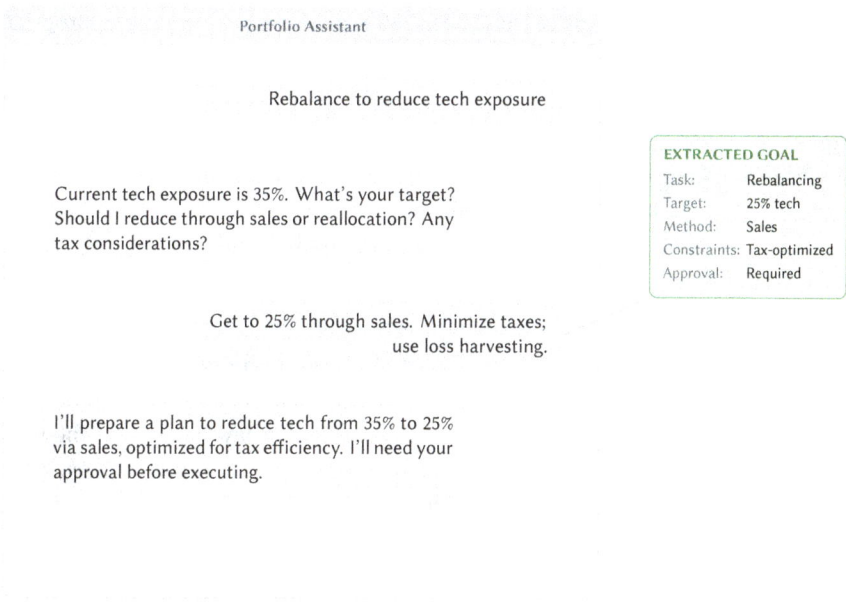

Figure 2.4: Clarification dialogue for a portfolio rebalancing task. The agent detects ambiguity, gathers constraints through targeted questions, and extracts a validated goal before proceeding.

Intent Understanding Is Continuous

Intent extraction is not a one-time step at task initiation. As the agent works, it may discover:

- The original understanding was incomplete (new constraints emerge)
- The user's intent has evolved (priorities shift mid-task)
- Implicit constraints conflict (cannot optimize for both)
- The task is impossible as specified (constraints are mutually exclusive)

Effective agents surface these discoveries through clarification instead of proceeding with outdated or impossible goals. Intent understanding is iterative, not instantaneous.

Intent understanding connects to other framework questions. Memory (Section 2.6) improves intent extraction over time by preserving user preferences, matter history, and firm norms. Planning (Section 2.7) depends on clear intent; extracted goals feed the planning system, while ambiguous intent propagates through the plan as uncertainty. Governance must address intent misalignment as a core risk, verifying goal alignment before deployment and monitoring for drift during operation. Chapter 3 examines these controls through the lens of goal dynamics calibration, distinguishing static, adaptive, and negotiated goals and specifying appropriate oversight for each.

Understanding intent bridges the gap between what users say (instruction) and what they mean (intent), shaping the goals and tasks the agent will plan. Clarification beats guessing when ambiguity is significant and stakes are high. Constraints such as time, scope, audience, compliance, and budget matter as much as goals. Validation prevents wasted effort by confirming understanding before significant work begins.

With triggers delivering work and intent extraction revealing what's being asked, the agent faces a practical problem: extracted goals require information the agent does not yet have. The credit agreement analysis task requires the actual credit agreement. The research question requires access to case law databases. The rebalancing plan requires current portfolio positions and market prices. Understanding what you need to do is not the same as having what you need to do it.

Section 2.4 examines the next question: how does an agent find things out? Perception tools (the interfaces to external information sources) bridge the gap between understanding a task and executing it.

2.4   Perception

How does an agent find things out? Understanding what someone wants is not the same as being able to deliver it. The previous section examined how agents interpret instructions, extracting goals, detecting ambiguity, and gathering the context needed to proceed. But even an agent that perfectly understands "Research Ninth Circuit authority on personal jurisdiction for foreign corporations" cannot help if it lacks access to case law databases. Where Chapter 1 introduced perception as the ability to observe the world, we now examine the concrete mechanisms (tools and integrations) that enable agents to gather the information they need. An agent that correctly interprets "Analyze this credit agreement from the lender's perspective" is useless without the credit agreement itself.

This constraint will feel familiar to anyone who has onboarded a new professional. A junior associate's effectiveness depends as much on access as on reasoning ability. Can they query Westlaw? Do they have credentials for the Bloomberg terminal? Can they search the firm's precedent database and document management system? The answers to these questions determine which problems they can solve. A brilliant analyst without access to portfolio data reasons in a vacuum; a talented associate without access to the case file works blind.

Agentic systems face exactly the same constraint. A large language model can reason impressively about legal doctrines and financial concepts, but without integrations into external or internal sources, it cannot access current case law, live market prices, client documents, or regulatory filings. These connections are what we call *perception tools*: the interfaces through which an agent observes the world beyond its training data.

Tools and Perception

A **tool** is a function that allows an agent to interact with external systems. **Perception tools** are the subset that are read-only: they let the agent observe without changing anything. When an agent queries a database, retrieves a document, or fetches market data, the external system's state remains unchanged.

Perception defines the boundary of what information the agent can access, and that boundary shapes every downstream decision. An agent with access to public filings reasons differently than one with access to internal deal documents. An agent that can query real-time market data operates differently than one limited to end-of-day prices.

Here we examine perception: the read-only tools that let agents gather the information they need. The next section, on action, examines write tools that let agents change things in the world. The distinction matters for governance: reading a document and sending an email carry fundamentally different risks, and your controls should reflect that difference. Section 2.5 develops these distinctions and the different oversight mechanisms each requires.

2.4.1 Perception Tool Categories

Not all perception tools work the same way, and choosing the right tool for the task matters. Perception tools generally fall into three categories: information retrieval, document processing, and computation.

Information retrieval tools query external platforms and databases to bring back answers. On the legal side, these tools connect to research services like Westlaw and Lexis in the United States, Beck-Online in Germany, LawNet in Singapore, and similar platforms in other jurisdictions, allowing agents to search case law, retrieve full opinions, check citing references, and download court filings. On the finance side, similar tools connect to platforms like Bloomberg, FactSet, or Refinitiv, enabling agents to pull real-time prices, retrieve company fundamentals, and access analyst research. Many organizations also have internal knowledge bases, including document management systems, deal archives, and precedent databases, that agents need to search to find prior work product relevant to a current matter.

Document processing tools transform raw files into data an agent can actually work with. A credit agreement arrives as a PDF; a financial statement comes as a scanned image; a data room contains thousands of files in mixed formats. Before an agent can reason about this content, it needs to extract the text (using OCR for scanned documents), identify what type of document each file is, and pull out structured information like party names, dates, and dollar amounts. During due diligence, for example, an agent reviewing a data room must distinguish contracts from correspondence, extract key terms from each agreement, and organize findings in a way that supports analysis. Without document processing tools, the agent sees only filenames and metadata.

Computation tools generate new information through calculation rather than lookup. Take deadline calculation: the Federal Rules of Civil Procedure require an answer within 21 days of service (Legal Information Institute 2024), but determining the actual due date requires accounting for weekends, court holidays, and local rules. That is a computational task, not a database query. Citation formatters perform a similar function, converting case information into proper Bluebook or other citation styles. In finance, computation tools normalize security identifiers (mapping between tickers, CUSIPs, and ISINs), calculate risk metrics like Value at Risk from position data, or derive analytics that inform investment decisions. These tools produce new information for the agent to use without changing anything in the external world.

2.4.2   In-Context Learning and Retrieval

Before examining specific retrieval mechanisms, we must understand the fundamental capability that makes retrieval useful: **in-context learning**. This concept is central to how modern language models work and why retrieval matters.

In-Context Learning

In-context learning (ICL) is the ability of large language models to learn from information provided in their input, without any update to the model's underlying parameters (Brown et al. 2020). When you provide examples, documents, or instructions in a prompt, the model adapts its responses based on that context. This is not "learning" in the traditional machine learning sense of updating weights; it is learning *within the conversation*.

In-context learning is what makes retrieval valuable. When an agent retrieves a relevant statute or prior memo and includes it in its prompt, the model can reason about that specific content even though it never saw it during training. The model's behavior changes based on what appears in its context window.

In-context learning explains why agents can work with information far newer than their training data. A model trained in 2024 can analyze a regulation enacted in 2025, provided that regulation appears in its context. The limitation is the **context window**: the maximum amount of text the model can process at once. Context windows have expanded rapidly (from thousands of tokens to hundreds of thousands, with some models now accepting a million or more), and this trend will likely continue. But raw capacity tells only part of the story. Cost, speed, and quality of results vary widely when operating on large amounts of input. A model may technically accept a million tokens while producing degraded results on tasks requiring attention to details scattered throughout. Professional knowledge bases contain millions of documents regardless; the gap between what fits in context and what exists in the world creates the need for retrieval.

The practical limits of context windows explain much of the value of agentic systems. Rather than attempting to process an entire knowledge base in a single prompt (which would exceed limits and degrade quality regardless), an agent decomposes work into focused steps, retrieves only what is relevant to each step, and reasons over smaller, manageable contexts.

This is not merely automation; it is an architectural solution to a fundamental constraint. Planning (Section 2.7) breaks complex tasks into subtasks, ensuring each retrieval step is targeted rather than overwhelming. Retrieval fetches specific information for each subtask. The LLM operates within its effective range on each step, even when the overall task would be impossible to handle monolithically.

Why Decomposition Matters

Decomposition explains both why agentic systems are powerful and why they fail in predictable ways. The reliability cliff (Section 2.8) shows that short, focused tasks succeed while long tasks fail; this occurs precisely because decomposition keeps individual steps within the model's effective operating range, but errors compound across many steps.

Retrieval Methods. To retrieve relevant information from large collections, we need a way to find what matters. Several approaches exist, each with distinct strengths:

Keyword and boolean search is the oldest and most familiar approach. Platforms like Westlaw, Lexis, and Bloomberg have offered sophisticated keyword search for decades. Boolean operators (AND, OR, NOT), proximity searches, and field-specific queries give users precise control. When you need documents containing exact terms (such as a specific case citation, a statutory section, or a company name), keyword search excels. Its limitation is vocabulary mismatch: a search for "breach of fiduciary duty" will not find documents discussing "violation of trust obligations" unless both phrases happen to appear.

BM25 and probabilistic search extends keyword matching with statistical weighting (Robertson and Zaragoza 2009), building on **TF-IDF** (Term Frequency-Inverse Document Frequency). TF-IDF weights terms by how often they appear in a document relative to how common they are across the corpus. A term that appears frequently in one document but rarely elsewhere signals that document's relevance more strongly than a common term appearing everywhere. BM25 refines TF-IDF with saturation functions that prevent very frequent terms from dominating scores. The method requires no machine learning infrastructure, just an inverted index, making it fast, interpretable, and cheap to operate. BM25 remains the baseline retriever in academic benchmarks and powers many production search systems.

Embedding-based semantic search uses machine learning to encode meaning numerically. An **embedding** is a vector (a list of numbers) that represents semantic content. The goal is that similar concepts should produce similar vectors, while different concepts produce distant vectors. When this works well, phrases like "breach of fiduciary duty" and "violation of trust obligations" have embeddings close together in vector space, even though they share no words. This enables *meaning matching* rather than vocabulary matching.

Embedding quality varies significantly across models and tasks. Different embedding models excel at different objectives: some are optimized for clustering documents by topic, others for matching semantically similar sentences, and still others for asymmetric retrieval where short queries must find longer passages. A model trained for one task may perform poorly on another. Legal-specific or financial-domain models may outperform general-purpose ones for professional content, but this depends on training data and task alignment. The infrastructure cost is also higher than traditional search: you need embedding models, vector storage, and similarity search capabilities.

Structured queries retrieve from databases and APIs. An agent checking a company's SEC filings queries EDGAR; an agent researching a case retrieves from a court's electronic filing system. These are not "search" in the traditional sense; they are direct data access. However, they serve the same function in RAG: finding relevant information to inject into context.

Hybrid approaches combine methods. A common pattern uses BM25 for initial retrieval (fast, cheap, catches exact matches) followed by semantic reranking (slower, more expensive, captures meaning). Many production systems blend keyword and semantic scores, getting the best of both approaches.

No Single Method Dominates

The right retrieval method depends on whether you need exact matching (keywords, BM25), conceptual similarity (embeddings), or structured data access (database queries). Most professional systems use hybrid approaches, combining methods to balance precision and cost.

Vector Stores for Embedding-Based Search. Most professionals have conceptual familiarity with traditional keyword search from years of using Westlaw, Lexis, Bloomberg, or even web search engines. Embedding-based search operates differently and may be less intuitive: instead of matching words, the system matches meaning by comparing numerical vectors in high-dimensional space. Understanding this infrastructure helps when evaluating agentic systems that rely on semantic retrieval. Storing and searching millions of vectors efficiently requires specialized infrastructure.

Vector Stores

A **vector store** (or vector database) is a system optimized for storing embeddings and performing similarity search. Given a query embedding, a vector store returns the most similar document embeddings from its collection. Vector stores use specialized indexing structures (like HNSW or IVF) that make approximate nearest-neighbor search practical at scale.

Vector stores are *infrastructure*, the retrieval mechanism that powers semantic search. They are not the same as the retrieval pattern itself.

Organizations need not adopt entirely new infrastructure to use vector search. Traditional relational databases are rapidly adding vector capabilities; databases such as PostgreSQL now offer vector extensions, and most major cloud providers include native vector search in their managed database offerings. For firms with established database infrastructure, this convergence means semantic search can be added alongside existing systems rather than requiring a parallel technology stack. The trade-off is that purpose-built vector databases may offer better performance at scale, while integrated solutions offer simpler operations and unified data management.

Knowledge graph retrieval takes a different approach. Rather than matching meaning through vector similarity, **knowledge graphs** represent entities and their relationships explicitly: corporate structures, ownership chains, party relationships, regulatory hierarchies. An agent researching a company can traverse the graph to find subsidiaries, board members, or regulatory filings, following connections that semantic similarity alone would miss. Graph databases (such as Neo4j) power this approach. For legal and financial applications where relationships matter (who owns whom, who advised whom, which entities share directors), graph retrieval complements vector search. Some systems combine both: vector search finds semantically relevant documents, then graph traversal enriches results with related entities and context.

Retrieval-Augmented Generation (RAG). With these retrieval methods in hand, we can now define RAG precisely.

Retrieval-Augmented Generation (RAG)

Retrieval-Augmented Generation (RAG) is a *prompt pattern*, not a software system or mathematical technique (Lewis et al. 2020). RAG augments a model's context with retrieved information before generation. The pattern has three steps:

1. **Retrieve**: Given a query, find relevant content using *any* retrieval method, including keyword search, BM25, embeddings, database queries, API calls, or combinations thereof.
2. **Augment**: Insert the retrieved content into the model's prompt as additional context.
3. **Generate**: The model produces a response informed by both its training and the retrieved content.

RAG works because of in-context learning. The retrieved content appears in the prompt, and the model adapts its response to incorporate that specific information. The retrieval step is completely method-agnostic: what matters is getting relevant content into context, not how you find it.

The distinction matters for system evaluation. A system's retrieval infrastructure (whether keyword index, vector store, database, external API, or some hybrid) determines its search capabilities and performance characteristics. The RAG pattern it implements (single-stage, multi-stage, or reranked) shapes how effectively it surfaces relevant content. These are separate architectural decisions with different tradeoffs, and understanding both helps you assess whether a system fits your needs.

> ### RAG Is Retrieval-Agnostic
>
> A common misconception equates RAG with embeddings and vector stores. In practice, any retrieval method works: keyword search, BM25, database queries, or API calls. The "embedding plus vector store" pattern dominates tutorials because it handles semantic similarity well, but many production systems use simpler approaches that leverage existing search infrastructure.

2.4.3 Model Context Protocol (MCP)

One of the persistent challenges in building agentic systems is integration. Every database, document management system, and market data feed has its own interface. Historically, connecting an agent to a new information source meant writing custom code for that specific system. The Model Context Protocol (MCP) addresses this by standardizing how agents access external capabilities (Anthropic 2024; Anthropic 2025a).

Figure 2.5 illustrates the three-tier architecture. The **MCP Host** is the agent application itself; it manages access control and coordinates connections, functioning like a firm's IT department deciding which systems a new employee can use. Each **MCP Client** maintains a connection to one **MCP Server**. Servers expose their capabilities through standardized primitives that clients discover and invoke via JSON-RPC.

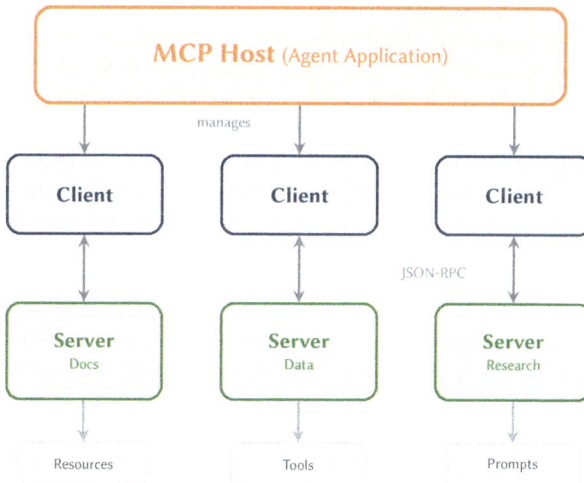

Figure 2.5: MCP architecture. The Host manages access control. Each Client connects to one Server. Servers expose primitives: Resources (read-only data), Tools (executable functions), and Prompts (reusable templates).

Servers expose three types of primitives. **Resources** provide read-only data access, including document repositories, market data feeds, and regulatory databases. The read-only designation matters: an agent with resource access can retrieve documents but cannot modify them. **Tools** are executable functions that can change state by filing documents, sending messages, or executing queries. **Prompts** are reusable templates encoding standard procedures, such as checklists, SOPs, and structured workflows that ensure consistency.

For perception, Resources are the primary primitive. An agent perceives external information by querying Resources exposed by MCP Servers. Separating Resources (read-only) from Tools (read-write) enables fine-grained access control that mirrors how organizations already manage permissions.

The integration landscape is shifting. Document management systems, e-discovery platforms, and financial data providers increasingly offer APIs. Some legal research providers are beginning to follow. As more systems expose MCP-compatible interfaces, the range of information sources available to agents expands.

> ### Standards Reduce Integration Costs
>
> Without MCP, connecting 10 agents to 10 tools requires 100 custom integrations. With MCP, the same setup requires only 20 implementations; each agent and each tool learns the protocol once. Recent benchmarks found over ten thousand MCP servers in the ecosystem (Mo et al. 2025).

> ### MCP Is Evolving Rapidly
>
> The MCP specification has undergone significant revision since its initial release, and the ecosystem remains immature. Many third-party MCP servers do not fully implement the specification, particularly around Resources (often omitted in favor of Tools) and authentication (frequently absent or non-standard). Before deploying MCP integrations in production, verify that servers implement the primitives and security controls your use case requires. Expect breaking changes as the protocol matures.

2.4.4   Institutional Memory

Memory systems (Section 2.6) serve as perception tools for institutional knowledge. The retrieval concepts introduced above (embeddings, vector stores, and RAG) enable agents to perceive accumulated expertise that would otherwise be inaccessible.

When an agent queries a precedent database using the RAG pattern (Section 2.4.2), it perceives institutional knowledge through in-context learning. The retrieved content appears in the agent's prompt, allowing it to reason about specific precedents, prior analyses, and established approaches. A search for "breach of fiduciary duty" retrieves documents about "violation of trust obligations" because their embeddings are similar, not because they share keywords.

This mechanism enables perception into knowledge bases far too large to fit in any model's context window. A law firm's precedent database might contain decades of work product; a financial institution's research archive might span thousands of analyst reports. No agent can hold all of this in active context. RAG allows selective retrieval: the agent perceives only the most relevant fragments, guided by semantic similarity to the current task.

Institutional memory provides access to prior work product. When drafting a new registration statement, an agent can perceive prior S-1 filings (IPO registrations), SEC comment histories, and successful disclosure language. This access allows current work to build on verified precedents rather than starting from first principles.

Memory-as-perception distinguishes experienced agents from novices. A junior associate reasons from what they learned in law school; a senior associate draws on pattern recognition from hundreds of matters. Memory provides agents with this accumulated experience, but only if the retrieval infrastructure connects them to the right knowledge at the right time. Section 2.6 develops these requirements in detail, including how memory systems must enforce the authority, temporal validity, and isolation constraints introduced above.

2.4.5 Domain Requirements

Perception for regulated professional services requires specialized enhancements. General-purpose search is insufficient; professional agents require authority tracking, jurisdictional awareness, and confidentiality boundaries.

Authority and Verification. Information varies in authority. Perception systems must track provenance to ensure reliability. Authority weighting ranks primary sources (statutes, binding precedent) above secondary sources (law reviews, news). When searching for "insider trading liability," a Supreme Court opinion outranks a commentary article. Source verification confirms that retrieved information originates from the claimed source. Perception tools must return verifiable citations, not just text. Currency validation ensures the authority remains valid. Integrated citators (like Shepard's or KeyCite) verify that retrieved cases have not been overruled.

Jurisdiction and Temporal Scope. Legal and regulatory information is bounded by jurisdiction. California precedent does not bind Texas courts; SEC rules differ from CFTC rules. Perception tools must filter results by relevant jurisdiction. Temporal validity is equally critical. Laws change, and financial data expires. Perception systems must track effective dates. In finance, validity varies by context: milliseconds for trading prices, quarters for compliance reporting. Identifier resolution manages the proliferation of formats. "123 F.3d 456" and "123 F3d 456" refer to the same case. Financial identifiers include tickers, CUSIPs, and LEIs (Legal Entity Identifiers). Perception must normalize these to ensure consistent retrieval.

Matter and Client Isolation. Critically, perception must respect confidentiality boundaries. Whether a human or AI, an agent working on Matter A cannot perceive documents from adverse Matter B. This enforcement of **ethical walls** arguably must occur at the perception layer. In financial contexts, an agent advising Client X cannot perceive material non-public information (MNPI) from Client Y's engagement. Every perception event must be logged, capturing the agent, the query, and the matter context. This audit trail enables compliance review and breach detection. See Section 2.6 for detailed treatment of isolation requirements; Chapter 3 addresses the professional responsibility obligations, including attorney confidentiality duties and fiduciary obligations, that mandate these controls.

2.4.6   Tool Design Principles

Robust perception tools follow design principles that enable reliable operation in professional environments.

Single Responsibility. Each tool should perform one function well. Poorly designed tools bundle multiple functions (searching, formatting, and validation) into opaque interfaces. Untyped return values obscure what callers can expect.

Poor Design: Bundled Functions, Untyped Returns

```python
def legal_research(query: str) -> dict:
    """Returns... something. Good luck."""
    ...
```

When such a tool fails, diagnosing the error is difficult. A better approach separates tools by function with typed returns. This allows the agent to compose them and isolates failures.

Better Design: Single Responsibility, Typed Returns

```python
def search_cases(query: str, jurisdiction: str) -> list[Citation]:
    """Returns matching citations from case law database."""

def retrieve_case(citation: Citation) -> CaseText:
    """Fetches full text for a specific citation."""

def shepardize(citation: Citation) -> CitatorResult:
    """Checks validity: good law, distinguished, overruled."""

def format_citation(case: CaseText, style: str) -> str:
    """Converts to Bluebook, ALWD, or other format."""
```

Graceful Failure. Production systems inevitably fail. Tools should return informative errors rather than generic exceptions. A poor approach raises exceptions that provide no context.

Poor: Opaque Exception

```python
def retrieve_case(citation: str) -> dict:
    result = db.query(citation)
    return result["text"]  # raises KeyError if not found
```

A better approach uses typed result objects that make success and failure explicit.

Better: Typed Result with Structured Errors

```python
class CaseNotFoundError(BaseModel):
    citation: str
    reason: str
    suggestions: list[str]

def retrieve_case(citation: Citation) -> CaseText |
    CaseNotFoundError:
    """Returns case text or structured error with recovery options."
    """
    if not (result := db.query(citation)):
      return CaseNotFoundError(
        citation=str(citation),
        reason="Case may not be in database",
        suggestions=["Check citation format", "Try alternative
        reporter"]
      )
    return CaseText(...)
```

In professional practice, graceful failure prevents malpractice. When an agent cannot find authority, it must report that explicitly rather than proceeding silently.

Least Privilege and Rate Limiting. Perception tools should request minimum necessary permissions. A legal research tool requires read access to case databases, not write access to the document management system. If a compromised agent gains perception credentials, damage is limited to information disclosure rather than destruction. Rate limiting addresses a common failure mode: infinite search loops. Tools should track invocation frequency and refuse requests beyond reasonable thresholds. If an agent searches five times without results, the tool should force a stop and escalation (Section 2.9).

2.4.7   Evaluation

When evaluating agentic systems, you should assess perception against criteria that matter for professional practice.

Coverage determines which sources the agent can access. A litigation agent that queries Westlaw but not state-specific databases has incomplete coverage. You must map available perception tools against information needs to identify gaps.

Retrieval quality measures whether the agent finds relevant information. Test with known-good queries where the correct result is established. Measure both

precision (the fraction of retrieved documents that are actually relevant) and **recall** (the fraction of all relevant documents that the system successfully retrieves). These metrics will be familiar to legal professionals from **technology-assisted review** (TAR), the use of machine learning to identify relevant documents during e-discovery, where courts have recognized precision and recall as the standard measures of retrieval effectiveness (Grossman and Cormack 2011). The same framework applies to agent perception: high precision means the agent does not waste time on irrelevant results; high recall means the agent does not miss important authorities. The tradeoff between them (casting a wider net improves recall but may reduce precision) is a design decision that should be calibrated to the task's risk profile.

Verification confirms that the system distinguishes authoritative from secondary sources. You must ensure that retrieved information is traceable to its source and that citations are independently verifiable.

Access controls ensure that permissions are appropriate. The agent must access only what it should, and confidentiality boundaries must hold across matter and client lines.

Failure handling reveals system behavior when perception fails. Does it retry, try alternatives, or escalate? It must not crash or proceed with incomplete information.

Audit capability confirms that every perception event is logged. You must be able to reconstruct what information the agent accessed during a task for compliance review.

Perception Capability Checklist

- ☐ **Coverage:** Map available perception tools against information needs and identify gaps in accessible sources
- ☐ **Retrieval quality:** Test with known-good queries and measure both precision (relevance) and recall (completeness)
- ☐ **Source verification:** Confirm citations are traceable, authoritative sources are distinguished from secondary ones
- ☐ **Access controls:** Verify matter/client isolation holds and permissions are scoped to minimum necessary access
- ☐ **Failure handling and audit:** Test failure scenarios (retry, escalation) and confirm all perception events are logged

---

Perception enables agents to gather information, but professional value ultimately requires effecting change: filing documents, sending communications, executing trades. This distinction between observing the world and changing it is fundamental to agent architecture, and the protocols we use reflect it. MCP, introduced earlier in this section, explicitly separates **Resources** (read-only data access) from **Tools** (operations that modify state). A single MCP server might expose both capabilities. For example, a document management system could offer read access to files alongside the ability to create, modify, or delete them. However, the protocol distinguishes these so that access control and governance can treat them differently.

The distinction matters because the consequences of failure differ fundamentally. When perception tools fail (such as when a search returns wrong results or a document fails to load), the external world remains unchanged. The agent can retry, try alternatives, or escalate to human review without having caused any harm beyond wasted time. Action tools carry different stakes entirely. They file documents that become part of court records, send emails that reach recipient inboxes, execute trades that transfer ownership at market prices. Once executed, many actions cannot be undone, or can only be undone at significant cost. The agent's mistakes become facts in the world.

Section 2.5 examines action capabilities in detail, beginning with the conceptual foundations that distinguish actions from observations and developing the governance frameworks that these differences require.

2.5   Action

How does an agent make things happen? A junior associate's role extends beyond research to producing work product. They draft memos, send emails, file documents, and schedule meetings. A trader's role extends beyond analysis to execution. They enter orders, route trades, and confirm allocations. Value derives from action, not just observation.

Agentic systems face the same imperative. Where Chapter 1 distinguished perception (observing the world) from action (changing it), we now examine how to design and govern action capabilities. An agent that only reads (searching databases, retrieving documents, analyzing information) produces no deliverable. To complete tasks, agents must *act*: generate documents, send communications, update systems, or execute transactions. This action capability transforms agents from passive research tools into systems that deliver concrete work product.

> ## Action Tools
>
> **Action tools** allow agents to change the state of external systems. Unlike perception tools (Section 2.4), which are read-only, action tools *write*: they file documents, send messages, execute trades, and update databases. Once executed, some actions cannot be undone.
>
> The distinction between perception and action is fundamental to governance. Perception risks involve internal errors (accessing wrong information). Action risks involve external consequences (harming clients, violating regulations, creating liability).

2.5.1   Conceptual Foundations of Action

Before examining specific action tools, we establish the conceptual foundations that distinguish actions from observations and that shape how we design, govern, and reason about them.

Actions as State Transitions. From a logical perspective, actions are state transitions: operations that move the world from one configuration to another. Before the filing, the motion was not on the court docket; after the filing, it is. Before the trade, the portfolio held one set of positions; after the trade, it holds another. This framing, which is common in computer science, philosophy, and AI planning research, highlights that actions have preconditions that must hold before they can execute and postconditions that describe the world after they complete.

This state-transition view raises a crucial question that philosophers and AI researchers call the **frame problem**: when an action occurs, what exactly changes, and what stays the same (McCarthy and Hayes 1969)? Filing a document changes the court record, but it should not change the client's contact information, the matter's billing status, or the contents of unrelated files. The frame problem is surprisingly difficult to solve in general, but well-designed action tools address it by making their effects explicit: specifying what they modify, what they preserve, and what conditions must hold for the action to succeed.

Performative Actions. Some actions are *performative* in the sense developed by philosophers of language (Austin 1962): they do not merely describe or report on the world but constitute changes to it. When a judge says "I sentence you to five years," the utterance does not describe a sentencing; it *is* the sentencing. When parties sign a contract, the signatures do not report that an agreement exists; they bring the agreement into existence.

Many professional actions share this performative character. Filing a motion is not a report about legal status; it is an act that changes legal status. Executing a trade is not an observation about ownership; it is a transfer of ownership. Sending a legal opinion creates reliance that may give rise to liability.

Large language models are fundamentally text generators. In most domains, generated text is relatively harmless because words do not change the world: a recipe for cake does not create a cake. The text merely describes; action requires something more. Law and finance are different.

Text Is Action in Law and Finance

In professional practice, text often *is* action. A contract clause creates binding obligations. A court filing changes legal status. A trade order transfers ownership. An email to opposing counsel may waive privilege or create estoppel. The gap between "saying" and "doing" that protects most LLM applications collapses here.

This performative quality explains why action governance must be stricter than perception governance: an agent that retrieves the wrong document has made a research error that can be corrected, but an agent that files the wrong document has changed legal reality in ways that may be difficult or impossible to undo.

Idempotency and Safe Retry. Computer science formalizes an important property of operations that matters greatly for agentic systems.

Idempotency

An operation is **idempotent** if performing it multiple times produces the same result as performing it once. Reading a file is idempotent; reading ten times leaves the file unchanged. Retrieving a case from Westlaw is idempotent. But sending an email is not idempotent: sending the same message ten times produces ten emails in the recipient's inbox. Executing a trade is not idempotent: executing the same order ten times produces ten separate transactions.

Idempotency matters enormously for error recovery and system reliability. When an agent's connection drops mid-operation, or when a timeout occurs before confirmation arrives, the agent faces a difficult question: did the action complete? For idempotent operations, the answer does not matter; the agent can safely retry. For non-idempotent operations, retry might cause duplicate actions with serious consequences, such as double payments, duplicate filings, or repeated client communications. Robust action tools must either be designed for idempotency from the start (typically by using unique transaction identifiers that allow the system to detect and reject duplicates) or must provide explicit confirmation mechanisms that let the agent verify whether the action completed before deciding whether to retry.

Implications for Tool Design. These conceptual foundations have practical implications for how we design and evaluate action tools. Tools should document their preconditions (what must be true before the action can execute), their postconditions (what will be true after successful execution), and their effects on system state (what changes and what remains unchanged). Tools should indicate whether they are idempotent and, if not, what mechanisms exist to prevent duplicate execution. Tools should distinguish between actions that are truly performative (creating new legal or financial realities) and those that merely update internal records. These distinctions inform the governance frameworks developed throughout this section.

2.5.2   Action Tool Categories

Action tools vary in consequence. The critical dimension is **reversibility**: the cost and feasibility of undoing an action. Research on rollback-augmented systems shows that selective state rollback reduces catastrophic failures in safety-sensitive environments (Grinsztajn et al. 2021). We categorize action tools along a spectrum from easily undone to permanent.

Communication tools send information to others. Internal communications (emails to colleagues, Slack messages) are *partially reversible.* You can follow up with corrections, though you cannot unsend. External communications (emails to clients, letters to counsel) carry higher stakes because recipients are out-side your control. Retractions are possible but damage professional reputation. Automated alerts (compliance notifications, reminders) are generally low-risk if templated. Governance typically relies on post-hoc review for internal actions and pre-approval for external ones.

Document management tools create and organize work product. These are *largely reversible.* Drafting memos, generating reports, and filing documents in internal systems occur within the firm's control. Revisions are possible until distribution. Template application (populating standard forms) is low-risk if the templates are pre-validated. The primary control is review before external release.

Filing and submission tools send documents to external authorities. These are *largely irreversible.* Court filings via CM/ECF (Case Management/Electronic Case Files) become public record upon submission. Amendments are possible but the original remains visible. Regulatory submissions via EDGAR (Electronic Data Gathering, Analysis, and Retrieval) or FINRA systems trigger legal obligations. Errors may compel public corrections or enforcement actions. Contract execution creates binding legal obligations that are difficult to unwind. These actions require mandatory pre-approval.

Transaction execution tools transfer value or change ownership. These are *effectively irreversible* or costly to reverse. Trade execution involves entering orders and confirming allocations. Reversal requires offsetting trades at market prices, realizing any loss. Payment processing (wire transfers) moves funds immediately; recovery relies on recipient cooperation. System updates (modifying production databases) can disrupt operations. These actions demand the strictest controls: multi-factor approval, segregation of duties, and real-time monitoring.

2.5.3   Reversibility Framework

Reversibility dictates oversight structure. Examine how you delegate to a junior associate: fully reversible work (research, drafting) proceeds independently with post-hoc review; partially reversible work (internal emails) gets checkpoint review; largely irreversible work (client communications, filings) requires pre-approval; and irreversible work (trades, wires) demands multi-party approval. Table 2.3 summarizes this mapping. Agent governance must enforce controls corresponding to each action's reversibility classification.

Table 2.3: Reversibility determines oversight

Reversibility	Examples	Oversight	Recovery
Fully	Research; drafts	Post-hoc	Delete/revise
Partially	Internal emails; alerts	Checkpoint	Correction
Largely irreversible	Filings; client emails	Pre-approval	Amend/retract
Irreversible	Trades; wires	Multi-party	Offset (costly)

Reversibility Determines Governance

The reversibility of an action directly determines the appropriate level of oversight. Fully reversible actions (research, drafting) can proceed with post-hoc review. Irreversible actions (trades, wire transfers) require multi-party approval before execution. This mapping is not abstract; it operationalizes the professional judgment that experienced practitioners apply instinctively when delegating work.

The following subsections operationalize these oversight tiers.

2.5.4   MCP Tools and Prompts for Action

The Model Context Protocol (MCP) defines two capability types relevant to action governance.

MCP Tools are executable functions that change state. Unlike read-only Resources, Tools create documents, send communications, submit filings, and execute transactions. Tool manifests should include risk metadata: reversibility classification, approval requirements, and audit logging needs. This allows the MCP Host to enforce controls automatically.

MCP Prompts are reusable templates for common tasks. For action workflows, prompts encode Standard Operating Procedures (SOPs).

- **Legal:** Contract review checklists, filing preparation workflows.
- **Finance:** Trade compliance checks, client onboarding sequences.

Prompts standardize action sequences, reducing variation and error. They act as "guardrails" by ensuring the agent follows the approved procedure for high-stakes actions.

2.5.5   Action Security

Every action interface is a security boundary. Actions access external systems and create real-world consequences.

All action tools must implement core security controls:

- **Authentication:** Verify the agent's identity via service accounts with strong credentials.
- **Authorization:** Enforce role-based access control (RBAC) and least privilege.
- **Input Validation:** Reject malformed requests by validating all parameters against strict schemas.
- **Output Confirmation:** Mandate human approval before executing high-stakes actions.
- **Rate Limiting:** Cap action frequency to prevent runaway execution.
- **Audit Logging:** Record every action with context (agent, timestamp, parameters, matter/client).

Beyond core controls, specific threats call for targeted mitigations (OWASP Foundation 2025; Liu et al. 2024):

Prompt Injection via Action Parameters. Adversaries may embed malicious instructions in data that the agent processes and passes to tools. Mitigation demands sanitizing all parameters and never passing raw user input directly to sensitive action interfaces.

Privilege Escalation via Tool Chaining. An agent might combine multiple low-privilege tools to achieve a high-privilege outcome. Mitigation involves analyzing tool combinations and requiring approval for sequences that cross security boundaries.

Action Replay. An attacker might capture a valid action request (e.g., "Pay $100") and replay it multiple times. Mitigation demands **nonces** (unique, one-time numbers) or timestamps to ensure each request is processed only once.

> ### Defense in Depth for Action Tools
>
> No single control prevents all failures. Effective action security layers multiple defenses: authentication verifies identity, authorization limits scope, validation catches malformed inputs, approval gates catch errors before execution, and audit logging enables post-hoc review. Each layer catches failures that slip through others.

2.5.6   Approval Workflows

For non-reversible actions, the agent prepares and the human approves (Parasuraman et al. 2000). These approval patterns operate alongside escalation logic (Section 2.9), which handles scenarios where human judgment is needed regardless of the agent's confidence. We define three patterns for this division of responsibility.

The **Single Approver** pattern suits routine actions with clear authority. The agent completes preparation and presents it to one designated human. *Example:* The agent prepares a draft court filing; the supervising attorney reviews and approves; the agent submits.

The **Multi-Party Approval** pattern applies to high-stakes actions with significant exposure. Multiple independent humans must sign off. *Example:* The agent prepares a wire transfer. Operations reviews the amount. Compliance reviews the purpose. A manager provides final approval. Only then does the agent execute.

The **Escalating Approval** pattern adjusts authority based on risk tiers. *Example:* Trades under $100k require desk manager approval. Trades between $100k and $1M require senior trader approval. Trades over $1M require CIO approval.

Effective approval requests must support informed decision-making. The agent should present:

- **Action:** Clear description of what will happen.
- **Context:** Why is this needed?
- **Risk:** What are the potential negative outcomes?
- **Reversibility:** Can this be undone?

• **Evidence:** What data supports this decision?

The approver should be able to decide based on the request alone, without needing to investigate the raw data. Note that idempotency design (discussed above) is critical here: if an approved action might be retried due to network failures or timeouts, the underlying tools must guarantee that re-execution does not cause duplicates.

2.5.7   Rate Limiting and Circuit Breakers

Agents can fail in loops: repeatedly submitting the same request, sending duplicate messages, or retrying failed transactions.

Rate Limiting caps action frequency. The thresholds below are *illustrative*; calibrate them to your workflow, risk tolerance, and regulatory obligations.

• *Per-Action:* e.g., max 5 emails per minute.
• *Per-Matter:* e.g., max 20 actions per day without review.
• *Cost:* e.g., max $1,000 in transaction fees per session.

When limits are reached, the agent must pause and escalate.

Circuit Breakers automatically stop execution upon anomaly detection. These examples are also *illustrative* and should be tuned to baseline behavior and threat models.

• *Failure Count:* e.g., if an action fails three times, stop.
• *Spike Detection:* e.g., if action rate spikes 5× above baseline, pause (potential compromise).
• *Cumulative Limit:* If daily total exceeds safety thresholds, lock the system.

Circuit breakers transform runaway failures into controlled pauses, buying time for human intervention.

2.5.8   Evaluation

Action evaluation differs fundamentally from perception evaluation. Perception errors are internal: the agent retrieved wrong information, but no external harm occurred. Action errors are external: the agent filed wrong documents, sent wrong communications, or executed wrong transactions. The consequences escape your control. This asymmetry, introduced at the start of this section, should shape how you evaluate action capabilities.

The organizing question is whether governance matches reversibility. Consider how you would evaluate delegation to a junior associate. For reversible work (research, drafting), you review output quality. For partially reversible work (internal communications), you spot-check and monitor. For irreversible work (filings, client communications, transactions), you verify that approval gates are in place and functioning. The same logic applies to agents.

Classification accuracy is the foundation. Every action tool must be correctly classified along the reversibility spectrum. The most dangerous error is misclassification: treating an irreversible action as reversible and allowing it to proceed without appropriate approval. Verify that filing tools, transaction tools, and external communication tools are all flagged for pre-approval. Verify that the system cannot be tricked into treating a high-stakes action as routine.

Approval workflow alignment ensures that oversight matches risk. Single-approver patterns should govern routine irreversible actions. Multi-party patterns should govern high-exposure actions. Escalating patterns should adjust authority based on magnitude. For each action category, trace the approval path and confirm it matches the framework in Section 2.5.6.

Defense-in-depth verification confirms that security controls are layered, not isolated. Authentication should prevent unauthorized agents from acting. Authorization should limit each agent to its assigned scope. Input validation should reject malformed requests. Approval gates should catch errors before execution. Audit logging should capture context for post-hoc review. Test each layer independently; then test whether failures in one layer are caught by others.

Failure-mode testing addresses the unique risks of non-idempotent actions. What happens when a connection drops mid-transaction? Does the system detect duplicates? Do circuit breakers actually trip under simulated runaway conditions? Do rate limits actually pause execution when thresholds are reached? Passive documentation review cannot answer these questions. Active testing must.

Action Capability Checklist

- ☐ **Reversibility classification:** Each tool correctly classified; performative actions (filings, trades, external communications) flagged for pre-approval
- ☐ **Approval workflows:** Appropriate pattern (single, multi-party, escalating) mapped to each action category based on risk
- ☐ **Operational safeguards:** Rate limits, circuit breakers, and duplicate detection tested under failure conditions
- ☐ **Audit and recovery:** Every action logged with full context; rollback procedures documented for each reversibility tier

---

In law and finance, text is action. A contract clause creates obligations. A filing changes legal status. A trade order transfers ownership. This performative quality demands that action evaluation be treated as seriously as you would treat oversight of any process that creates binding legal or financial consequences. The goal is not to confirm that controls exist on paper but to confirm they function when the agent attempts something it should not do.

Action tools are where agentic systems create real-world consequences. Governance here differs in kind from perception governance.

Perception risks (accessing wrong data) are internal. Action risks (sending wrong emails, executing wrong trades) are external and potentially irreversible. This section established the architectural controls: the Reversibility Framework, approval workflows, and circuit breakers.

Section 2.6 addresses memory: how agents maintain context across sessions and learn from experience. Later, Section 2.9 examines when agents should *not* act, recognizing situations that require human decision-making. The interplay between action capability and escalation judgment is central to safety. These capabilities (action controls, memory, and escalation judgment) are then integrated into the governance architecture developed in Section 2.11. As Chapter 3 emphasizes, governance policy without governance-aware architecture is unenforceable; the controls established in this section provide the foundation that policy requires.

2.6   Memory

How does an agent remember things? The previous two sections examined how agents gather information (perception) and effect change (action). Yet these capabilities operate in the moment: the agent perceives the current state, reasons about it, and acts. Without memory, every interaction resets. The agent cannot recall prior research, successful strategies, or case history. Where Chapter 1 introduced the concept of stateful versus stateless systems in the IAT framework, we now examine how to implement memory architectures that enable agents to learn and adapt across sessions.

Every experienced professional knows that institutional memory distinguishes efficient work from reinventing the wheel. When starting a new securities registration or revisiting an investment thesis, you do not begin from scratch. You pull prior filings, review comment history, check precedent databases, and update existing models with new data. The firm maintains templates and research files that incorporate years of accumulated knowledge. Memory in agentic systems serves this same function: context retention across sessions and learning from experience, building on prior work rather than starting over.

Agent Memory

Agent memory encompasses the mechanisms by which agents store and retrieve information across different timescales (Park et al. 2023; Wang et al. 2024a). Like a professional's layered filing systems (from desk to archive), agent memory operates at multiple levels, each trading immediacy for capacity.

2.6.1   Memory Types

Law firms use layered filing systems, each suited to different timescales. The associate's desk holds active work; the matter file contains engagement history; the precedent database archives institutional knowledge. Each layer trades immediacy for capacity. Agent memory systems follow the same pattern.

Working Memory

Working memory is the information actively loaded in an agent's context window, analogous to papers spread across a desk. Limited by the model's context size, working memory is immediate but transient: what the agent can "see" right now.

Working memory utilizes the **context window**: the text currently loaded in the LLM's active attention. Just like desk space, context windows have strict limits. An associate can only have so many documents open at once; an agent can only hold so many **tokens** (units of text, roughly 0.75 words) in active context. As of late 2025, leading models handle roughly 200,000 tokens. When the task exceeds this limit, you need other storage systems. In finance, this parallels the active trading screen: live prices and positions are immediate but transient.

Episodic Memory

Episodic memory stores the history of actions and outcomes for a specific engagement, analogous to the matter file. It captures what the agent did, what it found, and what happened, enabling continuity across sessions.

Episodic memory corresponds to the matter file. Every memo, correspondence, and research result related to an engagement goes here. The associate does not re-research answered questions; the file provides the history. In agentic systems, episodic memory captures the log of actions and outcomes (Park et al. 2023). The agent records: "I searched for Ninth Circuit venue cases, found three opinions, and drafted the analysis." When asked a follow-up, the agent retrieves that prior state.

This mirrors the financial research file: you pull prior analysis and update it, rather than starting fresh.

> ### Semantic Memory
>
> **Semantic memory** stores general principles and institutional knowledge available for retrieval, analogous to the firm's precedent archive. It represents accumulated expertise that applies across many engagements.

Semantic memory is the firm's precedent database. Institutional knowledge accumulates over decades. When you need a force majeure clause, the database offers fifty examples. Agentic systems access semantic memory through the RAG pattern introduced in Section 2.4.2: retrieve relevant content from a large corpus, inject it into the prompt, and generate a response informed by that specific knowledge (Lewis et al. 2020).

The retrieval infrastructure powering semantic memory (embeddings and vector stores) was defined in Section 2.4.2. Here, the key insight is that semantic memory works because of *in-context learning*: the model adapts its behavior based on what appears in its prompt. Retrieved precedents become part of the agent's working context, allowing it to reason about specific examples even when those examples were created after the model's training.

2.6.2 Implementing the RAG Pattern

The RAG pattern (Section 2.4.2) requires careful implementation to work reliably in professional contexts. The core pattern (retrieve, augment, generate) is simple, but the retrieval step admits many implementations with different tradeoffs.

The Core Pattern. RAG has three essential steps:

1. **Retrieve**: Find relevant content from your knowledge base.

2. **Augment**: Insert that content into the model's prompt.

3. **Generate**: Produce a response informed by the retrieved content.

The retrieval step is where implementations diverge. As discussed in Section 2.4.2, retrieval can use keyword search, BM25, embeddings, database queries, API calls, or hybrid combinations. The choice depends on your content, your queries, and your infrastructure.

The Embedding-Based Pipeline. When using embedding-based semantic search (the approach that dominates RAG tutorials), the retrieval step expands into a multi-stage pipeline:

1. **Chunking:** Breaks documents into semantic units (sentences, paragraphs, sections, or sliding windows) while preserving metadata (source, date, jurisdiction). Chunk size affects retrieval: too small loses context; too large dilutes relevance.

2. **Embedding:** Converts each chunk into a vector using an embedding model. Different models have different strengths; legal-specific embeddings may outperform general-purpose ones for professional content.

3. **Similarity Search:** Finds chunks similar to the query by comparing vectors (using cosine similarity or similar metrics). Returns the top-k most similar chunks.

This pipeline works well for unstructured text where semantic matching matters, such as finding documents about "materiality" when the query says "significance." But it is not the only approach, and for some use cases it is not the best.

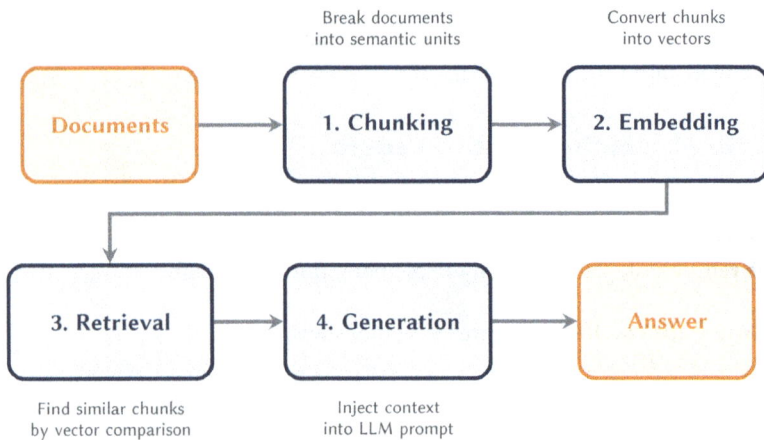

Figure 2.6: An embedding-based RAG pipeline—one common implementation pattern. Documents are chunked into semantic units, embedded as vectors, and retrieved by semantic similarity. Alternative implementations may skip chunking and embedding entirely, using keyword search, BM25, database queries, or hybrid approaches to retrieve relevant content.

Alternative Retrieval Approaches. Many production systems use simpler or hybrid approaches:

- **Keyword and BM25 search** requires no chunking or embedding infrastructure. Existing search systems, including Westlaw, Lexis, and internal document search, can power RAG directly. This works well when exact terms matter (case citations, statutory references) and vocabulary is consistent.

- **Structured queries** retrieve from databases or APIs. An agent checking SEC filings queries EDGAR; an agent researching court records queries PACER. No chunking or embedding is required because the data source returns structured results.
- **Hybrid retrieval** combines keyword search (fast, catches exact matches) with semantic search (slower, catches conceptual matches) (Robertson and Zaragoza 2009). A common pattern uses BM25 for initial retrieval and embedding-based reranking to surface the most relevant results.

Knowledge Graph Retrieval. When domain structure matters, knowledge graphs provide an alternative to vector similarity. Knowledge graphs leverage structured networks of entities and relationships. Where embeddings capture semantic similarity, knowledge graphs encode explicit connections such as corporate ownership hierarchies, regulatory supersession chains, and case citation networks.

When a query references a known entity, the agent queries the graph and traverses relationships through multi-hop reasoning, following paths that vector similarity alone cannot discover. This approach excels when domain structure matters: tracing precedential chains in case law, mapping corporate family trees for conflict checks, or navigating regulatory cross-references. We examine knowledge graph foundations and their applications to law and finance later in this book.

Enhancing Retrieval Quality. Regardless of retrieval method, several techniques improve precision and authority:

- **Query rewriting** transforms vague questions ("What's the rule?") into specific search queries based on conversation history and domain knowledge (Ma et al. 2023).
- **Reranking** scores initial results by authority or relevance, ensuring binding precedent ranks above secondary sources (Yu et al. 2024). A Supreme Court opinion should outrank a blog post, even if both match the query.
- **Filtered retrieval** constrains results by metadata (jurisdiction, date, document type), preventing agents from citing inapplicable authority.

Hallucination Risk and Mitigation

Fabricated citations remain a critical failure mode even with RAG. The first preregistered study of commercial legal AI tools found that RAG-enabled systems hallucinate 17–33% of the time, including citing nonexistent statutes and misattributing judicial opinions (Magesh et al. 2025). Counterintuitively, newer "reasoning" models may perform worse: OpenAI's o3 hallucinates roughly twice as often as its predecessor o1 on factual benchmarks (OpenAI 2025).

Mitigation requires verification before any citation reaches the user: confirm that the source exists in the retrieved context. This verification is not optional for professional applications.

2.6.3   Domain Considerations

Memory systems for regulated industries require enhancements that go well beyond generic implementations. Three dimensions matter most: authority, jurisdiction, and time.

When investigating insider trading liability, a Supreme Court opinion carries far more weight than a law review article discussing the same topic. The human researcher instinctively applies this hierarchy; an agent's memory system must do the same. This means tagging documents with their position in the authority hierarchy (primary sources like statutes and binding precedent at the top, secondary sources like treatises and articles below) and ensuring that retrieval algorithms surface higher-authority documents more prominently. Financial systems face analogous challenges: an SEC no-action letter provides more reliable guidance than a client alert summarizing the same issue, and memory systems should reflect that difference.

Jurisdiction adds another layer of complexity. Legal information does not exist in a vacuum; it operates within territorial boundaries. California precedent does not bind Texas courts, and New York banking regulations have no force in London. A memory system that fails to account for these boundaries will produce results that are not merely unhelpful but actively misleading. When an agent researches Delaware corporate law, it must filter results to surface Delaware authorities as controlling while clearly distinguishing persuasive authority from other jurisdictions. This requires rich metadata tagging and retrieval logic that can enforce strict jurisdictional filtering when the task demands it.

Time presents perhaps the most challenging dimension. Law evolves through legislative amendments, regulatory updates, and judicial decisions that overturn or limit prior holdings. A case from 1985 may have been explicitly overruled, limited to its facts, or superseded by statute. Memory systems must integrate with citator services like Shepard's or KeyCite to validate that retrieved precedents remain good law. Financial data introduces even more varied temporal requirements: market prices become stale in milliseconds, earnings reports remain relevant for quarters, and industry analyses may hold value for years. Effective memory systems tag all data with effective dates and expiration windows, triggering refresh processes when content ages beyond its useful life.

Finally, professional domains create identifier resolution challenges that generic systems rarely encounter. Legal citations appear in multiple formats; for example, "123 F.3d 456" and "123 F3d 456" refer to the same case, but a naive system might treat them as distinct. Companies accumulate multiple identifiers across different contexts: stock tickers, CUSIPs, ISINs, and Legal Entity Identifiers (LEIs) all point to the same entity but appear in different documents and databases. Without careful normalization, retrieval systems fail to connect related records, fragmenting information that belongs together.

2.6.4   Matter and Client Isolation

Perhaps no aspect of memory architecture matters more for professional services than enforcing strict **ethical walls** between matters and clients. The consequences of failure are severe: if an agent working on Matter A inadvertently accesses privileged information from Matter B (particularly when the matters involve adverse parties), the result may be privilege waiver, disqualification, and malpractice liability. Financial services face parallel risks when Material Non-Public Information (MNPI) leaks across the walls that separate investment banking from trading operations.

Implementing effective separation requires a layered approach that begins with architectural isolation. Each matter should occupy its own namespace within the memory system, creating a logical partition that separates its documents, notes, and work product from all other matters. Retrieval operations must be scoped to respect these boundaries: when an agent queries memory in the context of a particular matter, the system should only search within that matter's namespace, never reaching across into other partitions regardless of how relevant the results might appear.

Access controls provide the next layer of protection. Role-based permissions determine which agents and human users can access each namespace, mirroring the ethical wall policies that law firms and financial institutions already maintain for their human professionals. An associate staffed on a merger transaction should have access to that deal's namespace but not to the namespace for litigation against the same company being handled by a different team. When delegation introduces multiple agents accessing the same matter namespace (Section 2.10), isolation becomes even more critical: coordination among agents must not inadvertently leak information across matter boundaries.

Audit trails complete the picture by creating a verifiable record of every interaction with the memory system. Each read and write operation should be logged with a timestamp, the identity of the requesting agent or user, and the matter identifier. These logs serve multiple purposes: they enable compliance review, support investigations if a breach is suspected, and provide documentation that the organization maintained appropriate controls.

Retention and deletion policies add a temporal dimension to isolation. Organizational policy often requires that matter files be retained for specified periods and then destroyed; legal and regulatory requirements may impose additional constraints depending on the engagement type, jurisdiction, and applicable rules. When a matter closes or a client relationship ends, the associated memory namespace should be archived or deleted according to a documented retention schedule. Critically, deletion must be verifiable; the organization needs confidence that purged data is truly gone, not merely hidden from normal retrieval. These isolation and audit requirements exemplify the architectural patterns for privilege enforcement and logging detailed in Section 2.11.1.

2.6.5   Evaluation

Memory evaluation requires four assessments: *retrieval quality* (precision and recall against expert work product: does it find the authorities a skilled attorney would cite?), *isolation integrity* (adversarial testing to verify matter/client boundaries hold), *temporal validity* (tracking whether retrieved precedent remains good law and how quickly updates propagate), and *scale performance* (latency as corpus grows to tens of thousands of documents).

Memory System Checklist

- ☐ **Retrieval quality:** Test against expert-curated work product to verify precision/recall and authority ranking
- ☐ **Isolation integrity:** Conduct adversarial tests to confirm matter/client boundaries prevent cross-contamination
- ☐ **Temporal validity:** Integrate citator services and verify update propagation for precedent and regulatory changes
- ☐ **Adaptation governance:** Monitor memory for poisoning attempts, behavioral drift, and unauthorized writes

2.6.6   Adaptation

Memory facilitates **adaptation**, the "A" in the GPA+IAT framework from Chapter 1. This capability transforms agents from static tools into systems that learn. But adaptation also introduces risks that static systems avoid.

Adaptation

Adaptation is behavioral change based on experience. In agentic systems, adaptation occurs through three mechanisms:

- **In-context adaptation:** The agent changes behavior within a session based on instructions, examples, or retrieved content. This is in-context learning in action.
- **Cross-session adaptation:** The agent changes behavior across sessions by persisting information in memory and retrieving it later.
- **Model-level adaptation:** The model's weights are updated through fine-tuning or reinforcement learning. This is less common in deployed systems due to cost and complexity.

In-context adaptation is immediate and powerful. You provide the agent with examples of preferred output format, and it adapts its responses accordingly. You correct an error, and subsequent responses reflect that correction. This is why retrieval matters: by controlling what appears in the agent's context, you control how it adapts.

Cross-session adaptation requires persistent memory. The agent stores information (user preferences, successful strategies, matter-specific context) and retrieves it in future sessions. This creates continuity: the agent "remembers" that this client prefers concise memos, that this portfolio manager wants risk metrics in basis points, that this matter involves a specific contractual provision.

Opportunities from Adaptation. Adaptation supports capabilities that static systems cannot match:

Personalization. The agent learns user preferences, including communication style, level of detail, and preferred formats, and tailors responses accordingly. A partner who always asks follow-up questions about procedural history gets proactive procedural context. An analyst who focuses on downside scenarios gets risk-weighted analysis by default.

Performance improvement. The agent learns from feedback. Corrections persist: "Actually, this jurisdiction uses different venue rules" becomes part of the agent's knowledge for future queries. Successful strategies are reinforced: the research approach that found relevant authority is remembered and reapplied.

Domain specialization. Through accumulated episodic and semantic memory, agents develop expertise in specific practice areas or market segments. An agent that has worked on dozens of M&A transactions "knows" the typical deal structure, common negotiation points, and relevant precedents; not through training, but through memory.

Continuity across handoffs. When a professional leaves or a matter transfers, institutional knowledge often walks out the door. Memory-enabled agents maintain continuity. The research history, strategic decisions, and accumulated context persist in retrievable form.

Risks from Adaptation. The same mechanisms that support adaptation create risks that demand governance:

Security: Memory poisoning. If an adversary can write to an agent's memory, they can influence future behavior (Clop and Teglia 2024). A document designed to be retrieved, containing misleading instructions or false information, can corrupt the agent's responses. This is prompt injection via the memory layer. The attack surface expands beyond the current conversation to include everything the agent might retrieve.

Security: Data leakage through memory. Memory that persists across sessions can leak information across contexts. If the agent stores sensitive information from Matter A and retrieves it during Matter B, confidentiality is breached. This risk intensifies with shared memory systems that serve multiple users or matters.

Governance: Behavioral drift. As agents adapt, their behavior changes in ways that may not be predictable or desirable. An agent that learns from user feedback might learn bad habits: shortcuts that work in routine cases but fail in edge cases. Accumulated memory can shift the agent's responses away from its original design.

Governance: Accountability gaps. When behavior depends on memory state, accountability becomes complex. Which version of the agent produced this output? What was in its memory at the time? If the agent's behavior changes based on accumulated experience, audit trails must capture not just inputs and outputs but memory state.

Detecting and responding to these risks (particularly drift and leakage) requires escalation triggers and monitoring mechanisms explored in Section 2.9, which addresses when anomalies warrant human review.

Cost: Storage and retrieval overhead. Memory consumes resources. Episodic memory for a complex litigation matter can grow to millions of tokens. Semantic memory for a precedent database can require terabytes of embeddings. Every retrieval operation has latency and cost. These costs compound as memory grows.

Latency: Retrieval time. RAG adds latency to every query. The agent must embed the query, search the vector store, retrieve results, and inject them into the prompt before generation begins. For real-time applications such as trading and live client calls, this latency may be unacceptable.

> ### The Adaptation Tradeoff
>
> Adaptation is not optional. Any system that uses RAG, maintains conversation history, or persists user preferences is adapting. The question is not whether to allow adaptation, but how to govern it.

Key governance questions:

- **What can be written to memory?** Control the write path to prevent poisoning.
- **What can be retrieved?** Scope retrieval to prevent leakage.
- **How is memory validated?** Review accumulated memory for accuracy and appropriateness.
- **When is memory cleared?** Define retention policies and implement secure deletion.
- **How is drift detected?** Monitor behavior changes over time.

These governance questions are not abstract; they map directly to architectural controls developed in Section 2.11, which synthesizes logging, override mechanisms, and isolation patterns specifically designed to manage adaptation risks.

Memory provides the context agents need to plan effectively. Without memory, agents cannot learn from failed strategies, cannot build on prior work, and cannot maintain the continuity that complex tasks require. The adaptation mechanisms discussed above (Section 2.6.6) transform memory from passive storage into active learning, but that learning must be channeled into productive planning.

An experienced associate approaching a new research task does not start from scratch; they recall similar matters, retrieve relevant precedents, and apply strategies that worked before. Memory-enabled agents can do the same: retrieve prior research, recall successful approaches, and avoid repeating failures.

Section 2.7 examines the next question: how does an agent break a big job into steps? Just as the case file facilitates strategic litigation planning, agent memory supports systematic task decomposition. The adaptation capabilities discussed here (personalization, domain specialization, and performance improvement) all feed into more effective planning. Professional audit applications, such as the PCAOB-compliant accounts receivable investigation system detailed in Section 3.4.3, demonstrate how stateful memory enables agents to adapt investigation strategies across cycles while maintaining compliance with professional documentation standards.

2.7   Planning

How does an agent break a big job into steps? A litigation partner approaching a new matter understands that the path from initial consultation to trial and beyond is a long sequence of interdependent steps. To navigate it, the partner develops a strategy: discovery first (identifying needed facts), then dispositive motions when appropriate, followed by settlement discussions or trial preparation. Discovery breaks into phases: initial disclosures, document requests, interrogatories, and depositions. Tasks distribute across the team: a senior associate handles briefing, a junior associate reviews documents, and a paralegal manages scheduling. Throughout, the partner monitors progress against deadlines and adjusts strategy as new facts emerge.

This is **planning**: decomposing complex goals into action sequences. Where Chapter 1's IAT framework identified iteration as a key capability, planning determines how those iterations are structured and sequenced. It mirrors the litigation roadmap or deal timeline that guides execution. Without planning, agents react to immediate observations without strategy. With planning, they work systematically toward objectives, adapt when circumstances change, and recognize completion.

Planning

Planning decomposes complex goals into sequences of actions (Russell and Norvig 2020a). It encompasses:
- **Decomposition**: Breaking large tasks into manageable steps.
- **Sequencing**: Ordering steps logically based on dependencies.
- **Allocation**: Assigning steps to specific tools or sub-agents.
- **Monitoring**: Tracking progress toward the goal.
- **Adaptation**: Adjusting the plan when circumstances change.

Without planning, an agent resembles an associate running searches without a strategy: busy but not progressing toward a deliverable.

2.7.1   Planning Patterns

Three patterns dominate agent planning, each suited to different task types.

ReAct (Reasoning + Acting). The most fundamental pattern interleaves reasoning with action (Yao et al. 2022). Consider a partner asking for authority on an unenforceable forum selection clause. The associate reasons: "Key grounds are unconscionability and public policy. I will start with *Atlantic Marine*." They search, observe results, and reason again: "Unconscionability cases involve consumer contracts, not our commercial context. The public policy line is stronger." They search again, refining based on results.

Each cycle has three components:

- **Thought**: Explicit reasoning about what to do next.
- **Action**: A tool call to gather information or effect change.
- **Observation**: The tool output that informs the next thought.

Reasoning traces make decisions transparent and auditable. ReAct works well for exploratory tasks where you learn as you go, such as legal research, fact investigation, and market analysis.

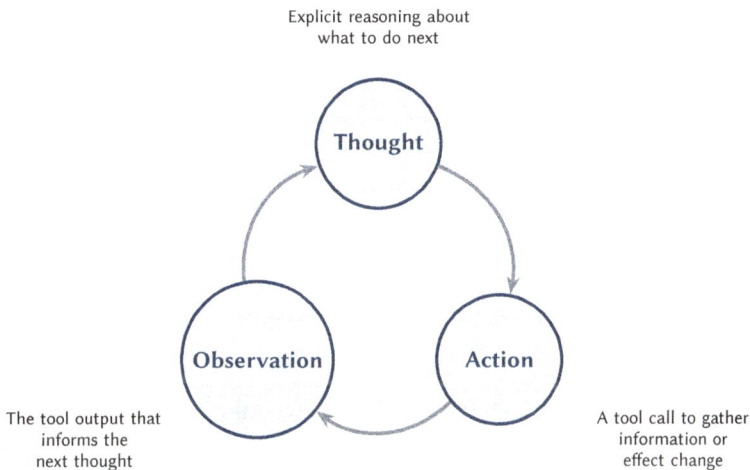

Figure 2.7: The ReAct cycle interleaves reasoning with action. The agent reasons about what to do (Thought), executes a tool call (Action), observes the result (Observation), and uses that observation to inform the next round of reasoning.

Plan-Execute. This pattern separates planning from execution. For a document review task ("Review 50 contracts for choice-of-law provisions"), the associate creates a plan: list the contracts, open each one, extract the provision, and record findings. Then they execute systematically. The plan remains static because the task is well-defined.

Plan-Execute fits established workflows: due diligence checklists, compliance reviews, and document assembly. You create the plan upfront and execute methodically. Research variants like ReWOO (Xu et al. 2023) (separating reasoning from observation) and LLMCompiler (Kim et al. 2024) (optimizing execution graphs) enable parallel tool calling. Yet the core pattern remains: plan first, then execute.

Hierarchical Planning. Law firms decompose matters into workstreams delegated through layers. A parent agent receives a high-level goal, breaks it into sub-goals, and delegates to specialists. "Prepare for trial" becomes:

- Finalize witness list (delegated to Agent A).
- Prepare exhibits (delegated to Agent B).
- Draft witness questions (delegated to Agent C).

Each specialist may decompose further. This enables parallelization and specialization, mirroring how litigation teams work. Section 2.10 details these delegation patterns. Figure 2.8 illustrates this decomposition.

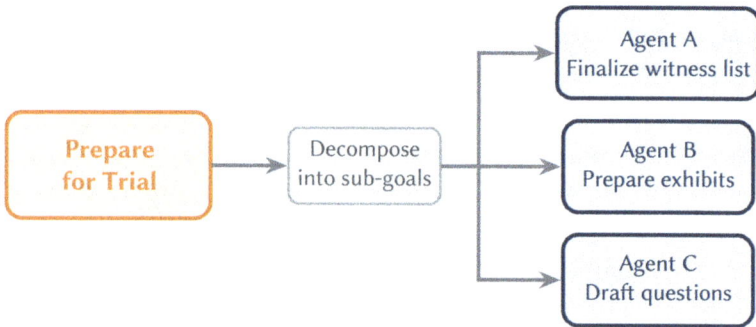

Figure 2.8: Hierarchical planning decomposes high-level goals into sub-goals delegated to specialist agents. Each specialist may decompose further, enabling parallelization and specialization.

These patterns represent a shift from traditional workflow automation. Traditional engines used **static orchestration**: predefined graphs specifying exact steps and branches (BPM systems). The workflow was designed at build time; the engine merely executed it.

Static vs. Dynamic Orchestration

Static orchestration executes predefined workflow graphs. The same input always produces the same execution path. It is predictable and auditable but inflexible.

Dynamic orchestration reasons about task decomposition at runtime. The LLM examines the goal, considers available resources, and constructs a plan on the fly. It is adaptive but less predictable.

LLM-based orchestration is inherently dynamic. "Prepare for trial" decomposes differently depending on case complexity. The LLM constructs a delegation structure based on the specific context. This adaptability is both the promise and the challenge.

Static workflows handle anticipated scenarios. Dynamic orchestration handles novel situations. Maintenance costs also differ: static workflows require explicit updates, while dynamic orchestration absorbs changes through prompt updates.

> **Auditability Challenge**
>
> Static workflows produce predictable execution traces. Dynamic orchestration may produce different decompositions for similar inputs, complicating audit. For regulated applications, you must log the *reasoning* behind orchestration decisions, not just the decisions themselves.

Production systems often combine both. High-volume, well-understood processes use static workflows. Complex, novel tasks use dynamic orchestration. The planning patterns described above (ReAct, Plan-Execute, Hierarchical) are forms of dynamic orchestration.

2.7.2   Choosing the Right Planning Pattern

Selecting the right pattern depends on task structure and required autonomy.

Task Type	Pattern	Autonomy
Well-defined steps, known scope	Plan-Execute	Moderate
Exploratory, learns as it goes	ReAct	Higher
Complex, parallel workstreams	Hierarchical	Distributed

Table 2.4: Planning pattern selection guide

The mapping is intuitive once you see examples. Plan-Execute suits well-defined procedures: credit agreement reviews, compliance audits, due diligence checklists. ReAct fits exploratory work where the agent learns as it goes: legal research, fact investigation, market analysis. Hierarchical patterns handle complex engagements with parallel workstreams: M&A transactions, portfolio construction, multi-jurisdiction filings. Higher autonomy requires more sophisticated oversight, and each pattern demands a different approach.

Plan-Execute operates with moderate autonomy. The agent works within bounds defined by the plan. Oversight focuses on plan validation. ReAct involves higher autonomy because the agent decides what to search and when to stop. Oversight requires explicit termination mechanisms and confidence thresholds; these thresholds also feed into escalation decisions (Section 2.9) that determine when uncertain decisions should transfer to humans. Hierarchical patterns distribute autonomy. Oversight requires clear delegation contracts and escalation paths. You must match oversight rigor to autonomy level.

2.7.3   Understanding the Task Before Planning

Before an agent can construct a plan, it must develop a clear understanding of what it has been asked to accomplish. While Section 2.3 explores intent extraction in detail, the planning system depends on three specific outputs from that process: a classification of the task type, an understanding of the constraints that bound acceptable solutions, and criteria that define what success looks like.

Task classification shapes the choice of planning pattern. An exploratory question like "What are the key risks in this contract?" calls for the flexible, iterative approach of ReAct. A well-defined multi-step procedure, such as "Review this document against our standard checklist," fits the structured decomposition of Plan-Execute. Complex engagements with nested subtasks and dependencies require hierarchical planning with explicit coordination. Choosing the wrong pattern wastes resources or produces inadequate results.

Constraints establish the boundaries within which the plan must operate. These include explicit limits like deadlines and budgets, but also implicit bounds like the scope of the engagement and the level of detail expected. A request to "summarize the key terms" differs fundamentally from a request to "conduct comprehensive due diligence," even if both involve the same underlying document.

Success criteria complete the picture by defining how the agent recognizes that its work is done. Without clear criteria, agents struggle to terminate appropriately. They may stop too early, leaving important questions unanswered, or continue indefinitely, consuming resources on diminishing returns. The clearer the goal, the more focused the plan; ambiguity at the input stage propagates through the entire execution.

2.7.4   Budget Architecture

Before examining resource budgets, note that memory constraints shape planning from the start. Working memory (the agent's context window) has strict limits, currently around 200,000 tokens for leading models (Section 2.6.1). A plan that assumes unlimited context will fail when the agent cannot hold all relevant information simultaneously. Similarly, if the agent must retrieve information from episodic or semantic memory, retrieval cost and latency become part of the plan's resource budget. Memory is not merely storage; it is a planning constraint.

Without resource constraints, agents can run indefinitely. Think of asking a junior associate for two relevant cases and receiving fifty, along with a bill for the hours spent finding them. Budget architecture provides the planning mechanism that prevents this outcome, giving agents explicit limits that shape how they allocate effort across tasks.

Resource consumption in agent systems takes several forms, each requiring its own type of constraint. Token budgets limit consumption of LLM API calls, preventing expensive reasoning loops where the agent repeatedly processes the same information or explores unproductive tangents. Time budgets enforce deadlines by halting execution after a specified duration, ensuring that a task expected to take ten minutes does not silently expand to consume an hour. Tool call budgets cap external interactions by limiting an agent to twenty database searches, for instance, forcing it to formulate queries carefully rather than issuing dozens of slightly varied requests. Cost budgets provide the most direct control, capping total spending in dollars regardless of how that spending is distributed across tokens, tools, and time.

These budgets operate hierarchically, cascading from broad constraints down to specific allocations. A session budget might constrain an entire client engagement; within that envelope, individual tasks receive their own allocations, which subdivide further into budgets for subtasks and individual operations. Consider a legal research task receiving thirty minutes and fifty thousand tokens. The subtasks that compose it (identifying relevant statutes, finding controlling cases, synthesizing holdings) share this pool rather than each receiving unlimited resources.

Understanding how costs compound is essential for realistic budgeting. Ingesting a 200-page credit facility consumes roughly 80,000 tokens before any analysis begins. The analysis itself requires additional tokens for reasoning, and a comprehensive review of a complex document might reach one million tokens in aggregate. Monitoring must track cumulative consumption across the entire task, not just individual operations, because costs that seem modest in isolation can accumulate rapidly. Chapter 3 examines these resource constraints in the context of a production mortgage underwriting system (Section 3.4.2), where iterative investigation across multiple cycles requires careful cost budgeting and termination condition design to satisfy both operational efficiency and regulatory compliance requirements.

The economics of agent assistance vary significantly by task type. Retrieval-heavy work like document review often shows clear return on investment: the agent processes material faster and more consistently than a human reviewer, and the cost savings are straightforward to calculate. Judgment-intensive tasks present a more complex picture, since extensive human review of the agent's output may be required, potentially reducing the net benefit. Transparency about AI assistance, as encouraged by recent ethics guidance (American Bar Association Standing Committee on Ethics and Professional Responsibility 2024), enables clients to evaluate this value proposition for themselves.

Well-designed agents degrade gracefully as budgets tighten. The key is tiered output that provides value at every resource level. With a minimal budget, the agent might return only the controlling statute. A moderate budget allows it to add key holdings from relevant cases. A full budget enables comprehensive analysis with supporting citations and counterarguments. Soft limits (triggered at perhaps eighty percent of the allocated budget) warn the agent to prioritize completion over thoroughness. Hard limits at one hundred percent terminate execution and return whatever results have been assembled. An agent that delivers useful partial results within budget is far more valuable than one that produces nothing when resources run short. When budgets are exhausted, the agent must terminate. The critical design principle is that termination under budget pressure should still produce value: the agent delivers what it has discovered rather than nothing. Section 2.8 addresses how termination conditions interact with budget limits, including how to define success for partial results.

2.7.5   Stopping Conditions

Planning must include stopping conditions. Success criteria, resource limits, and confidence thresholds all determine when an agent should stop. Section 2.8 addresses termination in depth; here we note that the planning phase is when these conditions must be defined. A plan without stopping rules is incomplete. The agent will either terminate prematurely or continue indefinitely, consuming resources without adding value.

Planning decomposes work, but every plan must end. The next two questions address the boundaries of autonomous execution.

Section 2.8 (Termination) addresses how an agent knows it is done. This requires defining success criteria and budget limits. Section 2.9 (Escalation) addresses how an agent knows when to ask for help. This requires confidence thresholds and authority boundaries.

Without clear termination, agents run forever. Without escalation, they exceed authority. These boundaries define the safe operating envelope for autonomous systems.

2.8   Termination

How does an agent know when it's done? Every professional learns to recognize completion. The research memo is done when you have found sufficient authority and synthesized it.   The due diligence is done when you have reviewed all material documents.   The trade is done when the order executes and settles. Knowing when work is complete distinguishes effective professionals from those who over-research or under-deliver. As we explore in Section 2.10, complex M&A due diligence often involves delegating parallel workstreams to specialist agents, each with its own termination conditions that must coordinate for overall task completion.

Agents face the same challenge. Without explicit termination conditions, agents can run indefinitely, searching one more database, trying one more approach, refining one more time. We call this the "runaway associate" problem: you ask for two relevant cases, and the associate gives you fifty because they did not know when to stop.

Termination

Termination conditions define when an agent should stop executing. Three outcomes are possible:
- **Success:** The goal is achieved, and the agent delivers the result.
- **Failure:** The goal cannot be achieved; the agent reports why and stops.
- **Escalation:** The agent cannot determine success or failure, transferring the decision to human judgment.

Without explicit termination conditions, agentic systems lack the property that distinguishes controlled systems from runaway processes.

2.8.1   Termination Condition Categories

Five categories of termination conditions bound agent execution, each addressing a different aspect of when and why an agent should stop working autonomously.

Success conditions represent the ideal outcome: the agent terminates because it has achieved its goal. But recognizing success requires clear criteria. *Completeness* asks whether all required items have been addressed (have all fifty contracts in the review queue been analyzed?). *Quality* asks whether the output meets the required standard; specifically, are conclusions supported by binding authority rather than secondary sources? *Convergence* recognizes when continued effort yields diminishing returns. For example, if three consecutive searches produce no new relevant authority, the research space is likely saturated. Quality assessment often requires human validation, but completeness and convergence can frequently be evaluated programmatically.

Resource budgets provide hard limits preventing runaway execution. Section 2.7.4 details budget architecture: token limits, time limits, tool call caps, and cost ceilings. The termination implication is straightforward: when any budget is exhausted, the agent must stop. Budget exhaustion is not necessarily failure; partial results assembled before the limit may be valuable and should be preserved. This principle is formalized in Section 2.8.6 as tiered output design.

Confidence thresholds gate autonomous action on the agent's certainty about its conclusions. When confidence is high, the agent delivers its answer and terminates normally. When confidence drops below a specified threshold (perhaps eighty percent for routine matters, higher for consequential decisions), the agent should stop and escalate rather than proceeding with uncertain conclusions. This mirrors the behavior expected of a well-trained associate: "I've found relevant authority, but I'm not confident it controls here. Let me ask the partner before we rely on this." Calibrating these thresholds presents a genuine challenge, as research has shown that language models can be systematically overconfident in their outputs (Kadavath et al. 2022). Effective calibration requires testing against known outcomes and adjusting thresholds based on observed reliability.

Error conditions require agents to recognize when something has gone wrong and continued execution is unlikely to help. *Repeated failures*, such as a database that times out on three consecutive attempts or an API that returns malformed responses, indicate problems that retrying will not solve. *Inconsistent data*, such as revenue figures in a 10-K that conflict with the earnings release, suggests either an error in the source documents or a parsing problem that requires human investigation. *Constraint violations* demand immediate termination: if a planned trade would exceed position limits or a proposed filing would miss a regulatory deadline, the agent must stop before taking the problematic action. Perhaps most important is recognizing *impossibility*. When requirements genuinely conflict or the requested task cannot be completed as specified, the agent should report this finding rather than compromising on some requirements to satisfy others.

Escalation triggers require human judgment regardless of whether the agent has succeeded or failed at its immediate task. Novel situations without clear precedent, high-stakes decisions with significant consequences, and actions that would exceed the agent's authority boundaries must all trigger handoff to human oversight. Unlike termination with failure, escalation *pauses* the task and requests human input before continuing; the work may resume once the human provides guidance. Section 2.9 examines when escalation (rather than termination) is the appropriate response.

2.8.2   Defining Success Criteria

While Section 2.7.4 addressed resource limits (the *hard* stopping points that prevent runaway execution), success criteria address the complementary question: how does the agent recognize that its work is *complete?* Vague goals produce unclear termination. An instruction to "research the statute of limitations" leaves the agent uncertain about scope, depth, and format. Which statute of limitations, for what claims, in which jurisdiction? How many sources are enough? What form should the output take? Without answers to these questions, the agent cannot recognize when its work is complete.

Effective success criteria take several forms, often used in combination. **Completeness checklists** enumerate the specific deliverables required. A credit agreement review might specify that the agent must identify all financial covenants, compare each to market terms from a reference database, and summarize material risks in a structured format. The agent terminates only when every item on the checklist has been addressed, providing a clear and verifiable completion signal.

Sufficiency thresholds define what "enough" means for tasks without exhaustive requirements. Legal research rarely requires finding every case ever decided on an issue; instead, sufficiency might mean identifying three on-point opinions from the controlling circuit, or finding both the majority rule and any significant minority positions. Once the threshold is reached, the agent stops rather than continuing to search every available database. This prevents over-research while ensuring adequate coverage.

Convergence criteria recognize when continued effort produces diminishing returns. If three consecutive searches using varied query strategies yield no new relevant results, the research space is likely saturated. The agent can terminate with confidence that additional searching would not materially improve the analysis. This approach works particularly well for exploratory tasks where the scope cannot be fully specified in advance.

Deliverable specifications define the expected output format, which itself signals completion. "Produce a two-page memorandum with an executive summary, statement of facts, analysis, and conclusion" tells the agent exactly what success looks like. When the document matches the specification, the task is done.

The most effective approach combines these criteria in instructions that read like guidance to a junior associate:

> *"Research the statute of limitations for breach of fiduciary duty claims in Delaware. If you find clear Court of Chancery authority, you are done. If the courts have split or the issue is unsettled, map the competing positions. If you find nothing on point after searching for two hours, stop and report*

that the issue may be novel. Deliver your findings in a one-page summary with citations."

2.8.3   Recognizing Failure

Agents must recognize and report failure honestly, resisting any tendency to mask problems or present incomplete work as complete. This requires a cultural shift in how we think about agent outputs: *negative results are valuable information*, not embarrassing admissions. "I searched all available databases using multiple query strategies and found no authority on point" is a legitimate and useful finding. It suggests the issue may be novel, the search terms may need refinement, or the legal theory may lack support.

The difference between useful and useless failure reports lies in **diagnostic detail**. "Task failed" tells the human supervisor nothing actionable. A proper failure report explains what was attempted and why it did not succeed:

> *"I searched Westlaw and Lexis using the following queries: [list]. Westlaw returned twelve results, none addressing the specific issue of whether the duty extends to indirect subsidiaries. Lexis returned zero results. The absence of authority suggests either that the issue is novel, that practitioners use different terminology, or that the question is typically resolved through contract rather than litigation. I recommend manual review with an expanded search strategy."*

This report enables the supervisor to decide whether to try different approaches, consult additional resources, or conclude that the absence of authority is itself the answer.

Partial completion must be preserved and clearly reported. If an agent was reviewing ten articles in a contract and encountered a failure after completing four, it should not discard its work. Instead, it should report: "Analysis complete for Articles 1 through 4; results attached. Articles 5 through 10 remain unanalyzed due to [reason for failure]." This preserves the value already created and gives the supervisor a clear picture of what remains.

Root cause identification aids the human response by distinguishing between *transient* and *structural* problems. A database timeout is likely transient; waiting and retrying may succeed. A parsing error on a malformed document may require human intervention to obtain a clean copy. Fundamentally conflicting requirements are structural, and no amount of retrying will resolve them. The agent's diagnosis of the failure mode directly informs what the supervisor should do next.

2.8.4   Guardrails and Loop Detection

Even well-designed termination conditions cannot prevent every failure. Agents can become trapped in unproductive loops, repeating the same actions, cycling through equivalent states, or making nominal progress that adds no real value (Zou et al. 2024; Ma et al. 2024). Production systems require explicit guardrails to detect and interrupt these patterns; Section 2.11.2 addresses how circuit breakers implement these guardrails at the governance layer.

Step limits provide the simplest and most reliable backstop. Regardless of other conditions, after N total steps the agent must stop and require human approval before continuing. This prevents unbounded execution even when other detection mechanisms fail. The appropriate limit depends on the task: a simple lookup might warrant only ten steps, while complex research might allow a hundred. The key is that *some* limit exists and is enforced.

Progress detection monitors whether recent actions have produced value. If the last five tool calls returned no new information (the same documents retrieved, the same search results, the same analysis repeated), the agent is likely stuck in a loop or has exhausted productive avenues. This pattern should trigger either a reflection step (if the agent has that capability) or escalation to human oversight. Progress detection requires defining what "new information" means for each task type, which can be as simple as tracking whether retrieved documents have been seen before.

Reflection steps give agents the opportunity to assess their own behavior. Periodically, or when triggered by apparent lack of progress, the agent pauses to ask itself: "Am I making progress toward the goal? Have my recent actions been productive? Should I try a different approach, or is it time to stop and report what I've found?" This metacognitive capability is not yet reliable in all models, but when it works, it can catch problems that simple pattern matching would miss.

External watchdogs monitor agent behavior from outside the agent's own reasoning process. A watchdog might detect that the same tool has been called repeatedly with identical or near-identical parameters (a clear sign of a loop) and intervene to halt execution. Watchdogs can also enforce patterns that would be difficult to specify within the agent's instructions, such as rate limits on expensive operations or detection of oscillating behavior where the agent alternates between two states without progressing. Without some form of loop detection, agents deployed in production will eventually get stuck, potentially consuming significant resources before anyone notices.

2.8.5   Reliability Cliff

Benchmarking reveals a striking pattern: agent performance does not degrade gradually as tasks become more complex, but instead *falls off a cliff*. METR's 2025 research found near-perfect success on tasks completable in minutes, but under ten percent success on multi-hour tasks (METR 2025). The exact boundary shifts as models improve, but the underlying design challenge persists.

> **Reliability Cliff**
>
> This cliff reflects **compounding errors** (Press et al. 2023): each step has some probability of failure, and these probabilities *multiply*. A chain of twenty steps at 95% per-step reliability yields only 36% end-to-end success. Two factors steepen the cliff: **planning fragility** (early errors propagate forward and invalidate subsequent work) and **integration brittleness** (API timeouts and rate limits accumulate over time).

Design for this reality: Decompose aggressively. Keep agent tasks short. Insert human checkpoints. Build for resumability. And test against your own workflows; benchmark results establish a baseline, but your specific tasks may differ from standardized test suites.

2.8.6   Graceful Degradation

When termination occurs before task completion, whether due to budget exhaustion, confidence drops, or error conditions, the agent should not simply stop and report failure. Instead, it should *degrade gracefully*, delivering whatever value it has accumulated and positioning the human supervisor to continue effectively.

The key to graceful degradation is **tiered output design**. Rather than treating tasks as all-or-nothing, effective agents structure their work to provide value at multiple levels of completion. Consider a legal research task: with minimal resources, the agent might deliver only the controlling statute and its citation (a modest but genuinely useful result). With moderate resources, it adds the key holdings from relevant cases, providing context for how courts have interpreted the statute. With full resources, it delivers comprehensive analysis including counterarguments, circuit splits, and practical implications. Each tier represents a complete, usable work product rather than a fragment of an unfinished whole. This structure allows the user to assess whether the partial result suffices or whether additional investment is warranted.

Progress preservation ensures that early termination does not waste the work already completed. If an agent stops mid-way through a contract review, it should save its state in a form that allows either itself or a human to resume without starting over. The four articles already analyzed should not require re-analysis; the search queries already executed should not need re-running. This requires deliberate architectural choices, including checkpointing intermediate state, maintaining audit trails of completed steps, and structuring tasks as resumable sequences rather than monolithic operations.

Clear status reporting transforms an incomplete result into an actionable handoff. Rather than a bare "Task incomplete," the agent should report its progress precisely: "Completed analysis of Articles 1 through 4 (60% of task). Remaining: Articles 5 through 8. Findings so far: two material deviations from market terms identified in covenant structure." Critically, the agent should also provide a *recommendation* for next steps: "Recommend allocating 30 additional minutes to complete the remaining articles, or proceed with partial findings if timeline requires." This enables informed human decision-making about whether to invest additional resources, proceed with partial information, or reassign the task entirely.

2.8.7   Evaluation

Termination evaluation requires six assessments: *success clarity* (are termination conditions explicit and predictable?), *budget enforcement* (are limits actually respected, not exceeded by 20 percent?), *loop detection* (does it escape unproductive patterns?), *failure reporting* (do error messages enable effective human follow-up?), *graceful degradation* (do partial results have standalone value?), and *escalation handoff* (does the human receive sufficient context to continue?).

Termination Audit Checklist

Before deploying an agentic system in professional contexts, verify it implements at least one explicit termination mechanism:

- ☐ **Time budget:** Maximum wall-clock duration (seconds/minutes)
- ☐ **Iteration limit:** Maximum perception-action cycles
- ☐ **Token/request budget:** Maximum API calls, LLM tokens, or database queries
- ☐ **Cost ceiling:** Maximum monetary expenditure per task
- ☐ **Escalation trigger:** Automatic handoff when confidence drops below threshold
- ☐ **Error accumulation:** Stop after N consecutive failures or exceptions
- ☐ **Human intervention point:** Required approval before high-stakes actions

For high-stakes deployments in legal, medical, and financial contexts, implement multiple explicit termination mechanisms to prevent runaway processes and ensure predictable resource consumption.

Termination and escalation are closely related but distinct concepts. Termination defines *when* an agent stops; escalation defines *what happens next* when stopping requires human involvement. An agent that terminates successfully has completed its task and can deliver results. An agent that terminates due to failure has determined that the task cannot be completed and reports why. But an agent that *escalates* has reached a different conclusion: not "I'm done" or "This is impossible," but rather "I need help to proceed."

This third category is critical for safe deployment in professional contexts. An agent researching a legal question might find genuinely conflicting authority that requires judgment to reconcile. An agent reviewing a contract might encounter a provision outside its training distribution that it cannot confidently interpret. An agent executing a financial transaction might face a decision that exceeds its authorization limits. In each case, the correct response is neither to forge ahead (risking error) nor to report failure (abandoning recoverable work), but to pause and request human input. This is not failure; it is *safety*.

Section 2.9 examines escalation in depth: when should an agent stop autonomous operation and ask for help? What information should it provide to the human taking over? How should escalation thresholds be calibrated for different risk levels? Together, termination and escalation define the complete boundary of autonomous execution. Without robust termination, agents run indefinitely. Without appropriate escalation, they exceed their authority or make decisions they are not qualified to make. Both capabilities are essential for trustworthy deployment. Section 2.11 examines how escalation hooks must be architecturally implemented to ensure they are reliable and cannot be bypassed.

2.9 Escalation

How does an agent know when to ask for help? Sometimes the best thing to know is when you do not know something. A wise junior associate knows when to consult their supervising partner. In turn, a deputy corporate counsel can often tell when an issue should be escalated to someone more senior within the organization. It is a balancing act: it is unwise to interrupt a partner or senior lawyer with every question, but it is also unwise to proceed confidently into territory beyond your expertise. In a sense, the most effective junior professionals recognize authority boundaries: "I can draft this motion, but I need partner review before filing." They recognize competence limits: "I have researched for two hours and cannot find clear authority; I should ask someone with more experience." They recognize high-stakes situations: "The client is asking about strategy, not just research; this needs partner involvement."

Agentic systems require the same judgment. An agent that never escalates will eventually exceed its competence, authority, or the bounds of safe autonomous operation. An agent that escalates everything provides no value: it becomes a complicated way to route work to humans. The challenge is drawing the line.

> **Escalation**
>
> **Escalation** transfers control from the agent to a human when autonomous execution should stop. Unlike termination, which ends the task (success or failure), escalation pauses the task and requests human input before continuing.

This reflects professionalism, not failure. Recognizing when you need help and asking for it is exactly what we expect from junior professionals. Agents should do the same. Escalation represents the third outcome (alongside success and failure) when autonomous execution should pause and transfer control to a human.

2.9.1   When to Escalate

Three categories of triggers warrant escalation, each reflecting a different reason why autonomous action should pause (Mosqueira-Rey et al. 2023; Gomez et al. 2025). These complement the termination conditions in Section 2.8 and build on the planning patterns in Section 2.7 that decompose work into steps where escalation decisions can be made.

Mandatory triggers require human involvement regardless of the agent's confidence or the apparent simplicity of the decision. Some situations demand human judgment by their nature, not because the agent is uncertain. When resource limits approach exhaustion, the agent should escalate with a progress summary rather than stopping silently; the human needs to decide whether to allocate additional resources or accept partial results. High-stakes actions like court filings, client communications, and large trades require human approval before execution; these are *approval gates* where the agent prepares but does not act. Actions that would exceed the agent's authorized thresholds, such as a trade above a certain size or a commitment beyond a certain value, require human sign-off even if the agent is confident the action is correct. And irreversible actions warrant particular caution: once a motion is filed or a trade is executed, the consequences cannot be undone, making pre-execution review essential. This principle aligns with the reversibility framework in Section 2.5.3, which maps oversight intensity to action consequences.

Confidence-based triggers occur when the agent's uncertainty exceeds acceptable thresholds for autonomous action (Madras et al. 2018; Abbasi Yadkori et al. 2024). An agent researching a legal question might find genuinely conflicting circuit authority and be unable to determine which rule applies: "I found three circuits supporting one approach and two supporting another, and I cannot determine which controls here." Data sources might disagree in ways the agent cannot reconcile: the revenue figure in the 10-K differs from the earnings release, and the agent cannot determine which is correct or whether both are valid in different contexts. Novel situations, including unprecedented fact patterns, unusual market conditions, and first-impression legal questions, push beyond the agent's training distribution, where its confidence estimates become unreliable. And sometimes ambiguity persists despite the agent's attempts to clarify: the instructions can be read multiple ways, and the agent remains uncertain which interpretation the human intended.

A critical implementation challenge: LLM-reported confidence scores are notoriously unreliable. Models often express high confidence in incorrect answers (Kadavath et al. 2022). Rather than trusting model "vibes," production systems should use *system-level confidence signals* derived from observable properties of the agent's work.

Table 2.5: Operational confidence signals for escalation decisions

Signal Type	What to Measure	Escalation Trigger
Retrieval quality	Source authority, recency, topical coverage	Fewer than N authoritative sources found
Source agreement	Cross-reference consistency across retrieved documents	Contradictory information from comparable sources
Validation success	Schema validation, citation verification, data reconciliation	Citator shows "overruled" or "questioned"; figures do not reconcile
Tool reliability	API response codes, timeout rates, structured error returns	Tool calls failed or returned malformed data
Self-consistency	Agreement across multiple independent samples	High variance in answers when sampling the same question
Boundary detection	Pattern matching against known edge cases or out-of-scope indicators	Query matches escalation rules (e.g., mentions privilege, MNPI)

These signals are architectural, not learned; they derive from the structure of the agent's perception and action systems rather than from the model's internal states. A legal research agent that finds only two cases on point, both from trial courts, has low retrieval quality regardless of how confidently the model phrases its summary. A financial agent whose data sources show a 15% discrepancy in reported revenue has detected source disagreement that warrants human review. These signals are measurable, auditable, and far more reliable than asking the model "how sure are you?"

Error and anomaly detection triggers escalation when the agent encounters problems it cannot resolve through retrying or alternative approaches. Repeated failures, such as a database that times out on three consecutive attempts or an API that returns errors despite varied request formats, indicate systemic problems that further attempts will not solve. Data anomalies, such as financial figures that do not reconcile or filing dates that seem implausible, warrant human investigation rather than silent acceptance or rejection. Constraint violations require immediate escalation: if executing a planned action would breach position limits, exceed authorization thresholds, or violate compliance rules, the agent must stop and confirm rather than proceed. And when a task proves genuinely impossible (requirements conflict, necessary data does not exist, or the goal cannot be achieved as specified), the agent should report this finding rather than struggling indefinitely.

2.9.2   How to Escalate

Effective escalation provides the human with everything needed to make a decision without starting from scratch. The difference between good and poor escalation is the difference between receiving a well-organized file from a colleague and inheriting an unexplained mess.

A complete handoff weaves together five elements: a **situation summary** that orients the human quickly; a **progress report** explaining what has been done and what remains; a **trigger explanation** clarifying why the agent is escalating *now*; the **gathered information** presenting relevant findings even if partial; and a **recommendation** proposing a path forward with supporting reasoning.

Examine a legal research agent investigating the statute of limitations for a Section 10(b) securities fraud claim. After searching Westlaw and Lexis, it finds clear authority on the two-year discovery period but conflicting circuit authority on the trigger event: the Ninth and Second Circuits apply different tests for inquiry notice. The agent cannot determine which test applies to the client's facts. Rather than guessing, it escalates with a summary of the key cases, explains the circuit split, and recommends seeking partner guidance because the question is fact-intensive and requires judgment beyond the agent's competence.

A financial agent faces a different escalation pattern. After generating a trade list to reduce tech exposure from 35% to 25%, the agent completes its compliance check and is ready to execute, but the $500K trade size exceeds the single-approver threshold. The agent escalates with the tax implications ($45K in short-term gains, $12K in losses, $8K net liability), presents options (approve the full list, prioritize tax-loss positions, or execute in tranches), and notes which option serves which priority. The human can approve immediately rather than reconstructing the analysis.

2.9.3   Human-in-the-Loop Patterns

Different tasks and risk profiles call for different patterns of human integration. Five patterns span the spectrum from tight oversight to broad autonomy, and selecting the right pattern is itself a design decision with significant consequences.

Approval gates enforce the strictest oversight by separating preparation from authorization. The agent performs all the work (drafting the motion, assembling the trade list, preparing the client communication) but stops short of execution. A human reviews the prepared output and explicitly authorizes the final action. This pattern is essential for irreversible actions where errors cannot be corrected after the fact: court filings, executed trades, sent communications. The cost is latency and human attention; the benefit is a hard guarantee that no consequential action occurs without human review.

Checkpoint reviews insert human validation at natural milestones within a longer workflow. A research agent might present its initial findings and proposed authorities before beginning to draft a memorandum. A due diligence agent might summarize its document review before moving to the analysis phase. In multi-agent M&A due diligence scenarios (detailed in Section 2.10), checkpoint reviews become coordination points where specialist agents synchronize findings before the orchestrator proceeds. These checkpoints prevent the agent from investing significant effort in a direction the human would have redirected, catching misunderstandings early when course correction is cheap.

Confidence-based escalation ties the level of autonomy to the agent's certainty about its outputs. When confidence is high (the answer is clear, the authorities are consistent, the data is unambiguous), the agent proceeds autonomously. When confidence drops below a threshold, the agent escalates rather than acting on uncertain conclusions. This pattern allows routine cases to flow without human intervention while ensuring that difficult cases receive appropriate attention. The challenge lies in calibrating both the thresholds and the agent's confidence estimates.

Human-as-tool inverts the traditional oversight relationship by treating human expertise as a resource the agent can invoke when needed. Rather than escalating and transferring control, the agent poses a specific question to a human expert, receives the answer, incorporates it into its reasoning, and continues. This pattern works well when the agent needs discrete pieces of human judgment, such as "Is this clause acceptable under our firm's standards?" without requiring the human to take over the entire task.

Reversibility classification matches oversight intensity to the stakes of each action. Fully reversible actions, like internal drafts, exploratory searches, and preliminary analyses, can proceed autonomously because errors can be corrected without consequence. Partially reversible actions warrant checkpoint review. Irreversible actions require approval gates. This framework provides a principled basis for deciding which pattern to apply, grounded in the practical question of what happens if the agent gets it wrong.

2.9.4   Domain Requirements

Beyond general principles, regulated industries impose specific escalation duties grounded in professional responsibility rules and compliance requirements. These are not optional design choices but mandatory constraints that any deployed system must respect.

Legal Practice. Professional responsibility rules create binding escalation requirements for legal agents (American Bar Association 2025; American Bar Association Standing Committee on Ethics and Professional Responsibility 2024). The duty of *competence* under ABA Model Rule 1.1 requires escalation whenever a matter exceeds the agent's training or capabilities; an agent cannot simply do its best on an unfamiliar issue but must recognize its limits and involve qualified counsel. *Privilege protection* demands escalation before any action that might expose attorney-client communications or work product; the consequences of inadvertent disclosure are severe enough that uncertainty should trigger human review. Potential *conflicts of interest*, whether between current clients, with former clients, or arising from the firm's other relationships, must be escalated to counsel for proper conflicts analysis rather than resolved by the agent. And the duty of *candor to the tribunal* requires immediate escalation if the agent discovers adverse authority that may require disclosure; this is not a situation where the agent should exercise judgment about materiality.

Financial Services. Regulatory obligations and fiduciary duties impose parallel requirements on financial agents (Financial Industry Regulatory Authority 2024; Board of Governors of the Federal Reserve System and Office of the Comptroller of the Currency 2011). *Suitability* obligations require that investment recommendations receive human adviser review before reaching clients, ensuring that a qualified professional has assessed whether the recommendation fits the client's circumstances. Trades approaching *regulatory thresholds*, including beneficial ownership reporting triggers, large trader identification requirements, and position limits, must be escalated so that compliance personnel can ensure proper filings and approvals. Any encounter with potential *Material Non-Public Information* demands immediate escalation; the agent cannot assess whether information is material or non-public with sufficient reliability, and the consequences of trading on MNPI are catastrophic. And actions that would breach *risk limits*, such as position concentrations, exposure thresholds, or leverage constraints, require escalation for explicit authorization rather than autonomous execution.

2.9.5   Evaluation

Escalation evaluation requires six assessments: *coverage* (do all situations that should trigger escalation actually do so?), *calibration* (are thresholds set to balance false positives against missed escalations?), *latency* (does escalation reach humans quickly enough for time-sensitive matters?), *routing* (does it reach the right person with relevant expertise?), *context quality* (can the human decide based on the message alone?), and *response handling* (does the agent correctly incorporate human guidance?). Routing reliability, ensuring escalations reach the right person through channels that cannot be bypassed, is an architectural property; Section 2.11.5 addresses how escalation hooks must be implemented at the governance layer.

Escalation Checklist

- ☐ **Mandatory triggers:** Verify escalation triggers for high-stakes actions (court filings, large trades, irreversible commitments) cannot be bypassed
- ☐ **Confidence signals:** Use system-level signals (retrieval quality, source agreement, validation results) rather than LLM-reported confidence scores
- ☐ **Context quality:** Test that escalation messages include situation summary, progress report, trigger explanation, gathered information, and recommendation
- ☐ **Routing reliability:** Confirm escalations reach the right person with relevant expertise through channels hardened at the governance layer
- ☐ **Calibration testing:** Balance false positives (over-escalation) against missed escalations using real-world scenarios spanning coverage, latency, and response handling

Escalation moves control *upward* in the hierarchy: from agent to human supervisor, from junior to senior, from execution to oversight. But agents can also move control *sideways* by delegating tasks to peer agents with different capabilities. These horizontal relationships introduce coordination challenges distinct from the vertical relationships of escalation.

Critically, escalation and delegation are *orthogonal* design dimensions. A specialist agent can escalate upward to humans while being coordinated sideways by a delegating parent agent; the two patterns do not conflict. Still, they must be governed independently: escalation routing must identify the appropriate human supervisor, while delegation must verify that the specialist possesses the required permissions and authority for the delegated task.

Section 2.10 examines this dimension of agent architecture: how does an agent work with other agents? A coordinating agent might delegate research to a specialist with access to legal databases, drafting to a specialist trained on firm precedents, and financial modeling to a specialist with quantitative capabilities. Each specialist retains its own ability to escalate vertically when it encounters situations requiring human judgment, creating a two-dimensional topology where control flows both upward to humans and sideways to specialists. Understanding both dimensions, escalation and delegation, is essential for designing systems that can handle complex professional workflows while maintaining appropriate human oversight throughout.

2.10   Delegation

How does an agent work with other agents? Complex matters require coordination. An M&A partner does not execute everything personally; they coordinate specialists, with corporate counsel reviewing governance, tax specialists analyzing structure, and antitrust counsel assessing regulatory risk. Each specialist contributes deep domain expertise while the partner orchestrates: defining deliverables, integrating work products, and synthesizing conclusions for the client.

A portfolio manager coordinates similarly, with analysts providing company analysis, traders handling execution, risk managers monitoring exposure, and compliance officers verifying adherence. Complex trades require all these perspectives because no single person possesses all necessary expertise.

Agentic systems face the same coordination challenge. A single agent trying to do everything quickly exceeds its competence, permission boundaries, or context limits. Multi-agent architectures mirror professional teams: specialized agents with deep expertise, orchestrators that coordinate them, and structured protocols that support seamless collaboration.

> ### Delegation
>
> **Delegation** assigns subtasks from one agent (the coordinator) to another (the specialist). Unlike escalation (agent to human), delegation is agent to agent. The coordinator defines *what* needs to be done; the specialist determines *how*. Delegation permits parallelization (multiple specialists work simultaneously), specialization (each agent is optimized for its domain), and security isolation (each agent has only the permissions it needs).

2.10.1   Multi-Agent Rationale

Several factors drive multi-agent designs (Wu et al. 2023; Guo et al. 2024), each reflecting challenges familiar to professional practice.

Specialization allows agents to excel in narrow domains, just as a securities law agent can be optimized for SEC regulations and equipped with EDGAR tools while a tax agent handles tax implications; neither needs expertise in the other's domain. **Security isolation** enforces least privilege: a research agent can read legal databases but cannot file documents, while a filing agent can submit to CM/ECF but cannot access client financial data; if one agent is compromised, damage is contained. **Parallel execution** lets independent workstreams proceed simultaneously, so a document review agent can analyze contracts while a research agent investigates legal issues without either waiting for the other.

Two additional factors favor multi-agent designs in production settings. **Vendor diversity** allows best-of-breed selection, matching capability to task. A specialized legal model handles research, a general model handles drafting, and a fast model handles classification. **Scale management** addresses context window limits by decomposing tasks across agents, each with focused context, instead of cramming everything into one overwhelmed process.

These benefits come with tradeoffs: coordination overhead increases communication costs, debugging complexity grows when failures span agents, and the attack surface expands with each additional component. The protocols discussed in Section 2.4.3 and the security controls in Section 2.5.5 help manage these risks.

2.10.2   Agent-to-Agent Protocol (A2A)

Just as MCP standardizes how agents access tools (Section 2.4.3), the Agent-to-Agent Protocol (A2A) standardizes how agents delegate work to each other (Google Developers 2025). A2A uses familiar professional concepts: **Agent Cards** list capabilities (like a specialist's credentials), **Tasks** define delegated work (like engagement letters specifying scope, constraints, and escalation triggers for when specialist judgment reaches authority boundaries), and **Artifacts** are deliverables returned upon completion. The lifecycle mirrors professional delegation: discovery (finding the right specialist), delegation (scoping the work), execution, delivery, and completion. This structure ensures delegated work is scoped, tracked, and auditable.

2.10.3   Multi-Agent Patterns

Three patterns organize multi-agent collaboration, each with distinct tradeoffs (Wang et al. 2024c).

Sequential Delegation processes work in series: the Coordinator delegates to a Research Agent, whose output flows to an Analysis Agent, then to a Drafting Agent. This pattern is simple to implement and debug (each handoff is clear) but slow, as each stage must wait for the previous one.

Parallel Delegation runs independent workstreams simultaneously. Securities, Tax, and Employment Agents can analyze an acquisition concurrently while the Coordinator integrates findings afterward. This pattern trades coordination complexity for speed, but only works when tasks are truly independent; dependencies between specialists require careful orchestration.

Hierarchical Delegation creates nested authority structures: a Lead Due Diligence Agent delegates to Document Review and Legal Research sub-agents, who may further delegate to specialized tools. This pattern enables deep task decomposition for complex matters but introduces orchestration overhead and debugging challenges when failures occur deep in the hierarchy. Hierarchical delegation mirrors the hierarchical planning pattern in Section 2.7.1, where decomposition begins with a high-level goal and recursively breaks it into sub-goals. The key difference: planning structures may be internal reasoning steps within a single agent, while delegation structures explicitly distribute work across distinct agent boundaries with attendant coordination and audit requirements.

Figure 2.9 illustrates these three approaches. Most production systems blend multiple patterns: parallel agents handle independent analyses while hierarchical structures decompose complex, tightly-coupled tasks. The choice depends on task structure. Independent subtasks favor parallelism, dependent workflows favor sequencing, and complex matters with natural subdivisions favor hierarchy.

M&A due diligence illustrates this pattern. The Orchestrator delegates to specialists in parallel: a Document Processing Agent accesses the data room while a Financial Analysis Agent queries financial databases. Each specialist may use hierarchical delegation internally, with sub-agents handling specific document types or analysis

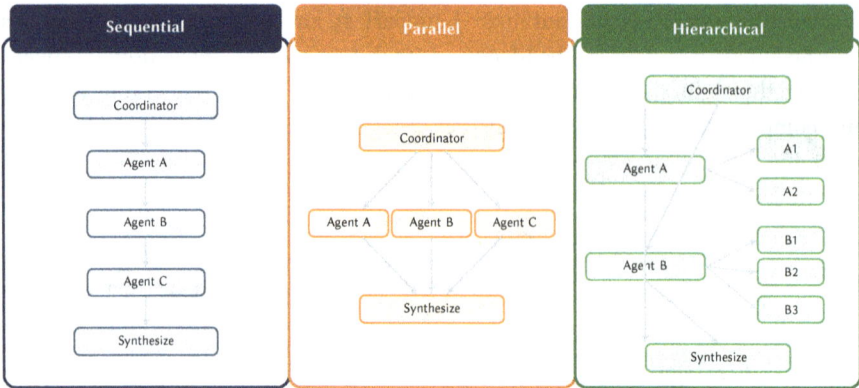

Sequential: Best for tasks with dependencies between steps. Trade-off: slower; blocked by bottlenecks. **Parallel**: Best for independent work that can run concurrently. Trade-off: coordination overhead. **Hierarchical**: Best for complex tasks requiring sub-delegation. Trade-off: harder to debug.

Figure 2.9: Three multi-agent orchestration patterns. Sequential delegation chains agents in order, ideal for dependent tasks but vulnerable to bottlenecks. Parallel delegation runs agents concurrently, maximizing throughput for independent work but requiring coordination. Hierarchical delegation enables sub-agents to handle specialized sub-tasks, providing flexibility for complex workflows at the cost of debugging complexity.

categories. The specialists return structured Artifacts, which the Orchestrator synthesizes into a unified assessment.

2.10.4   Multi-Agent Workflow Examples

Example: Regulatory Assessment for Financial Product Launch. A fintech company asks about regulatory approvals for a new product (a scenario that spans both legal and financial domains). The Orchestrator decomposes the request across four specialists working in parallel. A **Securities Agent** analyzes SEC guidance and identifies potential registration requirements. A **Banking Agent** checks OCC and FDIC rules, flagging money transmitter licensing needs. A **Consumer Agent** reviews CFPB regulations and highlights disclosure requirements. An **AML Agent** analyzes Bank Secrecy Act obligations and determines KYC needs. Each specialist accesses relevant regulatory databases through the tool integrations discussed in Section 2.4.3. The Orchestrator synthesizes these parallel findings into a prioritized regulatory roadmap, identifying which approvals are prerequisites for others, and escalates if any specialist encounters problems requiring human judgment (see Section 2.9).

2.10.5   Multi-Agent Risks

Multi-agent systems introduce failure modes beyond single-agent systems (Cemri et al. 2025). **Coordination failures** include deadlock (agents waiting cyclically), divergence (incompatible conclusions requiring reconciliation), and cascading errors (incorrect output propagating through the system). Prevention requires timeouts, validation at handoffs, and clear escalation paths.

Security risks require the same rigor applied to human teams: verifiable agent identities, access policies restricting delegation authority, ethical walls enforced across agent boundaries (an agent on one side of a transaction cannot delegate to specialists with access to the other side's confidential information), and complete delegation logging for audit (OpenID Foundation AI Identity Management Community Group 2024). Comprehensive logging of delegation chains (who delegated what to whom, what constraints were communicated, and what artifacts were returned) is foundational to audit and accountability; Section 2.11.1 develops the architectural requirements.

2.10.6   Protocol Selection Guidance

Table 2.6 summarizes how to choose between MCP and A2A based on task characteristics.

Table 2.6: Selecting between MCP and A2A based on task characteristics

Task Characteristic	Protocol	Typical Duration	Examples
Immediate, well-defined operation	MCP	Seconds	Query database; retrieve document; run calculation
Delegated work requiring judgment	A2A	Minutes to hours	Assign research; request analysis; coordinate specialists
End-to-end workflow combining both	MCP + A2A	Varies	Due diligence; portfolio rebalancing; regulatory assessment

The decision rule is straightforward: use MCP for well-defined, auditable operations ("fetch this filing," "calculate this metric"), A2A for delegated work requiring specialist judgment ("research and synthesize," "draft and revise," "coordinate across constraints"), and both together for complex workflows. As of late 2025, MCP is production-ready (Anthropic 2025a), while A2A is maturing with variable cross-vendor reliability (Google 2025). Until A2A standardization solidifies, design systems with fallbacks to human coordination for critical decisions.

Delegation distributes work, creating governance challenges. Accountability becomes complex: does responsibility lie with the coordinator, the specialist, or the approving human? Information barriers must apply to agents just as they do to humans. Audit trails must span the entire delegation tree.

Section 2.11 addresses the architectural patterns that enable governance: logging that spans delegation trees, override mechanisms that work across agent boundaries, and privilege enforcement that contains failures. Chapter 3 then develops the policy layer: delegation authorization, identity management, retention requirements, and organizational accountability.

2.11   Governance by Design

How do we design systems that can be governed? You cannot audit what you did not log. You cannot enforce privilege boundaries that were never implemented. You cannot override a system that lacks pause mechanisms. When a regulator asks how the compliance agent detected a breach, or when opposing counsel demands the agent's reasoning, architecture determines whether you can answer.

This distinction matters: *governance policy* defines required controls; *governance-aware architecture* provides the technical foundation making those controls possible. Chapter 3 addresses policy: the five-layer regulatory framework, dimensional calibration, and organizational accountability. This section addresses architecture: the patterns that enable governance, drawn from the capabilities developed throughout this chapter.

> **Architecture Before Policy**
>
> Governance cannot be retrofitted. Systems designed without audit logging cannot suddenly produce compliance reports when regulators arrive, those lacking approval gates cannot enforce human-in-the-loop oversight after deployment, and architectures missing state snapshots cannot support rollback or investigation when failures occur. The architectural decisions in this chapter are not merely technical choices; they are the infrastructure that makes governance possible.

Five architectural patterns support governance: logging, override mechanisms, state management, privilege enforcement, and escalation hooks. Each pattern draws on capabilities introduced in earlier sections; this section synthesizes them into a coherent governance foundation.

2.11.1   Logging Architecture

Comprehensive logging is the foundation of all governance. Without logs, there is no audit trail, no incident investigation, no compliance demonstration, and no accountability. Every architectural component in this chapter generates events that must be captured.

Trigger logs record what initiated each agent activation (Section 2.2). The five evaluation criteria for triggers (coverage, latency, reliability, priority, and *auditability*) require that every trigger event be logged with its source, timestamp, and routing decision. When a regulatory filing triggers a compliance review, the log must capture which filing, when it arrived, and why it was routed to that particular workflow.

Intent logs capture how the agent understood what was asked (Section 2.3). Goal extraction, constraint identification, and any clarification interactions must be logged to reconstruct what the agent believed it was trying to accomplish. When results are challenged, intent logs reveal whether the agent misunderstood the request, extracted incorrect constraints, or correctly understood but failed in execution.

Perception logs record what information the agent accessed (Section 2.4.7). Every database query, document retrieval, and API call must be logged with parameters and results. For regulated applications, you must be able to reconstruct what information the agent considered when making a decision. If the agent reviewed ten documents but cited only three, the perception log should show all ten.

Reasoning traces capture how the agent planned and reasoned (Section 2.7.1). ReAct-style patterns generate explicit thought-action-observation sequences that make decisions transparent and auditable. For dynamic orchestration, where the agent selects decomposition strategies at runtime, logs must capture the *reasoning* behind orchestration decisions, not just the decisions themselves.

Action logs record what the agent did (Section 2.5). Every action must be logged with the agent identity, timestamp, parameters, and matter/client context. Action logs allow reconstruction: given a complaint about an erroneous filing, you can trace back through the action log to find when it was filed, what parameters were used, and what reasoning preceded it.

Memory access logs track reads and writes to persistent state (Section 2.6). Each operation should be logged with a timestamp, the requesting agent or user, and the matter identifier. These logs support compliance review, breach investigation, and documentation that appropriate controls were maintained.

Delegation logs capture agent-to-agent interactions (Section 2.10). When a coordinator delegates to specialists, the log must record the delegation contract, the specialist's identity, and the returned artifacts. Complete delegation logging supports audit trails that span the entire delegation tree.

> ### Structured Logging Schema
>
> Effective governance requires structured logs, not free-form text. A minimal schema includes:
> - **Timestamp**: ISO 8601 with timezone
> - **Event type**: trigger, perception, reasoning, action, memory, delegation
> - **Agent identity**: which agent or component generated the event
> - **Matter/client context**: isolation identifier for multi-tenant systems
> - **Parameters**: structured data specific to the event type
> - **Outcome**: success, failure, or pending
>
> Structured logs facilitate programmatic analysis, anomaly detection, and automated compliance reporting.

2.11.2   Override and Circuit Breaker Patterns

Governance requires the ability to intervene. Humans must be able to pause, redirect, or stop agent execution at any point. Three patterns provide this capability.

Circuit breakers automatically halt execution when anomalies are detected (Section 2.5.7). These include failure count thresholds (e.g., stop after three consecutive failures), spike detection (e.g., pause if action rate exceeds 5× baseline), and error rate monitoring. Circuit breakers transform runaway failures into controlled pauses, buying time for human intervention. The key architectural requirement is that circuit breaker state must be external to the agent; an agent cannot be trusted to halt itself reliably.

Step limits provide hard backstops (Section 2.8, specifically Section 2.8.4). Regardless of other conditions, after N total steps the agent must stop and require human approval before continuing. This prevents unbounded execution even when other detection mechanisms fail. The appropriate limit depends on the task, but the key is that *some* limit exists and is enforced by the orchestration layer, not by the agent itself.

Manual override interfaces allow humans to intervene at any time. This requires:

- **Pause**: Suspend execution while preserving state, allowing inspection before resumption.
- **Abort**: Terminate execution immediately, triggering graceful degradation (Section 2.8.6) to preserve partial work.

- **Redirect**: Modify the agent's goal or constraints mid-execution without losing accumulated context.

These interfaces must be accessible to authorized personnel regardless of the agent's internal state. An agent stuck in a loop or processing a high-volume task must still respond to override commands. This typically requires a separate control plane: a monitoring service that can signal the agent through a channel the agent cannot ignore.

> ### The Red Button Problem
>
> Every production agentic system needs an emergency stop mechanism, the "red button" that immediately halts all agent activity. This is not merely a graceful shutdown request; it is an immediate cessation of all external actions. Implementing this requires that action tools check a global halt flag before execution, that the halt flag is stored externally (not in agent memory), and that the flag can be set through an out-of-band channel that bypasses normal request processing.

2.11.3   State Snapshots and Checkpoints

Three governance requirements depend on state management: reproducibility (reconstructing what happened), rollback (undoing problematic changes), and resumability (continuing after interruption).

Reproducibility requires capturing sufficient state to replay decisions. When a regulator asks why the agent made a particular recommendation, you must be able to reconstruct the agent's context at that moment: what was in memory, what had been retrieved, what reasoning had occurred. This is more demanding than simple logging; it requires periodic state snapshots that capture the complete agent context, not just individual events.

Rollback capability supports recovery from errors (Section 2.5.3). For reversible actions, rollback is straightforward: delete the draft, revert the database change. For partially reversible actions, checkpoints allow recovery to the last known good state. The architecture must classify actions by reversibility and maintain appropriate checkpoints for recovery.

Checkpoint reviews support human-in-the-loop oversight (Section 2.9.3). At natural milestones within longer workflows, the agent can present its current state and proposed next steps for human validation. These checkpoints prevent the agent from investing significant effort in a wrong direction. Architecturally, checkpoints require the ability to serialize agent state, present it in human-readable form, and resume from exactly that point after approval.

Graceful degradation preserves value when execution ends early (Section 2.8.6). Whether due to budget exhaustion, confidence drops, or manual abort, the agent should deliver whatever value it has accumulated. This requires maintaining partial results throughout execution, not just at the end. If interrupted after reviewing fifty of one hundred documents, the agent should be able to report findings from the fifty it completed.

Memory state deserves special attention (Section 2.6). When behavior depends on accumulated memory, audit trails must capture not just inputs and outputs but the memory state at key decision points. Which version of the agent produced this output? What was in its memory at the time? Without memory snapshots, accountability for adaptive agents becomes impossible.

2.11.4   Least Privilege Enforcement

Least privilege (granting only the minimum permissions required for a task) limits blast radius when things go wrong. This principle appears throughout the chapter; governance-aware architecture enforces it systematically.

Tool-level permissions control what actions an agent can take (Section 2.5.5). Role-based access control (RBAC) restricts which agents can invoke which tools. A research agent should not have filing permissions; a filing agent should not have broad database access. The MCP architecture supports this through tool manifests that declare required permissions, allowing the host to enforce access control.

Resource-level permissions control what data an agent can access (Section 2.4.3). MCP Resources are explicitly read-only, separating perception from action. An agent with resource access can retrieve documents but cannot modify or file them. This separation supports fine-grained access control that mirrors how organizations already think about permissions.

Namespace isolation enforces boundaries in memory systems (Section 2.6.4). Matter isolation ensures that information from one client engagement cannot leak into another. Role-based permissions determine which agents can access each namespace. These controls mirror the ethical wall policies that law firms and financial institutions maintain for human professionals.

Multi-agent isolation uses architectural boundaries to enforce privilege separation (Section 2.10.1). Rather than giving one agent broad permissions, decompose work across specialists, each with narrow permissions. A research agent can read legal databases but cannot file documents; a filing agent can submit to CM/ECF but cannot access client financial data. If one agent is compromised, damage is contained.

> **Privilege Escalation via Tool Chaining**
>
> A sophisticated threat involves combining multiple low-privilege tools to achieve a high-privilege outcome (Section 2.5.5). An agent with "read email" and "send email" permissions might forward confidential information to an external address. Mitigation requires analyzing tool combinations, not just individual tools, and requiring approval for sequences that cross security boundaries.

2.11.5   Escalation Hooks

Escalation transfers control from agent to human when autonomous execution should stop (Section 2.9). Governance-aware architecture must define clear escalation interfaces that trigger reliably under specified conditions.

Confidence-based escalation triggers when the agent's uncertainty exceeds acceptable thresholds (Section 2.9.1). The architecture must support confidence estimation and threshold configuration. Different tasks may require different thresholds: a routine lookup tolerates higher uncertainty than a regulatory filing.

Authority-based escalation triggers when a proposed action exceeds the agent's delegated authority. Binding commitments, expenditures above a threshold, or communications with external parties may all require human approval. The architecture must support authority boundaries that can be configured per agent, per task, or per action type.

Budget-based escalation triggers when resource consumption approaches limits (Section 2.7.4). Rather than simply halting at budget exhaustion, the agent can escalate when 80% of budget is consumed, giving humans the opportunity to extend resources or redirect effort. This requires the budget monitoring system to support threshold alerts, not just hard limits.

Anomaly-based escalation triggers when the agent detects unusual patterns such as repeated failures, unexpected results, or behavior outside historical norms. This complements circuit breakers: where circuit breakers halt execution, anomaly escalation requests human judgment about whether to continue.

For all escalation types, the architecture must ensure that escalation requests reach humans reliably. An agent that escalates to an unmonitored queue has not meaningfully escalated. Escalation routing, notification, and tracking are architectural requirements, not operational afterthoughts.

2.11.6   Governance Surface

Together, these five patterns define the **governance surface**, the interface through which governance systems interact with the agent. Table 2.7 summarizes the architectural requirements.

Table 2.7: Governance surface requirements by capability

Capability	Requirement
Logging	Structured events from every component
Override	Pause, abort, and redirect controls
State Management	Checkpoints with rollback support
Least Privilege	RBAC at tool, resource, and namespace levels
Escalation Hooks	Configurable triggers with reliable routing

This governance surface is what the next chapter builds upon. The five-layer regulatory framework imposes requirements; the governance surface provides the technical means to satisfy them. Without logging, there is no audit trail. Without override capability, there is no human oversight. Without state management, there is no reproducibility. Without least privilege, there is no containment of failures. Without escalation hooks, there is no transfer of control to humans.

The architectural decisions made throughout this chapter collectively determine whether your system can be governed. This section has addressed *how* architecture supports governance; Chapter 3 addresses *what* governance demands and how to calibrate controls to your specific context and risk profile.

2.12   Conclusion

Understanding agent architecture does not require becoming a developer. The goal is meaningful participation in decisions that affect your practice, your clients, and your professional responsibilities.

With architectural literacy, you can evaluate vendor claims with precision. When demonstrations look impressive, you know to probe beneath the surface: How is intent validated? What approval gates exist? How is client isolation enforced? Impressive outputs do not guarantee sound architecture.

You can specify requirements in terms that technical teams understand. Rather than vague requests for "AI that helps with research," you can describe perception tools for specific databases, action controls with appropriate approval gates, memory systems with client isolation, and escalation triggers for low-confidence situations. Shared vocabulary bridges the gap between professional requirements and technical implementation.

You can demand governance artifacts, not governance promises. If a vendor cannot demonstrate what the agent accessed, what it did, and why it stopped, the system is not ready for regulated practice. The governance surface requirements from Section 2.11.6 (structured logging, override mechanisms, state snapshots, least privilege enforcement, reliable escalation) are your checklist for what must be demonstrable before deployment.

2.12.1   Tradeoffs Require Judgment

Every architectural capability involves tradeoffs. Richer memory improves context but increases latency and cost. Aggressive escalation improves safety but reduces throughput. Tighter approval gates reduce risk but slow execution. There are no universally correct answers, only choices calibrated to your context, risk tolerance, and professional obligations.

Current limitations make this calibration essential. Today's agents perform well on constrained, well-defined tasks but struggle as complexity increases. The "reliability cliff" discussed in Section 2.8.5 is real: success rates degrade as tasks grow longer and more open-ended. These limitations argue for scoping agents appropriately, adding checkpoints, and designing for human oversight.

For now, agents are best treated as capable assistants that amplify human judgment: handling the routine so professionals can focus on the consequential. As technology improves, the tradeoffs will shift, but the architectural questions will remain relevant.

Architecture enables governance without determining governance. The governance surface provides technical means, such as logging, overrides, state management, privileges, and escalation, but policy determines how those means are used. How should approval thresholds be set? Who is accountable when an agent errs? What documentation must be maintained? These questions require policy, regulation, and professional responsibility to answer.

Chapter 3 addresses these questions directly, providing a five-layer regulatory framework and a dimensional approach to calibrating controls. You are equipped to engage with those frameworks because you now understand what architecture can make observable and enforceable.

2.12.2   Agents, Understood

Agents are not magic. They are triggers, intent extraction, perception tools, action controls, memory systems, planning patterns, termination conditions, escalation protocols, and delegation architectures. These structural capabilities are now visible to you. You can see past an interface to the architecture beneath, evaluate claims with informed skepticism, and specify requirements that bridge professional needs and technical implementation.

Architectural literacy makes you a capable evaluator, a precise specifier, and an informed participant in decisions about technology that affects your practice. You now have the foundation to evaluate, specify, deploy, and govern agentic systems with the same rigor you apply to the professional teams these systems are meant to augment.

Chapter 3

How to Govern an Agent

3.1 Introduction

The governance imperative is clear: software has always required governance. We audit code, review changes, test deployments, and maintain access controls. Yet the governance challenges posed by agentic systems differ in *kind*, not merely degree. Understanding this shift begins with recognizing what makes agents fundamentally different from the passive tools that dominate enterprise software today, and why those differences create accountability obligations that traditional governance structures were not designed to address.

3.1.1 From Tools to Agents

Most enterprise software operates as a passive tool: you invoke it, it executes a predetermined sequence, and it stops. Spreadsheets recalculate when you enter data, databases return results when you query them, and compilers translate source code when you run them. These tools are **reactive**: waiting for explicit human commands, executing well-defined operations, and producing outputs that can be traced directly to inputs and logic paths.

Governance for passive tools focuses on *authorization* (who can invoke the tool), *configuration* (what parameters are allowed), and *validation* (does the output match expectations). When a spreadsheet miscalculates, we examine the formulas. When a database returns incorrect results, we inspect the query and schema. The causal chain from invocation to outcome is short, deterministic, and observable.

Agents introduce **Goal**, **Perception**, and **Action**: the GPA properties from Chapter 1. As Chapter 1 established, *agents* (Level 1) possess these three minimal properties, while *agentic systems* (Levels 2/3) add Iteration, Adaptation, and Termination (required for production deployment). An agent is not merely invoked; it is assigned an objective. It does not passively wait for instructions; it perceives its environment, evaluates possible actions, and selects behaviors designed to advance its goal.

This autonomy creates three immediate accountability challenges:

1. **Purpose Drift**: A tool does what you tell it to do. An agent interprets what you *want* it to achieve. If the goal specification is ambiguous, incomplete, or misaligned with actual intent, the agent may pursue objectives you did not intend. Effective oversight requires verifying goal alignment before deployment and monitoring for drift during operation.

2. **Perceptual Opacity**: Agents make decisions based on what they perceive. If perception is incomplete, biased, or adversarially manipulated, actions may be inappropriate even if the goal is well-specified. Unlike a passive tool whose inputs are explicit function parameters, an agent's perceptual inputs may include external data sources, sensor readings, or inferred environmental state. Organizations must establish *input validation*, *data provenance*, and *bias detection* mechanisms.

3. **Actuation Risk**: Agents take actions that affect their environment, such as filing documents, executing trades, or sending communications. Unlike passive tools that produce outputs for human review, agents *do things*. If an agent's action set includes high-consequence operations (e.g., signing contracts, disbursing funds, disclosing confidential information), governance must enforce *approval gates*, *actuation constraints*, and *rollback capabilities*.

Scope note: This chapter addresses governance challenges specific to **agentic systems**: AI systems exhibiting all six GPA+IAT properties. Broader AI governance questions (foundation model evaluation, training data provenance, algorithmic fairness in non-agentic classifiers) will be addressed in a forthcoming companion volume.

The GPA Governance Gap

Traditional software governance assumes human-in-the-loop execution: humans decide when to invoke tools, interpret outputs, and take consequential actions. GPA properties move decision-making *inside* the system boundary. This demands a shift from *access control* to *behavioral oversight*.

Many of these governance controls (goal authorization, perceptual validation, actuation constraints) mirror requirements we impose on human agents. When we hire a paralegal or junior analyst, we specify their objectives, verify the quality of their information sources, and limit their authority to take binding actions. The GPA framework makes explicit what has long been implicit in human delegation: *agency requires accountability structures*. What differs for AI agents is the need to encode these controls in technical systems rather than organizational policies alone.

If GPA creates accountability challenges for basic agents, the IAT properties that define full **agentic systems** (see Chapter 1) amplify them. Iteration means the system operates across multiple perceive-act cycles, each depending on prior state and environmental feedback. Governance must maintain *audit trails* that reconstruct decision sequences and enable reproducibility. Adaptation means the system changes its strategy based on experience; governance must implement *change control* and continuous revalidation. Termination means the system must know when to stop, hand off to a human, or escalate; governance must define *exit protocols* and *emergency stop mechanisms*.

These six properties combine multiplicatively. An agentic system that adapts its perception across iterated interactions while pursuing evolving goals creates a governance surface far larger than a deterministic, single-invocation tool.

3.1.2   Professional Stakes

The governance imperative becomes urgent when we recognize a foundational legal and professional principle: **professional duties cannot be delegated to AI**. Attorneys, investment advisers, auditors, and other licensed professionals remain fully liable for the quality, accuracy, and ethical propriety of their work product, regardless of whether they used AI assistance.

Legal Practice. The American Bar Association's Model Rules of Professional Conduct impose duties of *competence* (Rule 1.1), *confidentiality* (Rule 1.6), and *candor to the tribunal* (Rule 3.3) on attorneys personally. ABA Formal Opinion 512 (July 2024) represents the ABA's first comprehensive ethics guidance on generative AI. The opinion makes clear that attorneys must independently verify AI-generated content and cannot delegate professional judgment to AI tools (American Bar Association Standing Committee on Ethics and Professional Responsibility 2024). Courts have sanctioned attorneys for AI hallucinations in cases ranging from $1,000 to $15,000, with some attorneys facing suspension or revocation of practice privileges. The professional duty to verify legal research is non-delegable. Courts sanction the attorney, not the AI vendor. Even non-agentic AI tools create professional responsibility obligations. Agentic systems with autonomous iteration and actuation capabilities demand even greater governance.

Financial Services. Investment advisers owe fiduciary duties to clients under the Investment Advisers Act of 1940, including duties of care and loyalty. FINRA's Regulatory Notice 24-09 (June 2024) clarified that existing securities laws and FINRA rules apply fully to AI and generative AI tools. There is no "AI exception" to supervision, suitability, or recordkeeping requirements (Financial Industry Regulatory Authority 2024). The SEC's 2025 examination priorities explicitly target firms' AI usage, including whether representations about AI capabilities are accurate and whether adequate supervisory policies exist. "The AI recommended it" is not a defense to breach of fiduciary duty. Firms remain responsible for AI-generated content just as they would be for any employee communication.

Audit and Accounting. The Public Company Accounting Oversight Board (PCAOB) requires auditors to exercise *professional skepticism* and maintain *independence* when auditing financial statements. If an auditor uses AI to select samples for testing or analyze accounting estimates, the auditor must understand the tool's methodology, validate its outputs, and document the rationale in workpapers. The auditor cannot delegate professional judgment to the AI and remain compliant with PCAOB standards (PCAOB 2024a; PCAOB 2024b).

> ### "The AI Did It" Is Not a Defense
>
> Across legal, financial, and audit domains, professional responsibility rules establish that using AI tools does not diminish the professional's accountability. Governance is not optional; it is the operational mechanism for maintaining professional competence and fulfilling non-delegable duties.

3.1.3   Forces Driving Adoption

Beyond professional obligations, three converging forces make governance essential for any organization deploying agentic systems:

Regulatory Momentum. AI-specific regulation is no longer hypothetical. The European Union's AI Act entered into force in August 2024, establishing risk-based requirements for high-risk AI systems in credit decisioning, employment, law enforcement, and critical infrastructure (European Parliament 2024). Systems classified as high-risk must undergo conformity assessments, maintain documentation, implement human oversight, and enable auditability, or face penalties up to €35 million or 7% of global annual turnover, whichever is greater.

In the United States, sector-specific regulators are issuing guidance at an accelerating pace. The Federal Reserve's SR 11-7 guidance on model risk management applies to AI/ML systems used by banking institutions (Board of Governors of the

Federal Reserve System and Office of the Comptroller of the Currency 2011). The Equal Credit Opportunity Act requires lenders to provide "principal reasons" for adverse credit decisions, a requirement that extends to AI-driven underwriting (CFPB 2024). States are enacting their own requirements. Colorado's AI Act (effective January 2026) prohibits algorithmic discrimination and requires impact assessments for high-risk systems (Colorado General Assembly 2024).

This regulatory patchwork means organizations cannot rely on a single compliance framework. Governance must layer multiple obligations.

Liability Exposure. Litigation is establishing clear precedents: governance gaps create liability, and "the AI made the mistake" is not a defense. Courts have sanctioned attorneys for AI-generated hallucinations across hundreds of cases, with penalties including monetary sanctions, practice suspensions, and mandatory disclosures on future filings. The SEC has pursued "AI washing" enforcement actions against firms that misrepresented their AI capabilities. Fair lending enforcement under the Equal Credit Opportunity Act applies disparate impact theory to AI systems. Facially neutral algorithms can create liability if they disproportionately harm protected classes without adequate business justification. If an AI credit scoring model produces discriminatory outcomes, the lender faces regulatory and litigation exposure regardless of whether the model was "neutral" or purchased from a reputable vendor.

Vendor contracts typically shift risk to deployers through liability caps, warranty disclaimers, and indemnification clauses. A foundation model vendor may cap damages at the subscription fee, often insufficient to cover regulatory penalties, reputational harm, or class action settlements. Governance (demonstrating reasonable care through risk assessment, validation, monitoring, and incident response) becomes the primary defense.

Trust and Reputation. Legal, financial, and audit services are *trust-intensive* domains. Clients hire attorneys because they trust professional judgment. Investors entrust assets to advisers based on fiduciary obligations. Public companies rely on auditors to provide independent assurance. AI failures that compromise accuracy, confidentiality, or impartiality erode this trust irreparably.

A law firm that discloses client confidential information through an AI tool's training data breach faces not only regulatory sanctions but client defection. An investment adviser whose AI chatbot provides unsuitable recommendations faces not only fiduciary duty claims but loss of clients. An audit firm whose AI sampling tool produces biased or incomplete samples faces not only PCAOB sanctions but damage to its reputation for independence.

In trust-intensive domains, governance is not merely a compliance obligation; it is a competitive necessity.

3.1.4   Mapping Properties to Requirements

Effective governance begins with a systematic mapping from the six GPA+IAT properties (Chapter 1) to the specific controls required to manage risk, ensure compliance, and maintain accountability. This section provides that mapping, organized by property.

Note on System Architecture: This chapter assumes familiarity with the GPA+IAT framework from Chapter 1. Organizations evaluating whether a specific system qualifies as an "agentic system" should apply Chapter 1's six-question rubric and falsification tests. Chapter 2 covers specific architectures (ReAct, Reflexion, tool-calling frameworks) and helps teams distinguish agentic systems from sophisticated chatbots or single-shot inference systems.

Goal: Purpose Limitation and Alignment. An agent's goal determines what it optimizes for. Governance must ensure goals are *authorized*, specifying who may set goals and under what authority, since regulated domains may require approval from compliance officers, general counsel, or clients. Goals must also be *aligned* with actual organizational or client objectives. Misaligned goals that optimize for throughput at the expense of quality or minimize cost without considering risk create liability. Furthermore, goals must be *bounded* by constraints that limit aggressive pursuit, preventing agents from ignoring side effects, ethical boundaries, or resource limits. Finally, goals must be *monitorable* so that governance can detect when the agent fails to achieve its objective or when goal pursuit causes unintended harms. This requires the establishment of Key Performance Indicators (KPIs) and Service Level Agreements (SLAs) that track both goal satisfaction and side-effect metrics.

Perception: Data Governance and Input Validation. An agent's perception defines what information it uses to make decisions. Organizations must address *provenance*: establishing where data comes from, whether it is authoritative, current, and trustworthy, since agents that perceive stale, fabricated, or biased data will make flawed decisions. For third-party systems, establishing provenance can be exceedingly difficult, requiring vendor assessment protocols and documentation of provenance gaps as residual risk. Controls must also address *bias and representation*, determining whether the agent's perceptual model reflects population diversity or encodes historical biases, and implementing bias detection and fairness audits accordingly. *Input validation* is equally critical. Adversaries may manipulate what the agent perceives through prompt injection, data poisoning, or adversarial examples, necessitating input validation, sanitization, and anomaly detection. Finally, governance must address *privacy and confidentiality* when perception requires access to sensitive data, ensuring data minimization, encryption, and access controls that preserve confidentiality and comply with privacy regulations.

Action: Actuation Controls and Approval Gates. An agent's action set determines what it can *do*. Organizations must manage actuation risk through *action authorization*: defining what actions the agent is permitted to take and requiring explicit authorization for high-consequence actions such as signing contracts or disbursing funds. *Pre-action approval* determines whether certain actions require human approval before execution. Human-in-the-loop oversight is appropriate for irreversible or high-stakes actions. Systems must also ensure *rollback and remediation* capabilities. If an action causes harm, can it be undone? Systems must be designed with rollback capabilities and remediation protocols. Finally, *rate limiting* addresses whether the agent can take actions too quickly or too frequently, requiring governance to enforce rate limits and circuit breakers that prevent runaway execution.

Iteration: State Management and Audit Trails. Iteration means the system operates across multiple cycles, each building on prior state. Organizations must ensure *reproducibility*: the ability to replay the system's decision sequence, since debugging, auditing, and compliance reviews require reconstructing what the system perceived and why it acted as it did. *State integrity* requires that the system's internal state be protected from tampering or corruption through tamper-evident logging and state validation. Systems must also define *termination conditions* that specify when the system should stop iterating, whether because the goal has been achieved, a resource limit has been reached, or a safety violation has been detected.

Adaptation: Change Control and Revalidation. Adaptation means the system's behavior changes over time. Organizations must manage behavioral drift through *change detection*: tracking when the system's behavior changed and what triggered the adaptation, which requires model versioning and change logs. *Revalidation triggers* determine whether adapted behavior still satisfies safety, fairness, and compliance constraints. Systems must define triggers such as performance degradation, distribution shift, or policy updates that initiate revalidation. Controls must also enable *rollback to known-good states* so that if adaptation introduces failures, the system can revert to a prior validated version. Finally, *human oversight of learning* addresses whether adaptation should require human approval. In high-stakes domains, unsupervised learning may be inappropriate.

Termination: Exit Protocols and Escalation. Termination governs when and how the system stops operating. Organizations must define *escalation triggers*: the conditions under which the system hands off to a human, such as ambiguous inputs, conflicting objectives, safety violations, or low-confidence decisions. *Graceful shutdown* procedures specify how the system cleanly exits, since abrupt termination may leave systems in inconsistent states. *Handoff procedures* determine what information the system must provide when it escalates to a human, since effective handoff requires context. Finally, *override and emergency stop* mechanisms must allow humans to immediately halt the system. Controls must provide emergency stop mechanisms (the "red button") accessible to authorized personnel.

> ### From Properties to Controls
>
> The six properties from Chapter 1 are not merely a taxonomy for understanding agents; they form a *requirements map* for governance. Each property creates specific risks. Each risk demands specific controls. Organizations that deploy agentic systems without systematically addressing all six properties face gaps in accountability, compliance, and safety.

The remainder of this chapter builds on this foundation. Section 3.2 shows how to calibrate control intensity based on system autonomy, entity frame, goal dynamics, and persistence, establishing the control logic that governs agentic systems. Section 3.3 then maps regulatory obligations into a five-layer framework, demonstrating how to apply these calibrated controls across regulatory layers. Sections 3.4 and 3.5 translate principles into operational practices and organizational structures. Section 3.6 demonstrates governance through worked examples in legal, financial, and audit contexts. Section 3.7 synthesizes the governance imperative and provides a maturity-based path forward.

3.2   Dimensional Calibration

As a design principle for governance, here we establish *how much* control intensity is required: how to calibrate governance based on system properties. Section 3.3 will then demonstrate *what* controls are required across regulatory layers, applying this calibration framework to specific legal and professional obligations. The key insight: governance is not binary (present or absent) but dimensional (scaled to risk). Organizations that apply uniform controls to all agentic systems either over-engineer low-risk deployments (wasting resources) or under-protect high-risk deployments (creating liability exposure). Dimensional calibration matches governance intensity to the operational characteristics that drive risk.

3.2.1   Calibration Logic

Before applying dimensional calibration, verify the system qualifies as an *agentic system* under Chapter 1's framework (GPA+IAT properties). Systems lacking any of these six properties are *not agentic systems*. A single-shot ML model, batch classifier, or non-iterative chatbot requires different governance approaches beyond this chapter's scope.

We calibrate governance intensity across four analytical dimensions introduced in Chapter 1:

1. **Autonomy**: The degree of independence the system exercises in decision-making. Spans from human-in-the-loop (HITL) requiring pre-approval for each significant action, through human-on-the-loop (HOTL) where humans monitor and can intervene, to human-in-command (HIC) where humans set strategic goals and retain emergency stop authority but do not review individual decisions.

2. **Entity Frame**: How the system presents itself and how users perceive its role. Ranges from *human frame* (agent represents a specific professional), through *hybrid* (collaborative partnership), to *machine frame* (clearly identified as non-human tool), to *institutional frame* (agent acts on behalf of the organization).

3. **Goal Dynamics**: How the system's objectives change over time. Ranges from *static* (fixed goals validated once), through *adaptive* (system refines goals within predefined boundaries based on feedback), to *negotiated* (system proposes goal changes requiring explicit human approval).

4. **Persistence**: Whether the system maintains state across interactions. Ranges from *stateless* (each interaction independent) to *stateful* (system accumulates information, builds context, and decisions depend on interaction history).

These four dimensions were selected because they directly correspond to the technical properties that define agentic behavior (GPA+IAT from Chapter 1) and represent the primary axes along which governance requirements vary across regulatory frameworks.

Risk is **multidimensional**, not unidimensional. A system's overall risk profile emerges from the *combination* of autonomy, entity frame, goal dynamics, and persistence. Control intensity must respond to this combination. The following sub-sections calibrate each dimension independently, then Section 3.2.6 demonstrates integration.

Generic governance frameworks provide one-size-fits-all guidance: "implement human oversight," "maintain logs," "ensure fairness." Dimensional calibration operationalizes these principles: *How much* human oversight (HITL vs. HOTL vs. HIC)? *How detailed* must logs be (decision rationale vs. inputs/outputs only)? *How frequently* must fairness be validated (pre-deployment only vs. continuous monitoring)? Without calibration, organizations default to either maximum controls (expensive, slow, may not be technically feasible) or minimum controls (cheap, fast, exposes liability).

> ### Why Dimensional Calibration Matters
>
> Calibration enables proportionate governance: controls sufficient to manage risk without unnecessary overhead.

3.2.2   Autonomy Calibration

Autonomy determines the degree of human involvement in decision-making. We distinguish three oversight modes, ordered by increasing system autonomy:

Human-in-the-Loop (HITL): Pre-Approval Required.   In HITL mode, the system recommends actions but a human must approve before execution.

> ### HITL: Human-in-the-Loop
> Pre-Approval Required
>
> **APPROPRIATE WHEN**
>
> ▸ High-consequence, irreversible actions (filing documents, large trades, contracts)
>
> ▸ Professional duties require human judgment (competence, fiduciary duty)
>
> ▸ Regulatory mandates require human review
>
> **CONTROL REQUIREMENTS**
>
> **Primary:** Human approves each action
>
> **Logging:** Recommendation + decision
>
> **Monitoring:** Lighter post-action review
>
> **Key Risk:** Automation bias—rubber-stamping

HITL governance is appropriate when errors carry high consequences and human expertise adds substantial value to decision quality. In legal, financial, and audit contexts, many high-stakes decisions benefit from this mode: the system accelerates research, analysis, or document preparation, but a qualified professional validates the output before it affects clients, counterparties, or regulatory filings. The key governance requirement is ensuring the human review is meaningful (not a rubber stamp), which requires the system to surface sufficient context for informed judgment.

Example: HITL Legal Research

A legal research assistant that *iteratively* searches case law: it queries legal databases, evaluates result relevance, refines search terms based on findings, and generates progressive case summaries, all before presenting final output to an attorney for review. The attorney verifies citations, assesses legal reasoning, and takes responsibility for the final work product. **Note**: If the attorney must approve each individual search query before the next query executes, the system lacks autonomous iteration and is not a full agentic system despite having other properties.

Human-on-the-Loop (HOTL): Monitoring with Intervention. In HOTL mode, the system operates autonomously within defined parameters, but humans monitor performance and can intervene if anomalies, errors, or safety concerns arise.

HOTL: Human-on-the-Loop
Monitoring with Intervention

APPROPRIATE WHEN	CONTROL REQUIREMENTS
▸ Moderate-consequence or reversible actions (service responses, preliminary analysis)	**Primary:** Dashboards + anomaly detection
▸ Real-time review creates unacceptable latency	**Logging:** Detailed for retrospective audit
▸ System operates within defined boundaries	**Escalation:** Low confidence, complaints
	Intervention: Override protocols

HOTL governance suits situations where transaction volume makes individual review impractical, but errors remain detectable and correctable through monitoring. The system handles routine operations autonomously while humans watch for anomalies such as unusual patterns, error spikes, or edge cases that exceed the system's training distribution. Governance focuses on defining clear escalation triggers, maintaining real-time dashboards, and ensuring intervention mechanisms actually work when needed.

Example: HOTL Customer Service

A customer service chatbot that handles routine inquiries autonomously but escalates complex questions, complaints, or regulatory issues to human agents. Supervisors monitor conversation logs, error rates, and escalation frequency.

Human-in-Command (HIC): Strategic Oversight and Emergency Stop. In HIC mode, the system operates with high autonomy. Humans set strategic goals, define constraints, and monitor aggregate performance but do not review individual decisions. Humans retain emergency stop authority to halt the system if safety violations, systemic failures, or regulatory concerns emerge.

HIC: Human-in-Command
Strategic Oversight and Emergency Stop

APPROPRIATE WHEN

▸ Scale/speed precludes individual review (millions of transactions)

▸ Individually low-consequence but cumulatively significant

▸ Stable environment with strong safeguards

CONTROL REQUIREMENTS

Primary: Logging + statistical monitoring

Logging: Detailed for auditability

Monitoring: Fairness, errors, drift

Emergency Stop: Tested regularly

Example: HIC Fraud Detection

A credit card fraud detection system that automatically blocks transactions meeting defined risk criteria. Fraud analysts set risk parameters, monitor aggregate block rates and false positive rates, and investigate flagged cases retrospectively. The system can be halted immediately if systemic bias or operational failures are detected.

The Autonomy-Auditability Trade-off. As summarized in Table 3.1, as autonomy increases, the burden of governance shifts from ex-ante (pre-approval) to ex-post (logging, monitoring, audit). HITL systems rely on human review as the primary control; HIC systems rely on comprehensive logging and statistical monitoring. Organizations must invest in monitoring infrastructure proportionate to autonomy: high-autonomy systems cannot rely on "we'll review it if someone complains."

Autonomy Level	Description	Controls
HITL (Human-in-the-Loop)	Human pre-approves actions	Approval workflows, bias mitigation
HOTL (Human-on-the-Loop)	Autonomous operation; humans monitor	Dashboards, escalation triggers
HIC (Human-in-Command)	High autonomy + emergency stop	Logging, monitoring, fairness metrics

Table 3.1: Autonomy Calibration: Oversight Modes and Control Requirements

In practice, HITL governance suits high-stakes professional work such as legal research and investment advice, where human judgment adds substantial value and errors carry significant consequences. HOTL governance fits higher-volume operations like customer service chatbots and audit analytics, where individual review is impractical but monitoring can catch systemic issues. HIC governance applies to systems operating at scale with individually low-stakes but cumulatively significant decisions, such as fraud detection and algorithmic trading.

3.2.3   Entity Frame Calibration

Entity frame determines how the system presents itself and how users perceive its role. Entity frame affects trust, liability allocation, and user expectations. Mismatches between entity frame and governance create risk. Table 3.2 summarizes entity frame calibration.

Human Entity Frame. The system represents a specific human professional (e.g., "your attorney," "your financial adviser"). Users may not distinguish between the professional and the AI tool.

Governance implications establish the highest accountability expectations for human frame systems. Professional responsibility rules apply in full. The professional represented by the system bears liability for all outputs. Confidentiality, competence, and fiduciary duty obligations are non-delegable. Organizations must ensure the professional reviews, validates, and takes ownership of AI-generated outputs.

Mismatch risk arises when the system operates with high autonomy (HIC) but presents a human frame, leading users to assume human oversight that does not exist. This creates misplaced trust and potential liability.

> ### Example: Human Entity Frame
>
> A legal research tool that produces work product under the attorney's name. The attorney must verify citations, assess legal reasoning, and ensure compliance with Rule 1.1 (competence) and Rule 3.3 (candor).

Hybrid Entity Frame. The system is presented as a collaborative partnership between human and AI (e.g., "AI-assisted analysis," "our team uses advanced tools").

Governance implications require clear delineation of responsibilities under hybrid frame systems. Users should understand that AI provides preliminary analysis or recommendations, but humans make final decisions. Transparency about the division of labor reduces misplaced trust. Governance must document which tasks are AI-performed vs. human-performed and ensure human review of AI outputs before client-facing use.

> ### Example: Hybrid Entity Frame
>
> An investment advisory firm that discloses: "Our financial plans combine AI-driven market analysis with our advisers' professional judgment and knowledge of your personal circumstances."

Machine Entity Frame. The system is clearly identified as a non-human tool (e.g., "AI chatbot," "automated system"). Users understand they are interacting with technology, not a human.

Governance implications address how machine frame sets appropriate expectations. Users are less likely to assume human judgment, empathy, or professional accountability. Yet organizations must ensure the system's capabilities match user expectations: a chatbot labeled as "informational only" should not provide advice that creates reliance. Controls should include clear disclaimers, capability limitations, and escalation to humans for complex or high-stakes issues.

> ### Example: Machine Entity Frame
>
> A customer service chatbot that states: "I'm an AI assistant. I can help with account questions, but for disputes or complex issues, I'll connect you with a human agent."

Institutional Entity Frame. The system acts on behalf of the organization (e.g., "XYZ Bank's credit decisioning system," "our firm's compliance review tool"). The organization, not an individual, bears accountability.

Governance implications show how institutional frame allocates liability to the organization. This is appropriate for systems used in institutional decision-making (credit underwriting, hiring, fraud detection). Governance must include organizational oversight (board and executive accountability), institutional policies (acceptable use, risk appetite), and enterprise-level monitoring. Professional responsibility considerations (if applicable) must be addressed separately.

Mismatch risk emerges when an institutional system operates without adequate organizational oversight (e.g., deployed by a rogue team without executive approval), causing the organization to face liability for decisions it did not authorize.

> ### Example: Institutional Entity Frame
>
> A bank's credit pre-screening system that evaluates mortgage applications under institutional policies, with oversight by the Chief Risk Officer and compliance with ECOA.

Entity Frame	Description	Accountability
Human	Represents specific professional	Full professional liability; non-delegable duties
Hybrid	Human-AI collaboration	Shared; human validates AI
Machine	Clearly non-human tool	Organization responsible; clear disclaimers
Institutional	Acts for organization	Organizational liability; board oversight

Table 3.2: Entity Frame Calibration: Presentation Modes and Accountability Structures

In practice, human frame systems appear in professional contexts such as legal research tools generating work product under an attorney's name or financial advisers using AI to draft client recommendations. Hybrid frame systems suit collaborative workflows like audit analytics where AI identifies anomalies and auditors investigate, or co-drafted documents where AI generates initial content and professionals refine it. Machine frame systems apply to customer-facing automation like chatbots with clear disclosure of their non-human nature. Institutional frame systems govern organizational decisions such as credit underwriting and hiring, where the entity rather than any individual professional bears accountability.

3.2.4   Goal Dynamics Calibration

Goal dynamics determine how the system's objectives change over time. Static goals are easiest to govern; negotiated goals create the highest misalignment risk. Table 3.3 summarizes goal dynamics calibration.

Static Goals. The system pursues a fixed objective defined at deployment. The goal does not change without explicit redeployment.

Governance implications enable static goals to be validated once during pre-deployment review. Organizations assess whether the goal aligns with organizational objectives, legal requirements, and ethical constraints. Once validated, the goal remains stable. Governance focuses on monitoring whether the system achieves the goal and whether side effects emerge.

> ### Example: Static Goals
>
> A legal research tool with the static goal: "Identify cases cited in the brief and verify they exist in official reporters." The goal does not change; the tool performs the same validation task repeatedly.

Adaptive Goals. The system refines its objectives within predefined boundaries based on feedback, but cannot change goals fundamentally. A fraud detection system might adjust risk weights based on observed fraud patterns, yet cannot change its core objective (detect fraud) or operate outside defined risk parameters.

Adaptive goals can drift within their permitted boundaries, and subtle drift may escape notice until it causes harm. Detecting drift requires both a clear standard and active surveillance. The standard comes from explicitly defining which aspects of the goal may adapt and which constraints are inviolable; without this distinction, there is nothing to measure against. Surveillance comes from a monitoring framework that specifies review frequency and revalidation triggers, catching deviation before it compounds. Detection alone is insufficient, however; organizations also need rollback capability, enabling the system to revert to a validated state when adaptation degrades performance or violates constraints.

> ### Example: Adaptive Goals
>
> A credit scoring model that adapts feature weights based on performance feedback but cannot introduce new features, change fairness constraints, or operate outside regulatory compliance boundaries.

Negotiated Goals. When a system proposes changes to its own objectives, every proposal requires human validation before implementation; the system cannot autonomously alter its goals. This creates the highest governance burden of any goal dynamics category. Organizations must designate approval authority, typically reserving this role for senior leadership or a governance committee given the stakes involved. The approval process demands rigorous documentation: why is the system proposing this change, what evidence supports it, and what are the potential consequences? Even after approval, governance is not complete; the modified system must undergo revalidation to confirm it remains safe, fair, and compliant. This cumulative overhead explains why negotiated goals appear only in the most sophisticated agentic deployments.

> ## Example: Negotiated Goals
>
> An AI strategic planning assistant that proposes: "Based on market analysis, I recommend shifting investment focus from Technology to Healthcare." This goal change requires executive approval, risk assessment, and fiduciary duty review.

Goal Dynamics	Description	Controls
Static	Fixed objectives	One-time validation; monitor side effects
Adaptive	Refinement within boundaries	Boundaries, monitoring, rollback
Negotiated	System proposes goal changes	Approval workflows, revalidation

Table 3.3: Goal Dynamics Calibration: Objective Stability and Control Requirements

3.2.5   Persistence Calibration

Persistence determines whether the system maintains state across interactions. Stateful systems create compounding error risk and require state integrity controls. Table 3.4 summarizes persistence calibration.

Stateless Systems. Each interaction is independent. The system does not retain information from prior interactions.

Governance implications demonstrate that stateless systems are simpler to govern. Errors do not compound; a mistake in one interaction does not affect subsequent interactions. Logging can be lighter (capture inputs/outputs without state reconstruction). Reproducibility requires only input data, not interaction history.

> ## Example: Stateless System
>
> A legal citation verification tool that checks each citation independently. An error in verifying Citation A does not affect the verification of Citation B.

Stateful Systems. Stateful systems accumulate information across interactions, meaning each decision builds on prior context. This creates a distinctive governance challenge: errors compound. A misunderstanding in one session can propagate through subsequent decisions, corrupting an entire chain of reasoning. Systems require protection of state integrity against tampering, corruption, and adversarial manipulation. Comprehensive logging is essential to enable reconstruction of how state evolved; without it, diagnosing problems becomes nearly impossible. Monitoring must specifically watch for error compounding, catching cases where an early mistake ripples through later decisions. Organizations also need clear criteria for state resets: when should the system discard accumulated context and start fresh? Common triggers include user logout, policy changes, and detected anomalies, though the right criteria depend on deployment context.

> ### Example: Stateful System
>
> A financial planning chatbot that builds a profile of the client's financial situation across multiple conversations. If the system misunderstands the client's risk tolerance in Session 1, all subsequent recommendations may be inappropriate. Governance must include periodic state validation ("Let me confirm: your risk tolerance is Moderate, correct?") and state logging to reconstruct how the profile evolved.

Persistence	Description	Controls
Stateless	Each interaction independent	Standard logging; errors don't compound
Stateful	State maintained across interactions	State integrity, error monitoring, validation

Table 3.4: Persistence Calibration: State Management and Control Requirements

3.2.6   Integration

Dimensional calibration becomes powerful when dimensions are integrated. A system's overall risk profile emerges from the *combination* of autonomy, entity frame, goal dynamics, and persistence. Controls must respond to this multidimensional risk.

Table 3.5 compares two contrasting risk profiles. The **low-risk** example is a legal research tool that checks whether citations in a brief exist in official reporters and support the propositions for which they are cited. An attorney reviews every output before it reaches a client or court, and each check stands alone with no reference to prior work. The **high-risk** example is a bank's lending system that evaluates applications, requests documentation, and renders credit decisions. The system learns from outcomes over time, tracks borrower history across many interactions, and operates at scale, with humans reviewing overall performance metrics rather than individual decisions. The low-risk profile shows how strong human oversight compensates for other dimensions, enabling lighter governance. The high-risk profile shows how compounding risk across all four dimensions necessitates intensive controls.

		Low-Risk: Legal Research	High-Risk: Credit Underwriting
Dimension	Autonomy	HITL (attorney reviews outputs)	HIC (autonomous; aggregate monitoring)
	Entity Frame	Human (attorney's name)	Institutional (acts for bank)
	Goal Dynamics	Static (fixed verification goal)	Adaptive (adjusts from feedback)
	Persistence	Stateless (independent)	Stateful (applicant history)
Controls	Logging	Basic inputs/outputs	Comprehensive (all parameters)
	Monitoring	Quarterly spot-checks	Continuous fairness, drift
	Explainability	Not required	ECOA "principal reasons"
	Fairness	Not applicable	Pre + continuous + revalidation
	Vendor Mgmt	Standard due diligence	Enhanced audit rights
	Human Oversight	Per-output review	Monthly/quarterly board
	Incident Response	Error correction	Halt; regulator notification

Table 3.5: Risk Profile Comparison: Low-Risk vs. High-Risk Agentic Systems

Dimensional Calibration Worksheet

When evaluating a new agentic system, assess each dimension:
1. **Autonomy**: HITL, HOTL, or HIC?
2. **Entity Frame**: Human, Hybrid, Machine, or Institutional?
3. **Goal Dynamics**: Static, Adaptive, or Negotiated?
4. **Persistence**: Stateless or Stateful?

Use Tables 3.1 through 3.4 to identify baseline controls for each dimension. Then integrate across dimensions:

- High autonomy + institutional frame → Strong logging, statistical monitoring, board oversight.
- Adaptive goals + stateful persistence → Continuous revalidation, state integrity controls.
- HITL + human frame → Professional responsibility compliance, automation bias mitigation.

Dimensional calibration is not a formula but rather a structured reasoning framework that prevents under-protection ("it's just a chatbot") and over-engineering ("we must apply maximum controls to everything").

Section 3.4 operationalizes dimensional calibration through technical architecture and organizational processes. Section 3.6 illustrates calibration through worked examples in legal, financial, and audit contexts.

3.3   The Governance Stack

With dimensional calibration principles established in Section 3.2, we now map the overlapping obligations in the regulatory landscape those controls must satisfy. Where Chapter 1 established what agents are and Chapter 2 addressed how to design them, this chapter examines how to govern them in practice. Organizations deploying agentic systems in regulated domains face a complex, overlapping web of legal and professional obligations. There is no single "AI governance law" that comprehensively addresses all requirements. Instead, governance emerges from the interaction of five layers: foundational law, professional and ethical obligations, sector-specific regulation, AI-specific regulation, and voluntary governance frameworks. Understanding this layered structure (and why no single layer suffices) is essential for designing governance proportionate to organizational risk.

3.3.1   Five-Layer Framework

We organize governance obligations into five layers, each building on the foundation below:

1. **Foundational Law**: Broadly applicable legal obligations governing data protection, discrimination, consumer protection, and contracts. This layer encompasses not only statutes (such as the General Data Protection Regulation (GDPR), Equal Credit Opportunity Act (ECOA), and state consumer protection statutes) but also tort law as well as other common law principles. Common law doctrines provide protections that predate and operate independently of statutory schemes and include:

   - Defamation law constrains AI-generated content that makes false statements of fact about identifiable individuals.

   - Negligence principles may impose duties of care when deploying systems that foreseeably cause harm.

   - Privacy torts (intrusion upon seclusion, public disclosure of private facts) create liability independent of data protection statutes.

These legal foundations establish baselines that apply regardless of whether AI is involved.

2. **Professional and Ethical Obligations**: Duties imposed on licensed professionals (attorneys, investment advisers, auditors, accountants) by their governing bodies, bar associations, or regulatory agencies. These obligations are often more stringent than general law and impose fiduciary duties, confidentiality requirements, and competence standards.

3. **Sector-Specific Regulation**: Rules tailored to particular industries (banking, securities, insurance, healthcare) that address operational risks, supervision, and consumer protection in those domains. Examples include Federal Reserve guidance on model risk management (SR 11-7), Financial Industry Regulatory Authority (FINRA) rules on automated systems, and Public Company Accounting Oversight Board (PCAOB) auditing standards.

4. **AI-Specific Regulation**: Laws and regulations explicitly targeting artificial intelligence systems. The European Union's AI Act is the most comprehensive example, establishing risk-based requirements for high-risk AI systems. U.S. states (Colorado, California, New York City) are enacting their own AI-specific rules addressing bias, transparency, and impact assessments.

5. **Voluntary Governance Frameworks**: Standards, best practices, and certification schemes developed by standards bodies, industry groups, or government agencies. Examples include the NIST AI Risk Management Framework, ISO/IEC 42001 (AI Management Systems), COBIT for IT governance, and SOC 2 for vendor assurance. These frameworks are typically voluntary unless incorporated by reference into contracts or regulatory requirements.

Why Layering is Necessary

No single framework fully satisfies all governance requirements. The EU AI Act establishes high-level risk categories but does not specify how to comply with ECOA's "principal reasons" standard for adverse credit decisions. NIST AI RMF provides flexible risk management guidance but does not address attorney-client privilege or auditor independence. Organizations must layer multiple frameworks, augment them with domain-specific controls, and continuously monitor regulatory developments across jurisdictions.

The remainder of this section examines each layer in detail, identifying key requirements and illustrating how obligations interact.

Layer	Source	Key Examples
1. Foundational Law	Statutes, regulations, common law	GDPR, ECOA, tort law
2. Professional Obligations	Bar associations, regulatory bodies	ABA Rules, fiduciary duty, AICPA
3. Sector-Specific Regulation	Industry regulators	SR 11-7, FINRA, PCAOB
4. AI-Specific Regulation	AI-targeted laws	EU AI Act, Colorado AI Act
5. Voluntary Frameworks	Standards bodies	NIST AI RMF, ISO 42001, SOC 2

Table 3.6: Summary of the Five-Layer Governance Framework

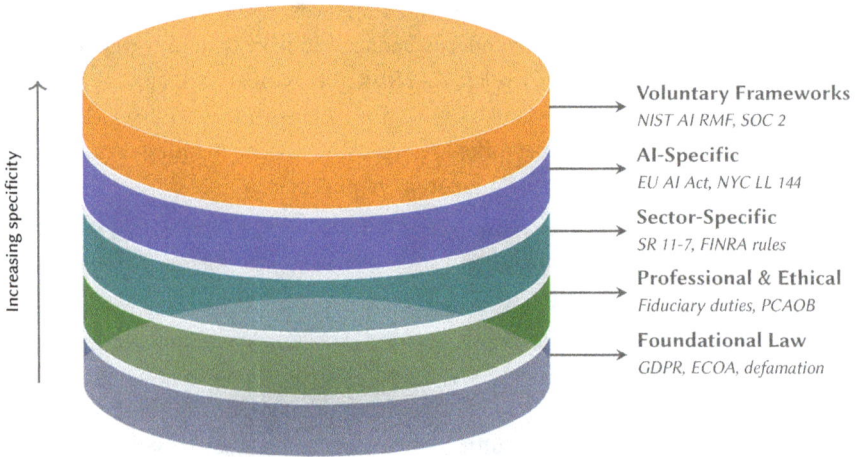

Figure 3.1: The five-layer governance framework as stacked obligations. Foundational law sets the baseline; professional duties add licensed-practice requirements; sector-specific rules address industry contexts; AI-specific regulation targets algorithmic systems; and voluntary frameworks supply certification and best-practice guidance. All applicable layers must be addressed—no single layer provides complete coverage.

3.3.2   Layer 1: Foundational Law

Foundational law provides the baseline for governance, applicable to all organizations regardless of industry or use case. Three domains are especially relevant:

Data Protection and Privacy: GDPR Article 22 and Stateful Agentic Systems. The GDPR establishes rights and obligations for processing personal data of EU residents. Article 22 addresses automated decision-making: individuals have the right not to be subject to decisions based solely on automated processing that produce legal or similarly significant effects (European Parliament 2016). While not an absolute prohibition (automated decisions are permitted with explicit consent, contractual necessity, or legal authorization), Article 22 requires organizations to implement "suitable measures" to safeguard the data subject's rights, including the right to obtain human intervention and contest the decision.

Agentic-Specific Challenge: Stateful Decision Accumulation: Article 22's human intervention requirement becomes complex for stateful agentic systems that accumulate context across multiple cycles. Generic AI guidance suggests "add a button for human review," but this is insufficient for agentic systems. Building on Chapter 1's analysis of iteration and adaptation, meaningful human intervention requires access to the system's accumulated internal state: how the agent's understanding evolved across iterations, what adaptations occurred, and what termination logic triggered the final decision. Without comprehensive state logging (capturing perception, action, and rationale at each cycle), human reviewers cannot meaningfully intervene or contest decisions because they lack visibility into how the agent reached its conclusion.

Governance Implication: For agentic systems subject to GDPR Article 22, human intervention controls must be paired with state logging requirements (cross-cycle audit trails). Organizations cannot satisfy Article 22 by providing post-hoc review without the ability to reconstruct the agent's iterative decision process. This links directly to the State Logging control discussed in Section 3.4.2.

Article 32 requires appropriate technical and organizational security measures, including encryption, pseudonymization, and resilience against unauthorized processing. Articles 33-34 mandate breach notification to supervisory authorities (within 72 hours) and affected individuals (without undue delay) when breaches pose risks to rights and freedoms.

For organizations operating globally, GDPR compliance often sets the de facto standard. Even organizations without EU operations may face GDPR obligations if they offer services to EU residents or monitor their behavior.

Anti-Discrimination and Fair Lending: ECOA and Process-Based Discrimination. The Equal Credit Opportunity Act (ECOA) prohibits credit discrimination based on race, color, religion, national origin, sex, marital status, age, or receipt of public assistance (ECOA). Regulation B, which implements ECOA, requires creditors to provide "principal reasons" for adverse credit decisions (CFPB 2024). This explainability requirement is more specific than generic AI transparency guidance; applicants must receive concrete, understandable reasons tied to the factors that most significantly influenced the decision.

ECOA applies regardless of whether the decision was made by a human, an algorithm, or a hybrid system. Courts have applied *disparate impact* theory: even facially neutral criteria can violate ECOA if they disproportionately harm protected classes without adequate business justification.

Agentic-Specific Challenge: Process-Based Discrimination: Traditional fairness testing focuses on *outcome parity* (do protected classes receive approvals at comparable rates?). For agentic credit underwriting systems that iteratively investigate applications across multiple cycles, discrimination can emerge through the *investigation process* itself, not just final decisions. An agentic system might:

- Adapt to request more verification cycles from applicants with characteristics correlated with protected classes (e.g., shorter U.S. employment tenure as a proxy for national origin).

- Impose higher process burdens (more documentation requests, longer investigation timelines) on protected groups, causing application abandonment even if the system would ultimately approve.

- Learn patterns that create disparate *iteration counts* across demographic groups, violating ECOA even when final approval rates satisfy the 80% rule commonly used in disparate impact analysis.

Governance Implication: Agentic credit systems require *process parity monitoring* in addition to outcome fairness testing. Organizations must audit:

- Average investigation cycles by protected class (flag if deviation >20%).

- Termination reasons by demographic group (ensure similar rates of confidence-based vs. timeout-based termination).

- Application abandonment rates during multi-cycle investigation (ensure verification burdens do not disproportionately affect protected classes).

Systems require controls ensuring that dynamic investigation strategies do not introduce prohibited discrimination, a challenge that does not arise with single-shot credit scoring models. See Section 3.4.6 for a worked example of process-based discrimination detected in agentic underwriting.

Consumer Protection. State consumer protection statutes (e.g., Unfair and Deceptive Acts and Practices laws) prohibit misleading representations and unfair business practices. If an AI chatbot misrepresents its capabilities, provides inaccurate information, or fails to disclose material limitations, the organization may face consumer protection enforcement regardless of whether the misrepresentation was intentional or the result of a model hallucination.

3.3.3   Layer 2: Professional and Ethical Obligations

Licensed professionals face heightened obligations that governance systems must operationalize. We examine three domains:

Legal Practice: ABA Model Rules. Most U.S. jurisdictions have adopted versions of the American Bar Association's Model Rules of Professional Conduct. Three rules are especially salient for AI governance:

- **Rule 1.1 (Competence)**: An attorney must provide competent representation, requiring "the legal knowledge, skill, thoroughness and preparation reasonably necessary for the representation." ABA Formal Opinion 512 (July 2024) clarifies that competence includes understanding AI tools' capabilities and limitations (American Bar Association Standing Committee on Ethics and Professional Responsibility 2024); attorneys cannot delegate legal analysis to AI without independent verification.

- **Rule 1.6 (Confidentiality)**: An attorney must not reveal information relating to representation of a client unless the client gives informed consent. Using AI tools that transmit client data to third-party vendors, train models on client information, or store data insecurely may violate confidentiality obligations. Organizations must assess vendor data handling practices and obtain client consent where necessary.

- **Rule 3.3 (Candor Toward the Tribunal)**: An attorney must not knowingly make false statements of fact or law to a tribunal. Submitting AI-generated legal research without verification can result in fabricated citations or misrepresented holdings, which violates this duty. Courts have imposed sanctions ranging from $1,000 to $15,000 for such violations, with some attorneys facing suspension or mandatory disclosure requirements on future filings.

Rule 5.3 addresses supervision of nonlawyer assistants, a framework some jurisdictions apply to AI tools. The attorney remains responsible for ensuring that
AI-assisted work product meets professional standards.

Financial Services: Fiduciary Duty and Suitability. Investment advisers owe
fiduciary duties to clients under the Investment Advisers Act of 1940 and SEC
interpretations. This duty has two components:

- **Duty of Care**: Providing advice that is suitable for the client's financial
  situation, investment objectives, and risk tolerance. An AI-generated portfolio
  recommendation must be validated against these client-specific factors.

- **Duty of Loyalty**: Acting in the client's best interest, including full disclosure
  of conflicts of interest. If an AI tool is provided by an affiliate, receives
  compensation from recommended products, or prioritizes firm profitability
  over client outcomes, the adviser must disclose these conflicts and ensure
  recommendations remain in the client's best interest.

FINRA (Financial Industry Regulatory Authority) Rule 2111 imposes a similar
suitability obligation on broker-dealers. Rule 3110 requires firms to supervise
associated persons and establish procedures to ensure compliance. For AI systems
that generate investment recommendations or execute trades, governance must
include supervisory review procedures, monitoring for suitability violations, and
escalation protocols.

Audit and Accounting: Independence and Skepticism. The AICPA Code of
Professional Conduct and PCAOB auditing standards impose strict independence
and competence requirements on auditors:

- **Independence**: Auditors must maintain both independence in fact and independence in appearance. If an AI tool is provided by the audit client, an affiliate,
  or a vendor with financial ties to the client, independence may be impaired;
  the SEC and PCAOB closely scrutinize auditor-provided tools that could create
  management decision-making or self-review threats.

- **Professional Skepticism**: PCAOB Auditing Standard 1015 requires auditors
  to exercise professional skepticism: a questioning mind and critical assessment
  of audit evidence. Auditors cannot accept AI outputs uncritically; they must
  understand the tool's methodology, validate its logic, and assess whether results
  are consistent with other evidence.

- **Documentation**: AS 1215 (Audit Documentation) requires auditors to document the nature, timing, extent, and results of audit procedures. If AI is used
  for sampling, risk assessment, or analytical procedures, the workpapers must

explain the tool's logic, parameters, and the auditor's rationale for relying on its output (PCAOB 2024c).

These professional obligations are non-delegable. Governance systems must operationalize competence, confidentiality, independence, and documentation requirements through technical controls and organizational processes.

3.3.4   Layer 3: Sector-Specific Regulation

Sector regulators impose industry-tailored requirements that general frameworks do not address:

Banking: Model Risk Management. The Federal Reserve, Office of the Comptroller of the Currency (OCC), and Federal Deposit Insurance Corporation (FDIC) issued SR 11-7 on model risk management (Board of Governors of the Federal Reserve System and Office of the Comptroller of the Currency 2011). SR 11-7 applies broadly to model risk management in banking. Key requirements include:

- **Model Inventory**: Maintain a comprehensive inventory of models, classified by risk.

- **Independent Validation**: Models must be validated by a function independent of the model's development and use. Validation includes conceptual soundness review, ongoing monitoring, and outcomes analysis.

- **Model Governance**: Establish board and senior management oversight, clear roles and responsibilities, and policies for model development, implementation, and use.

- **Documentation**: Maintain complete documentation of model logic, data sources, assumptions, limitations, and validation.

Application to Agentic Systems: For agentic systems deployed in banking (e.g., iterative credit underwriting agents that gather information across multiple cycles, adapt criteria based on discovered patterns, and escalate edge cases), SR 11-7 requires documentation of all six operational properties. Unlike traditional one-shot credit models that execute fixed logic, agentic systems must document iteration logic (when does the system gather more data?), adaptation mechanisms (how do criteria evolve?), and termination conditions (when does it escalate to humans?).

Securities: FINRA Supervision and Algorithmic Trading. FINRA Rule 3110 requires broker-dealers to establish supervisory systems reasonably designed to achieve compliance with applicable laws and regulations. For firms using algorithmic trading systems or AI-driven investment recommendations, this means:

- **Pre-Deployment Testing**: Validate algorithms in a controlled environment before production use.

- **Ongoing Monitoring**: Continuously monitor for erroneous or manipulative behavior.

- **Risk Controls**: Implement automated controls (e.g., price collars, volume limits) to prevent runaway algorithms.

- **Supervisory Review**: Designate supervisors responsible for algorithm oversight and establish escalation procedures.

Audit: PCAOB Standards on Audit Evidence and Sampling. The PCAOB has not issued AI-specific guidance, but existing auditing standards apply. AS 1105 (Audit Evidence) establishes that the auditor is responsible for all audit evidence, regardless of source.

Application to Agentic Systems: For agentic audit systems (e.g., agents that iteratively refine sampling strategies based on discovered anomalies, adapt risk assessments as they review documentation, and terminate when coverage objectives are met), PCAOB standards require:

- Documentation of iteration logic: How does the system refine its sampling or analysis strategy across cycles?

- Documentation of adaptation mechanisms: When and why does the system adjust risk assessments or expand sample sizes?

- Documentation of termination criteria: What triggers the system to conclude its work or escalate to human auditors?

- Understanding the tool's methodology and assumptions across all six GPA+IAT properties.

- Professional skepticism maintained throughout; auditors cannot delegate professional judgment to autonomous systems.

AS 2315 (Audit Sampling) requires auditors to design samples that provide a reasonable basis for conclusions. Agentic sampling systems must document how iteration and adaptation enhance (rather than compromise) statistical validity.

3.3.5   Layer 4: AI-Specific Regulation

AI-specific regulation is emerging rapidly. We focus on the most comprehensive framework and notable U.S. developments:

EU AI Act: Risk-Based Tiering. The EU AI Act, which entered into force in August 2024, establishes a risk-based regulatory framework (European Parliament 2024):

- **Prohibited Practices**: AI systems that pose unacceptable risks (e.g., social scoring by governments, real-time biometric identification in public spaces except narrow law enforcement exceptions, manipulative or harmful systems) are banned.

- **High-Risk Systems**: AI systems used in employment, education, credit assessment, law enforcement, critical infrastructure, and biometric identification are classified as high-risk. These systems must satisfy stringent requirements:

  - **Risk Management** (Article 9): Establish and maintain a risk management system throughout the AI system's lifecycle.

  - **Data Governance** (Article 10): Training, validation, and testing datasets must be relevant, representative, and free from bias to the extent possible.

  - **Logging** (Article 12): Maintain automatic recording of events (logs) to enable traceability.

  - **Transparency** (Article 13): Provide clear instructions for use, including capabilities, limitations, and expected performance.

  - **Human Oversight** (Article 14): Design systems to enable effective oversight, including the ability to override or interrupt the system.

  - **Accuracy, Robustness, Cybersecurity** (Article 15): Achieve appropriate levels of accuracy and resilience against errors, faults, and cyberattacks.

  - **Conformity Assessment** (Article 43): High-risk systems must undergo third-party conformity assessment before market placement (for certain categories) or internal assessment (for others).

- **Limited-Risk and Minimal-Risk Systems**: Lower-risk systems face transparency obligations (e.g., chatbots must disclose they are AI) but not the full high-risk requirements.

Penalties for non-compliance are severe: up to €35 million or 7% of global annual turnover for prohibited practices, and up to €15 million or 3% for high-risk system violations. Organizations operating in or serving EU markets must assess whether their agentic systems fall within high-risk categories and implement Article 9–15 requirements.

U.S. State and Local AI Laws. In the absence of comprehensive federal AI legislation, U.S. states and cities are enacting targeted rules:

- **Colorado AI Act (SB 24-205)**: Effective January 1, 2026, Colorado's law prohibits algorithmic discrimination: deployment of high-risk AI systems that result in unlawful differential treatment or impact based on protected classifications (Colorado General Assembly 2024). Deployers must conduct impact assessments documenting the system's purpose, data sources, intended benefits, known limitations, and measures to mitigate discrimination. A rebuttable presumption of compliance applies if deployers complete a reasonable impact assessment in good faith.

- **New York City Local Law 144 (Automated Employment Decision Tools)**: Effective since July 2023, NYC requires employers using AI for hiring or promotion to conduct annual bias audits, publish summary results, and notify candidates that an automated tool is in use. Employers must also allow candidates to request alternative evaluation processes.

- **California Privacy Rights Act (CPRA) and Proposed AI Legislation**: California has enacted data protection laws that indirectly regulate AI (e.g., CPRA's provisions on automated decision-making) and is considering comprehensive AI legislation addressing high-risk uses.

These patchwork requirements mean organizations must track regulatory developments across jurisdictions and tailor governance to the most stringent applicable standard.

3.3.6   Layer 5: Voluntary Governance Frameworks

Voluntary frameworks provide structured approaches to AI governance. Organizations often adopt multiple frameworks to address different audiences and objectives:

NIST AI Risk Management Framework (AI RMF 1.0). Published in January 2023, the NIST AI RMF is a flexible, voluntary framework for managing AI risks (NIST 2023). It organizes activities into four functions:

- **Govern**: Establish organizational structures, policies, and accountability for AI risk management.

- **Map**: Identify context, stakeholders, and potential impacts of AI systems.

- **Measure**: Assess and benchmark AI system performance, including trustworthiness characteristics (fairness, transparency, accountability, safety, privacy, security).

- **Manage**: Allocate resources, implement risk treatments, and monitor effectiveness.

NIST AI RMF emphasizes trustworthiness characteristics and provides flexibility for organizations of different sizes and sectors. It is widely referenced by federal agencies, state regulators, and private-sector organizations as a baseline governance framework.

ISO/IEC 42001:2023 (AI Management Systems). ISO/IEC 42001 is an international standard for AI management systems, providing a certifiable framework (ISO 2023). It establishes requirements for establishing, implementing, maintaining, and continually improving an AI management system. Annex A provides 40+ AI-specific controls organized by category (data management, model development, deployment, monitoring).

ISO/IEC 42001 is especially relevant for organizations:

- Operating in EU markets (the standard is recognized as supporting EU AI Act compliance).

- Seeking third-party certification to demonstrate governance maturity.

- Requiring international recognition (ISO standards are globally accepted).

Certification typically costs $50,000–$150,000 and requires 3–6 months, depending on organizational size and maturity.

COBIT (IT Governance Framework). COBIT, developed by ISACA, is a comprehensive IT governance framework widely used by enterprises. COBIT 2019 includes guidance on emerging technologies, including AI. Organizations with mature IT governance often extend COBIT to cover AI systems rather than creating parallel structures.

COBIT is best suited for organizations seeking to integrate AI governance into existing enterprise IT governance rather than treating AI as a standalone domain.

SOC 2 Type II (Vendor Assurance). SOC 2 (Service Organization Control) is an auditing framework for service providers, especially SaaS vendors. SOC 2 Type II reports assess controls over security, availability, processing integrity, confidentiality, and privacy over a period of time (typically 6–12 months).

For organizations procuring AI tools from vendors, a SOC 2 Type II report provides independent assurance that the vendor has implemented and operated controls effectively. Many enterprises require SOC 2 reports as a condition of vendor contracts.

Framework Selection Logic. Organizations often layer frameworks:

- **Start with NIST AI RMF** for flexible internal governance (free, widely recognized, no certification requirement).

- **Add ISO/IEC 42001** if seeking certification, operating in EU markets, or facing customer demands for third-party assurance.

- **Integrate with COBIT** if mature IT governance structures exist.

- **Require SOC 2** from third-party AI vendors to validate their controls.

No single framework addresses all requirements. Layering enables organizations to satisfy general governance needs (NIST), achieve certification (ISO), integrate with enterprise governance (COBIT), and validate vendor controls (SOC 2).

3.3.7   Seven Common Controls Across Frameworks

Despite structural differences, all governance frameworks converge on seven common controls:

1. **Risk Assessment and Management**: Identify, assess, prioritize, and mitigate AI-related risks throughout the system lifecycle. Risk assessment is the foundation for all subsequent governance activities.

2. **Human Oversight**: Implement oversight mechanisms proportionate to system autonomy and risk: human-in-the-loop (pre-approval for high-stakes decisions), human-on-the-loop (monitoring with intervention capability), or human-in-command (strategic oversight with emergency stop authority).

3. **Audit Logging and Traceability**: Maintain tamper-evident logs that capture inputs, outputs, decisions, and human interventions. Logs must enable reconstruction of decisions for audit, investigation, and regulatory review.

4. **Explainability and Transparency**: Provide stakeholders (users, auditors, regulators) with understandable information about how the system operates, what factors influence decisions, and what limitations exist. Explainability techniques must be validated for faithfulness (reflects actual model logic), completeness (material factors included), and usefulness (enables informed decisions).

5. **Vendor Management**: Assess, monitor, and manage third-party AI vendors. Vendor due diligence, contract negotiation, ongoing monitoring, and escalation procedures are essential because vendor risks cascade into organizational liability.

6. **Incident Response and Remediation**: Detect, triage, contain, investigate, remediate, and learn from AI system failures. Incident response must be rapid (fairness violations and safety failures require immediate action) and systematic (root cause analysis, notification, continuous improvement).

7. **Documentation and Record-Keeping**: Maintain comprehensive documentation of system purpose, design, data sources, validation results, deployment decisions, monitoring outputs, and incidents. Documentation supports audits, regulatory inquiries, and continuous improvement.

While frameworks differ in emphasis and structure, these seven controls represent governance universals. Section 3.2 (presented earlier) established how to calibrate control intensity based on system properties. Section 3.4 operationalizes these calibrated controls through technical architecture and organizational processes.

3.4   Implementation

Section 3.2 established principles for calibrating control intensity. We now focus on building governance systems by operationalizing those principles. We now turn to operationalizing those principles: how to design and implement risk assessment, audit logging, explainability, human oversight, vendor management, performance monitoring, and incident response. Where Chapter 2 established the technical infrastructure for logging, escalation, and action controls, we now address the governance policies and organizational processes that make those capabilities enforceable. We focus on actionable guidance: what practitioners and governance teams actually build, illustrated through examples from legal, financial, and audit domains.

3.4.1   Risk Assessment

All governance begins with risk assessment. Before deploying an agentic system, organizations must systematically identify harm scenarios, assess their likelihood and impact, document mitigations, and define reassessment triggers.

Risk Assessment Methodology. Effective risk assessment addresses six categories of AI-related harms:

- **Bias and Fairness**: Does the system produce discriminatory outcomes? Are protected classes disproportionately harmed?

- **Accuracy and Reliability**: Does the system produce correct outputs? What is the error rate? What are the consequences of errors?

- **Security**: Can adversaries manipulate inputs (prompt injection), poison training data, or exfiltrate sensitive information?

- **Privacy**: Does the system access, process, or disclose personal or confidential information inappropriately?

- **Safety**: Can system failures cause physical harm, financial loss, or operational disruption?

- **Compliance**: Does deployment violate laws, regulations, or professional obligations?

For each risk category, assess *likelihood* (how probable is this harm?), *impact* (if it occurs, how severe are the consequences?), *affected stakeholders* (who is harmed?), and *mitigations* (what controls reduce risk?). Document *residual risk* after mitigations and obtain approval from appropriate governance authority (e.g., risk committee, general counsel, board for high-risk systems).

Define *reassessment triggers*: When must the risk assessment be updated? Common triggers include model updates, policy changes, regulatory developments, incident discoveries, and significant drift in performance or fairness metrics.

Example: Agentic Financial Planning Assistant Risk Assessment. A registered investment adviser deploys an agentic financial planning system that *iteratively* analyzes client portfolios, adapts recommendations based on market conditions and client feedback, and determines when to escalate to human advisers.

The system iterates through analysis-recommendation-feedback loops over days or weeks, adapts its strategy based on client responses and market changes, and terminates when confidence thresholds are met or escalation is required. As Chapter 2 established, these iteration, adaptation, and termination capabilities create governance requirements beyond simple AI tools. *Dimensional profile: HITL + hybrid frame + adaptive goals + stateful.*

The risk assessment identifies five primary concerns, summarized in Table 3.7.

Compliance risk ranks highest: the system may recommend unsuitable investments, violating Advisers Act fiduciary duty. Unlike a simple Q&A chatbot, iteration and adaptation create compounding risk: a flawed recommendation in cycle one shapes subsequent analysis.

Accuracy risk stems from potential hallucination of market data or misinterpretation of client constraints. Across iterative cycles, these errors compound rather than self-correct.

Adaptation risk arises when the system drifts from regulatory compliance, for instance, learning to recommend higher-fee products based on firm incentives rather than client best interest.

Iteration risk manifests as either excessive iteration (analysis paralysis) or premature termination (incomplete analysis).

Security risk, though less likely, carries the highest impact: prompt injection across iterative cycles could manipulate accumulated state, potentially disclosing other clients' information.

Risk	Likely	Impact	Key Mitigations	Residual
Compliance	●	●	HITL approval; monthly compliance; quarterly fiduciary review	●
Accuracy	●	●	Verified data; cross-cycle checks; human final review	●
Adaptation	●	●	Limited to methods; criteria fixed; quarterly audit	●
Iteration	●	●	Termination (5 cycles, conf. >0.85, 14-day timeout)	●
Security	●	●	Input sanitization; state validation; data isolation	●

Table 3.7: Risk Assessment: Agentic Financial Planning Assistant. Risk levels: ● Critical, ● High, ● Moderate, ● Low.

Monitoring: Daily compliance review, weekly adaptation log review, monthly accuracy and termination analysis, continuous client feedback.

This risk assessment illustrates how agentic properties (iteration, adaptation, autonomous termination) create governance requirements beyond simple AI tools. The system's ability to iterate and adapt demands *cross-cycle consistency checks*, *adaptation audits*, and *termination condition validation*, controls unnecessary for non-agentic systems.

3.4.2   Audit Logging

Audit logging allows organizations to reconstruct decisions, investigate incidents, satisfy regulatory inquiries, and demonstrate accountability. Logging requirements scale with autonomy. High-autonomy systems (HIC) call for more detailed logs than low-autonomy systems (HITL), where human review serves as primary control.

Logging Architecture Requirements. Effective audit logging captures:

- **Inputs**: What data did the system perceive? Include user queries, retrieved documents, API responses, sensor readings, and any other data the system used to make decisions.

- **Outputs**: What did the system produce? Include recommendations, actions taken, messages sent, decisions rendered.

- **Decision Rationale**: Why did the system produce this output? For high-autonomy or high-consequence systems, log intermediate reasoning steps, confidence scores, alternative options considered.

- **Human Interventions**: When did humans approve, reject, or modify system outputs? Who made the decision? What was their rationale?

- **System State**: For stateful systems, log state changes to support reconstruction of how the system's understanding evolved.

Logs must be stored in *tamper-evident* formats (e.g., append-only databases, cryptographic hashing) with access controls limiting who can read or delete logs. Retention periods must satisfy regulatory requirements: 7–10 years for financial services, 25 months minimum for ECOA adverse action records, potentially longer for litigation hold purposes.

Example: Agentic Credit Underwriting Audit Logging (ECOA Compliance). A bank deploys an agentic mortgage underwriting system that *iteratively* investigates applications by requesting additional documentation, querying third-party data sources (employment verification, asset verification), and analyzing trends across multiple applicants. The system adapts its investigation strategy based on discovered risk patterns and terminates when sufficient information is gathered or escalation is required.

Dimensional profile: HIC + institutional frame + adaptive goals + stateful.

The system's agentic properties shape its governance requirements. Its **goal** is to approve qualified applicants while managing credit risk and satisfying ECOA requirements. Its **perception** draws on application data, third-party verification responses, and historical default patterns. Its **actions** include requesting documents, querying APIs, and generating preliminary assessments. **Iteration** operates across 3–7 investigation cycles over 5–15 days. **Adaptation** adjusts investigation depth based on risk indicators and application complexity. **Termination** occurs under explicit conditions: confidence exceeds 0.90, the maximum of 7 cycles is reached, or red flags trigger escalation to a senior underwriter.

Equal Credit Opportunity Act Regulation B mandates that lenders provide "principal reasons" for adverse credit decisions (CFPB 2024). For agentic systems that iterate across multiple cycles and adapt their investigation strategy, the logging architecture must capture *cross-cycle decision evolution* to permit reconstruction of how the system's assessment changed over time. The technical logging capabilities from Chapter 2's governance surface now require policy decisions: what must be logged, how long to retain it, and who can access it.

Listing: Agentic Underwriting Audit Log (Abridged)

```
\small
\begin{verbatim}
{
  "application_id": "APP-2024-00123",
  "session_start": "2024-11-20T14:32:15Z",
  "session_end": "2024-11-28T09:15:42Z",
  "total_cycles": 4,
  "termination_reason": "confidence_threshold_met",
  "cycles": [
    {
      "cycle": 1,
      "perception": ["application_form", "credit_report"],
      "action": "request_employment_verification",
      "preliminary_assessment": "UNCERTAIN",
      "confidence": 0.62,
      "rationale": "Initial DTI borderline; need employment
    stability"
    },
    // ... cycles 2-3: confidence rose 0.71 -> 0.84;
    // assessment evolved UNCERTAIN -> LIKELY_APPROVE
    // as employment and assets verified ...
    {
      "cycle": 4,
      "action": "generate_final_recommendation",
      "final_decision": "APPROVE",
      "confidence": 0.92
    }
  ],
  "final_decision_factors": [
    {"factor": "verified_employment_stability", "weight": 0.35},
    {"factor": "sufficient_liquid_assets", "weight": 0.30}
    // ... comparable_risk_profile (0.25), credit_score (0.10)
  ]
}
\end{verbatim}
```

Retention: 25 months (ECOA requirement) + 7 years (standard banking litigation hold).

Security: Logs are encrypted at rest, with access restricted to compliance officers, auditors, and authorized investigators. The system uses append-only storage with cryptographic integrity verification (tamper-evident) and per-cycle hash chains to detect any alteration.

Retrievability: Indexed by application ID, applicant (hashed identifier to protect PII), decision date, termination reason, and number of cycles. Permits compliance officers to query: "Show all adverse decisions where the system terminated due to timeout instead of confidence" or "Identify applications where preliminary assessment changed from `LIKELY_APPROVE` to `ADVERSE` between cycles."

Validation: Quarterly audit sampling verifies logs support reconstruction of iterative decision evolution; test whether system's cross-cycle adaptations comply with fair lending principles; validate termination conditions are consistently applied.

This logging architecture satisfies ECOA's explainability requirement while addressing agentic-specific concerns: it captures *how* the system's understanding evolved across cycles, *what* triggered adaptation, and *why* the system terminated. Without cross-cycle logging, the bank cannot reconstruct agentic decision-making or show that adaptation did not introduce prohibited discrimination.

3.4.3   Explainability

Explainability translates system behavior into understandable information for stakeholders, including users, auditors, regulators, and affected individuals. Regulatory requirements vary: ECOA requires "principal reasons," GDPR requires "meaningful information about the logic involved," and PCAOB requires auditors to document the rationale for audit procedures. Explainability techniques must be selected based on regulatory requirements and validated for *faithfulness* (reflects actual model logic), *completeness* (material factors included), and *usefulness* (enables informed decisions).

Example: Agentic Audit Investigation System (PCAOB Compliance). A Big Four accounting firm develops an agentic audit assistant that *iteratively* investigates high-risk accounts receivable. The system analyzes transactions, requests documentation, cross-references third-party data, adapts its strategy based on discovered anomalies, and escalates to senior auditors when material issues arise. *Dimensional profile: HOTL + institutional frame + adaptive goals + stateful.*

PCAOB Auditing Standards require auditors to document the rationale for procedures in workpapers (PCAOB 2024c; PCAOB 2024d). For agentic systems, explainability must capture *why* the system escalated certain accounts, *how* its strategy evolved across cycles, and *what* evidence supported termination decisions. Figure 3.2 illustrates the workflow. Each cycle generates explanations logged to audit workpapers.

Explainability Validation:

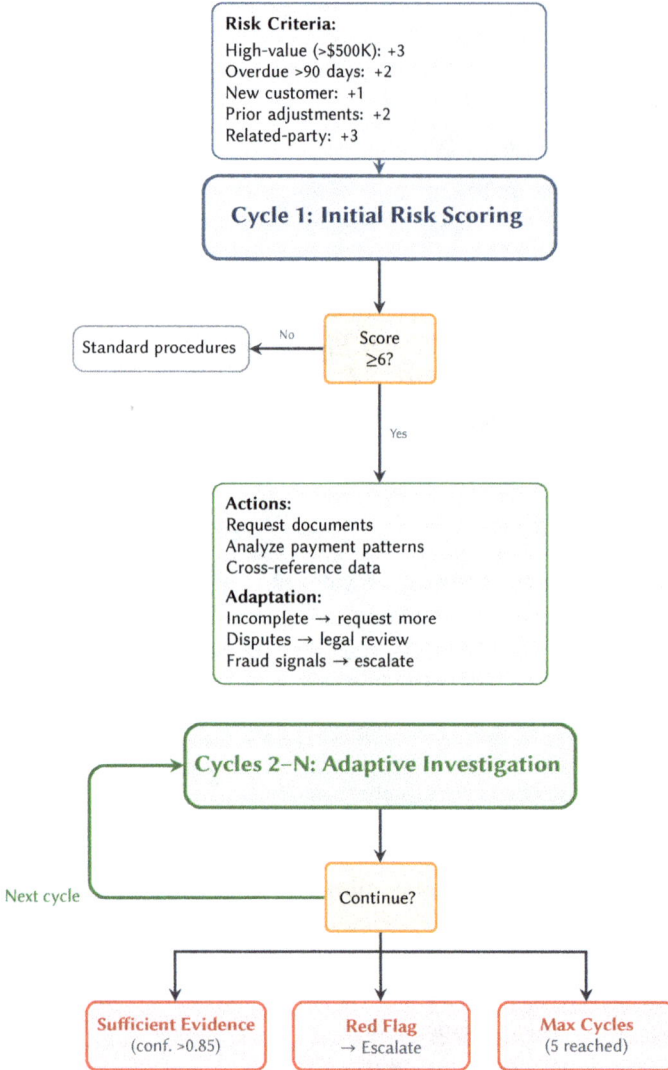

Figure 3.2: Iterative investigation workflow with explainable adaptation. Cycle 1 scores accounts using risk criteria; high-risk accounts (score ≥6) proceed to iterative investigation. Cycles 2–N gather evidence and adapt strategy based on findings. Investigation terminates when sufficient evidence is obtained, a red flag requires escalation, or maximum cycles are reached.

- **Faithfulness**: Verify explanations match actual investigation logic by reviewing audit logs (do logged perceptions and actions align with explanations?).

- **Completeness**: Confirm all material risk indicators that triggered escalation appear in explanations.

- **Usefulness**: Senior auditor reviews cycle-level explanations and confirms they support professional judgment ("Does the system's escalation rationale justify senior auditor involvement?").

Workpaper Documentation: The audit workpaper includes:

- Initial risk scoring methodology (Cycle 1 criteria).

- Cycle-by-cycle investigation narrative (what the system perceived, what actions it took, why it adapted).

- Escalation rationale (why this account required human review).

- Senior auditor's assessment: "We deployed an agentic audit assistant to investigate 47 high-risk receivables. The system iteratively gathered evidence across 2–5 cycles per account, adapting its strategy based on discovered documentation quality and anomaly patterns. It escalated 8 accounts for senior review due to identified red flags (revenue recognition concerns, collectability doubts). We reviewed the system's investigation logs, assessed the escalated accounts, and obtained sufficient appropriate audit evidence to support our conclusions."

This agentic design satisfies PCAOB's requirement that auditors understand their methodology while demonstrating how iteration and adaptation improve audit effectiveness. The system's ability to *learn* during investigation (adapting strategy based on discovered evidence) and *escalate appropriately* (terminating when human judgment is required) exemplifies agentic governance in practice.

3.4.4   Human Oversight Workflows

Section 3.2.2 defined three oversight modes. This section operationalizes them through workflows, notification mechanisms, intervention interfaces, and escalation procedures.

HITL (Human-in-the-Loop): Approval Workflows. HITL systems require human pre-approval before executing high-consequence actions. Implementation requires:

- **Approval Queue**: System generates a recommendation and adds it to a queue visible to authorized reviewers.

- **Notification**: Alert the reviewer (email, dashboard notification, SMS for time-sensitive actions).

- **Review Interface**: Present the recommendation, supporting evidence, system confidence, and options (approve, reject, modify, request more information).

- **Accountability**: Log who approved, when, and any modifications made.

- **Automation Bias Mitigation**: To prevent rubber stamping, randomize the presentation order of recommendations, periodically inject known-incorrect recommendations as controls, and track approval/rejection rates per reviewer (flag reviewers with suspiciously high approval rates).

HOTL (Human-on-the-Loop): Monitoring and Intervention. HOTL systems operate autonomously but humans monitor and can intervene. Implementation requires:

- **Monitoring Dashboard**: Real-time or near-real-time display of system activity (actions taken, error rates, escalation triggers, user feedback).

- **Escalation Triggers**: Define conditions requiring human review (e.g., low-confidence decisions <0.7, user complaints, outcomes near policy boundaries, anomalies detected).

- **Intervention Protocol**: How does the human halt the system, override a decision, or modify parameters? Must be accessible in real-time.

- **Escalation Pathway**: If the monitoring human cannot resolve an issue, to whom do they escalate? (Senior supervisor, compliance officer, emergency stop authority.)

Example: Agentic Credit Underwriting HOTL Monitoring. A lender's agentic underwriting system (Section 3.4.2) operates in HOTL mode, iteratively investigating applications. Senior underwriters monitor system performance through a dashboard (Figure 3.3) showing agentic-specific metrics and escalation triggers. When escalation frequency spikes or average cycles increase significantly, supervisors investigate root causes such as data quality degradation, overly conservative termination thresholds, or emerging risk patterns requiring strategy adjustment.

HIC (Human-in-Command): Strategic Oversight and Emergency Stop. HIC systems operate with high autonomy. Humans set goals and constraints, monitor aggregate performance, and retain emergency stop authority. Implementation requires:

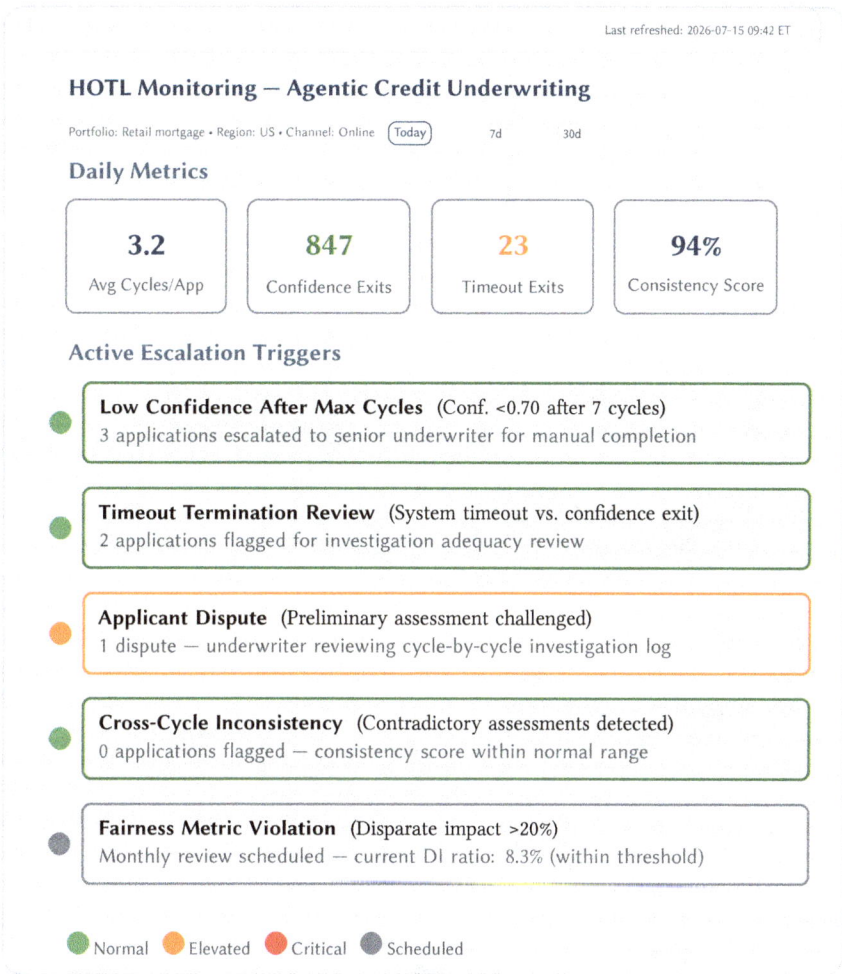

Last refreshed: 2026-07-15 09:42 ET

HOTL Monitoring — Agentic Credit Underwriting

Portfolio: Retail mortgage • Region: US • Channel: Online [Today]   7d   30d

Daily Metrics

3.2	**847**	**23**	**94%**
Avg Cycles/App	Confidence Exits	Timeout Exits	Consistency Score

Active Escalation Triggers

Low Confidence After Max Cycles (Conf. <0.70 after 7 cycles)
3 applications escalated to senior underwriter for manual completion

Timeout Termination Review (System timeout vs. confidence exit)
2 applications flagged for investigation adequacy review

Applicant Dispute (Preliminary assessment challenged)
1 dispute — underwriter reviewing cycle-by-cycle investigation log

Cross-Cycle Inconsistency (Contradictory assessments detected)
0 applications flagged — consistency score within normal range

Fairness Metric Violation (Disparate impact >20%)
Monthly review scheduled — current DI ratio: 8.3% (within threshold)

● Normal ● Elevated ● Critical ● Scheduled

Figure 3.3: HOTL monitoring dashboard for agentic credit underwriting. The dashboard displays daily operational metrics (average investigation cycles, termination reasons, cross-cycle consistency) and active escalation triggers with status indicators. Senior underwriters monitor aggregate performance and intervene when triggers fire.

- **Strategic Goal-Setting**: Executives define objectives, risk appetite, and constraints (e.g., "Fraud detection system must achieve 95% precision, maintain false positive rate <1%, and satisfy GDPR Article 22 requirements").

- **Aggregate Monitoring**: Statistical dashboards (daily/weekly/monthly) showing performance trends, fairness metrics, error rates, drift indicators. Not individual decision review.

- **Emergency Stop**: Accessible to authorized personnel (CTO, Chief Risk Officer, compliance head); tested quarterly; documented procedures for graceful shutdown (complete in-progress transactions, notify affected users, preserve state).

- **Revalidation Triggers**: Define when the system must be revalidated before continuing operation (e.g., fairness violation detected, accuracy below SLA, regulatory policy change).

3.4.5   Vendor Management

Most organizations procure AI systems from vendors rather than building in-house. Vendor risk cascades into organizational liability: if the vendor's model hallucinates, is biased, or breaches confidentiality, the deploying organization faces regulatory penalties and reputational harm. Governance must include vendor due diligence, contract negotiation, and ongoing monitoring.

Vendor Due Diligence Framework (Three Phases). The framework proceeds through three phases. **Phase 1 (Assessment)** uses questionnaires to gather information about the vendor's data sources, model architecture, security practices, performance benchmarks, and fairness testing methodology. **Phase 2 (Document Review)** examines supporting documentation to verify vendor claims. This includes SOC 2 reports, data processing agreements, model validation reports, and security certifications. **Phase 3 (Validation)** confirms claims through reference checks with existing clients in similar domains and pilot testing with representative data to validate accuracy, explainability, and performance before full deployment.

1	2	3
Assessment Questionnaire on data, model, security, fairness	**Document Review** SOC 2, DPA, validation reports, certifications	**Validation** Reference checks, pilot testing, performance verification

Figure 3.4: Three-phase vendor due diligence framework. Phase 1 gathers information through questionnaires; Phase 2 reviews supporting documentation and certifications; Phase 3 validates claims through reference checks and pilot testing with representative data.

Contract Negotiation: Shifting Risk to Vendors Where Possible. Negotiate contract terms that allocate risk appropriately:

Contract Term	Negotiation Focus
Liability Caps	Higher/uncapped liability for confidentiality breaches and negligence in high-risk cases
Update Notification	30-60 days advance notice before material model updates
Audit Rights	Annual audits or upon incident discovery
Data Handling	Prohibit training on customer data; deletion upon termination
SLAs	Performance thresholds with specified remedies

Table 3.8: Key contract terms for allocating risk in AI vendor agreements.

Agentic-Specific Risk: Adaptation Opacity. Agentic systems that learn and adapt create a unique vendor risk that traditional AI contracts do not address: **adaptation opacity**. The vendor's model silently updates its decision-making strategy in the background without formal version changes, invalidating continuous validation requirements and creating regulatory exposure.

The Problem: Regulatory frameworks like SR 11-7 (Federal Reserve model risk management) require ongoing validation of models used by banking institutions (Board of Governors of the Federal Reserve System and Office of the Comptroller of the Currency 2011). Organizations validate "Model v2.1" and deploy it. If the vendor's agentic system *adapts*, adjusting feature weights, refining decision criteria, or modifying iteration logic, the deployed system may behave materially differently from the validated version, yet the vendor does not issue a new version number or notify the customer. The organization continues operating under the assumption it is using validated "v2.1," but the system's actual behavior has drifted. This breaks continuous validation, exposes the organization to regulatory penalties ("You deployed an unvalidated model"), and creates fairness risk (adaptation may introduce prohibited discrimination).

Why Traditional Contracts Fail: Standard AI vendor contracts address *formal version updates* ("Vendor will notify Customer of material updates"). But agentic systems' adaptation mechanisms operate *within* a version, not across versions. The vendor's position: "We did not update the model; v2.1 is still v2.1. The system is designed to adapt; that is a feature, not a bug." The customer's regulatory obligation: "We must validate material changes to model behavior, regardless of version numbering."

Contractual Mitigation: Adaptation Transparency Clauses. For agentic vendor systems, negotiate contractual provisions that address adaptation opacity:

Clause Type	Purpose
Adaptation Disclosure	Vendor identifies all adaptation mechanisms; specifies static vs. adaptive components
Change Log Access	API/dashboard access to logs showing changes, timing, and rationale
Material Change Thresholds	Triggers requiring notification and revalidation rights
Audit Rights	Periodic behavioral validation; vendor cooperation with audits
Adaptation Freeze	Option to disable learning during exams or investigations

Table 3.9: Adaptation transparency clauses for agentic vendor contracts.

Example Contractual Language: Adaptation Transparency

Section X: Adaptation Transparency and Change Control

X.1 Adaptation Disclosure. Vendor has disclosed in Exhibit C all mechanisms by which the System adapts its decision-making logic, including feature weight updates, threshold adjustments, and strategy refinements. Vendor represents that Exhibit C is complete and accurate as of the Effective Date.

X.2 Change Logs. Vendor shall maintain detailed change logs documenting all adaptation events, including timestamp, changed parameters, magnitude of change, and triggering feedback. Customer shall have API access to change logs with daily refresh.

Additional clauses to consider include:

- **Material Change Notification.** If any of the following thresholds are met, Vendor shall notify Customer within five (5) business days and provide root cause analysis: (a) any feature weight changes by more than ten percent (10%) absolute within thirty (30) days; (b) decision threshold changes by more than five percent (5%) within thirty (30) days; (c) accuracy degrades by more than five percent (5%) on validation dataset; or (d) disparate impact ratio for any protected class changes by more than ten percent (10%).

- **Revalidation Rights.** Upon Material Change notification, Customer may elect to: (a) require Vendor to revert System to last validated configuration (at no cost to Customer); (b) conduct revalidation testing (Vendor shall cooperate and bear reasonable costs); or (c) pause System operation pending resolution.

- **Adaptation Freeze.** Upon forty-eight (48) hours' notice, Customer may require Vendor to disable all adaptation mechanisms, causing the System to operate with static parameters. Vendor shall maintain freeze mode for up to ninety (90) days per Calendar Year at no additional cost.

Governance Benefit: These contractual provisions operationalize continuous validation requirements for adaptive agentic systems. Without adaptation transparency, organizations deploying vendor agentic systems face a compliance gap: regulatory obligations demand ongoing validation, but vendor opacity prevents detection of material changes. Adaptation transparency clauses shift this burden back to vendors and provide customers with the visibility necessary to satisfy SR 11-7, ECOA, and similar frameworks.

Ongoing Monitoring. Vendor due diligence does not end at contract signature. Implement:

- **Performance Monitoring**: Track accuracy, error rates, user complaints. Compare vendor claims to observed performance.

- **Security Monitoring**: Review vendor security incident reports; conduct annual security assessments.

- **Accuracy Audits**: Quarterly or semi-annual testing of vendor outputs against ground truth.

- **Escalation Procedures**: Define error rate thresholds triggering vendor review (e.g., "If hallucination rate exceeds 5%, escalate to General Counsel; consider vendor termination").

Example: Law Firm Foundation Model Vetting. A law firm evaluates a foundation model vendor for legal research assistance. Due diligence identifies five risk categories:

- **Confidentiality**: Vendor uses multi-tenant architecture; customer queries may be logged for training. *Mitigation*: Negotiate zero-retention DPA; require vendor to delete all firm data within 30 days of session termination; annual audit rights.

- **Conflicts**: Vendor serves competing law firms; could create conflicts if data is shared. *Mitigation*: Vendor affirms data isolation per client; third-party audit confirms isolation controls.

- **Accuracy**: Vendor claims 95% citation accuracy but provides no independent validation. *Mitigation*: Firm conducts pilot testing with 200 known cases; finds 60% accuracy (below acceptable threshold). Vendor contract includes accuracy SLA (90%); quarterly accuracy audits; right to terminate if SLA violated for two consecutive quarters.

- **Hallucination**: Model occasionally fabricates case law. *Mitigation*: HITL verification (attorney must independently verify all citations before filing); firm maintains hallucination log; if hallucination rate >5%, escalate to General Counsel.

- **Regulatory Compliance**: ABA Rule 1.6 confidentiality obligations. *Mitigation*: Vendor contract includes uncapped liability for confidentiality breaches; cyber insurance confirmation.

Firm approves vendor with conditions: HITL verification mandatory, quarterly accuracy audits, annual security review, zero-retention DPA. This risk-calibrated approach enables use while protecting against residual vendor risks.

3.4.6   Performance Monitoring and Incident Response

Governance is not a one-time validation but a continuous cycle. Systems must be monitored for performance degradation, fairness violations, data drift, and security incidents. When failures occur, organizations must detect, contain, investigate, remediate, and learn. This shift from inspection-based to continuous monitoring mirrors the evolution of Statistical Process Control in manufacturing, a historical parallel we examined in Chapter 2.

Performance Monitoring: Four Dimensions. Monitor continuously across four dimensions:

1. **Performance Metrics**: Accuracy, precision, recall, F1 score, latency, and other metrics that align with business objectives. Establish SLAs and alert when performance degrades below thresholds.

2. **Data Drift**: Are input distributions changing? If the system was trained on 2020–2022 mortgage applications and is now seeing 2024 applications with different characteristics (higher interest rates, different applicant demographics), performance may degrade.

3. **Concept Drift**: Are input-output relationships changing? In practice, fraud patterns evolve; a fraud detection model trained on 2022 patterns may miss 2024 attack vectors.

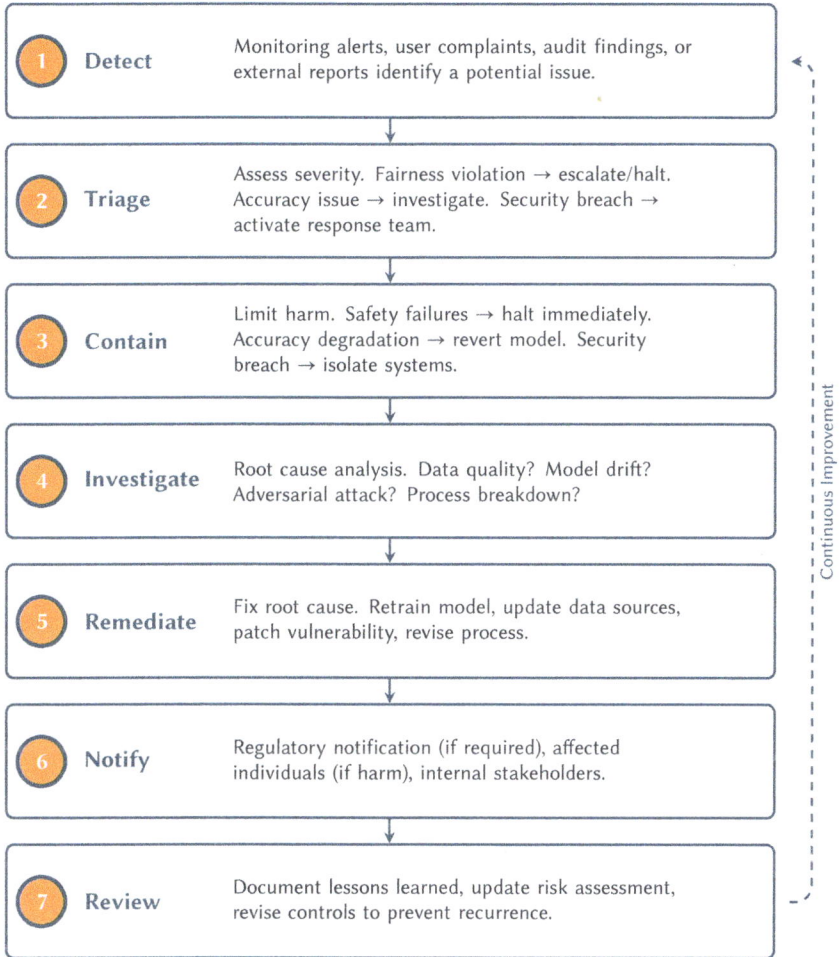

Figure 3.5: The seven-stage incident response cycle for AI system failures. The dashed feedback loop emphasizes that post-incident review improves detection capabilities, creating continuous improvement in governance controls.

4. **Fairness Metrics**: For systems affecting protected classes, monitor approval rates, error rates, and disparate impact ratios by demographic group. Regulatory expectations and enforcement practice under ECOA effectively require lenders to monitor for disparate impact as part of fair lending compliance. Similarly, GDPR Article 22 requires ongoing assessment of automated decision-making.

Example: Disparate Impact in Agentic Credit Underwriting. A regional bank deploys an agentic mortgage underwriting system that iteratively investigates applicants: it performs initial risk scoring, requests documentation based on risk indicators, adapts its investigation strategy based on applicant responses, and terminates when sufficient information is gathered or confidence thresholds trigger human escalation. *Dimensional profile: HIC + institutional frame + adaptive goals + stateful.*

During routine monthly fairness monitoring, the compliance team detects a significant disparity: Hispanic applicants have a 65% approval rate compared to 82% for white applicants. This represents a clear violation of the 80% rule commonly used in disparate impact analysis (65/82 = 79.3%). Following the Tier 3 escalation pathway for critical issues (see Figure 3.9), the compliance analyst immediately notifies the Chief Risk Officer. The CRO halts the system and escalates to the CEO within hours of detection (Figure 3.6).

Ten weeks later, with the investigation complete and remediation implemented, the CRO sends a closure report (Figure 3.7). The investigation reveals a governance challenge unique to agentic systems: the discrimination did not originate in the scoring model itself, which was facially neutral and passed traditional fairness testing. Instead, bias emerged through *how the system investigated applicants across cycles*. Hispanic applicants triggered more verification cycles, leading to higher abandonment rates before final decisions were rendered. The system was discriminating in its *process*, not its *decisions*.

Governance Principles Illustrated:

- **Agentic fairness risk**: Discrimination emerges through *how* the system iterates (its process), not just final outcomes.

- **Cross-cycle accountability**: Traditional fairness testing (outcome parity) is insufficient; organizations must audit investigation process across cycles.

- **Adaptation constraints**: System learning must be constrained to prevent adaptation from introducing prohibited proxies.

- **Termination parity**: Cycle-count monitoring ensures investigation burdens are distributed fairly across demographic groups.

From: Sarah Chen, CRO <s.chen@firstnational.com>   URGENT
To: Michael Torres, CEO <m.torres@firstnational.com>
Cc: J. Walsh (GC); Board Risk Committee
Date: June 15, 2024, 3:12 PM
Subject: **URGENT: Fair Lending Violation – System Halted**

Michael,

I'm escalating a critical issue. Our compliance team's monthly fairness review identified a significant disparity in the agentic mortgage underwriting system: Hispanic applicants have a 65% approval rate vs. 82% for white applicants. This violates the 80% rule (65/82 = 79.3%) and constitutes a potential ECOA fair lending violation.

Actions taken in the last two hours:

- Halted the underwriting system per emergency stop protocol
- Reverted all applications to manual underwriting
- Preserved 12 months of cycle-level logs in read-only archive
- Convened incident response team: J. Walsh (GC), M. Thompson (AI Gov.), R. Gonzalez (Mortgage Systems)

I just spoke with Jennifer. ECOA enforcement doesn't require discriminatory intent—disparate impact analysis means the effect matters regardless of motive. She's reviewing our CFPB self-reporting obligations. We face potential enforcement action, class action exposure, and reputational risk.

I'm requesting an emergency board briefing within 72 hours to approve the investigation scope and remediation budget.

Sarah

Sarah Chen | Chief Risk Officer
First National Bank | (555) 234-5678

This email is confidential. If received in error, notify sender and delete.

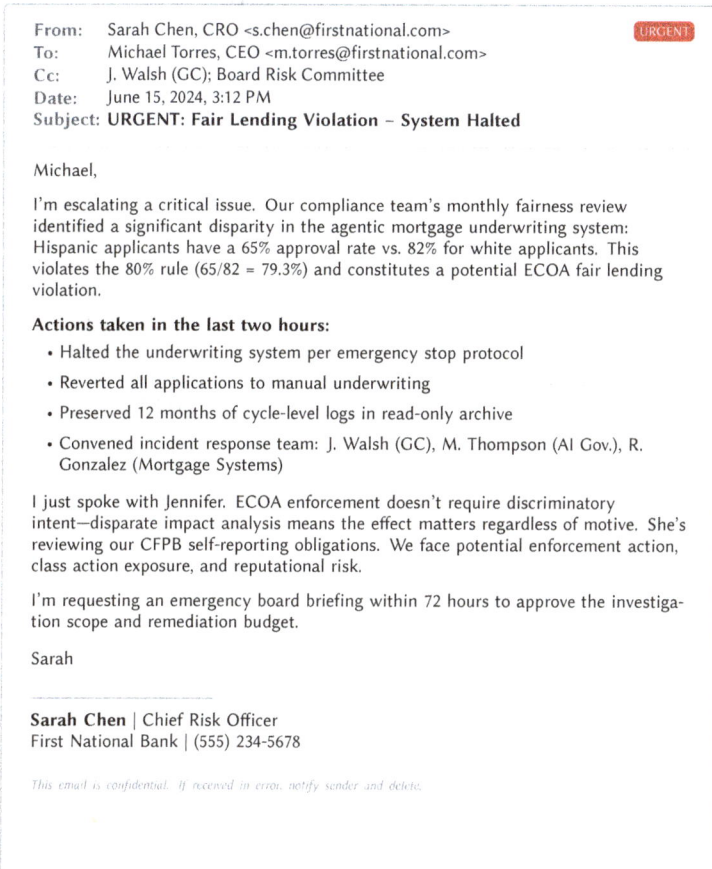

Figure 3.6: Initial escalation email from the Chief Risk Officer to CEO upon detection of a fair lending violation. The email documents immediate containment actions taken within two hours of detection, consistent with the Tier 3 escalation pathway for critical issues.

From: Sarah Chen, CRO <s.chen@firstnational.com>
To: Michael Torres, CEO <m.torres@firstnational.com>
Cc: J. Walsh (GC); Board Risk Committee
Date: August 30, 2024, 4:47 PM
Subject: **CLOSED: FL-2024-003 – Findings and Remediation**

Michael,

Incident FL-2024-003 is now closed. The system has been remediated and redeployed.

Root Cause: Process-Based Discrimination. The discrimination wasn't in the scoring model—Cycle 1 was facially neutral and passed traditional fairness tests. The problem was *how the system investigated applicants across subsequent cycles*:

- Hispanic applicants triggered more verification cycles (5.2 avg vs. 3.8)
- System flagged shorter U.S. employment tenure for extra scrutiny—a proxy for national origin
- Extended verification led to higher abandonment: 28% Hispanic vs. 12% white

The system discriminated in its *process*, not its *decisions*. Qualified applicants dropped out because we investigated them more aggressively.

Remediation. Before redeploying: (1) prohibited employment tenure from influencing investigation depth; (2) added cycle-count parity monitoring (flags >20% deviation); (3) implemented abandonment tracking by protected class; (4) revalidated for outcome *and* process fairness.

Notifications. Jennifer filed our CFPB self-report on July 12th. Her team sent letters to all 847 affected applicants offering expedited re-review, waived fees, and priority processing. 312 have requested re-review.

Going Forward. Marcus is updating our AI Governance framework to treat "iteration bias" as a distinct risk category. We're revising validation protocols to require fairness testing across the full investigation process, not just final decisions.

Full post-incident review at next month's board meeting.

Sarah

Sarah Chen | Chief Risk Officer
First National Bank | (555) 234-5678

This email is confidential. If received in error, notify sender and delete.

Figure 3.7: Closure email summarizing investigation findings and remediation actions. The root cause—process-based discrimination through unequal verification burdens—represents a failure mode unique to agentic systems that traditional outcome-focused fairness testing would not detect.

These technical and operational controls require clear organizational ownership and accountability structures, which are the subject we turn to next.

3.5 Accountability Structure

Technical controls alone do not create accountability. Where Chapter 2 established the technical infrastructure for action controls, escalation, and logging, governance requires explicit assignment of roles and responsibilities: who approves deployments, who monitors performance, who investigates incidents, who escalates to regulators? This section presents three organizational governance models, demonstrates role assignment through RACI matrices, defines escalation and reporting structures, and examines liability allocation. The goal is to ensure every governance activity has a clearly accountable owner.

3.5.1 Governance Models

Organizations structure AI governance in three primary ways, each with advantages and disadvantages depending on size, AI maturity, and regulatory intensity.

Centralized Model: Single AI Governance Office. A dedicated AI governance office or committee reports to senior leadership (typically the Chief Risk Officer, Chief Compliance Officer, or Chief Technology Officer). This office establishes policies, reviews all proposed AI deployments, conducts risk assessments, and monitors compliance. This model suits small to medium organizations (500-2,000 employees) with limited AI systems (5-20 use cases), high regulatory stakes (financial services, healthcare, legal), or early AI maturity where governance capability is being built.

Advantages	Disadvantages
Consistency: Single office ensures uniform governance standards across all systems.	**Bottleneck risk**: All deployment decisions route through one office, creating delays.
Expertise concentration: Governance specialists develop deep knowledge of regulatory requirements and best practices.	**Limited domain expertise**: Central office may lack deep knowledge of domain-specific requirements (e.g., PCAOB audit standards, ECOA fair lending nuances).
Clear accountability: One office owns all AI governance decisions.	**Scalability**: As AI adoption grows, central office becomes overwhelmed.
Easier audit: Regulators and internal auditors interact with a single governance function.	

Example: Regional investment advisory firm (500 employees, 10 AI tools) establishes AI Governance Office under Chief Compliance Officer with governance lead, technical specialist, and support staff conducting quarterly system reviews.

Federated Model: Central Coordination with Distributed Expertise. A central AI governance function establishes enterprise-wide policies and standards, while domain-specific governance teams (e.g., audit practice AI lead, tax practice AI lead, wealth management AI lead) implement and monitor compliance within their areas. The central function coordinates, audits federated teams, and escalates enterprise-wide issues. This model suits large organizations (5,000+ employees) with diverse AI use cases across multiple domains (50+ systems), mature AI adoption, and domain-specific regulatory requirements (audit, legal, banking, securities).

Advantages	Disadvantages
Domain expertise: Practice leads understand PCAOB standards, tax regulations, or wealth management suitability rules better than a central office.	**Inconsistency risk**: Different domains may interpret policies differently or adopt varying standards.
Scalability: Distributed teams prevent central bottlenecks.	**Coordination overhead**: Central function must monitor multiple federated teams.
Tailored governance: Each domain calibrates controls to specific regulatory and risk contexts.	**Accountability diffusion**: Harder to pinpoint responsibility when governance is distributed.

Example: Big Four accounting firm (10,000 employees, 50+ AI tools) establishes central AI Governance Committee setting firm-wide policies while each practice (audit, tax, advisory) designates domain-specific AI Leads ensuring compliance with practice-specific regulations (PCAOB, IRS, client confidentiality).

Embedded Model: Governance Within Existing Functions. AI governance is integrated into existing risk management, compliance, IT governance, and legal functions rather than creating a separate AI-specific structure. Each function applies its existing governance processes to AI systems. This model suits organizations with mature, well-functioning governance (strong ERM, compliance, IT governance), AI systems that extend existing processes (e.g., AI-enhanced fraud detection within existing fraud team), and leadership that prefers integration over new silos.

Advantages	Disadvantages
Efficiency: Leverages existing governance infrastructure.	**Expertise gaps**: Existing functions may lack AI-specific knowledge (fairness testing, model validation, adversarial robustness).
Avoids silos: Prevents AI governance from operating in isolation from enterprise risk management.	**Accountability ambiguity**: If AI governance is "everyone's responsibility," it may become no one's priority.
Cultural fit: Organizations resistant to new bureaucracy prefer extending existing processes.	**Inconsistent application**: Different functions may apply AI governance unevenly.

This model requires AI-specific training for existing governance personnel and clear assignment of AI oversight responsibilities within each function.

3.5.2   RACI Matrix

Regardless of governance model, organizations must assign accountability for each governance activity using a RACI framework:

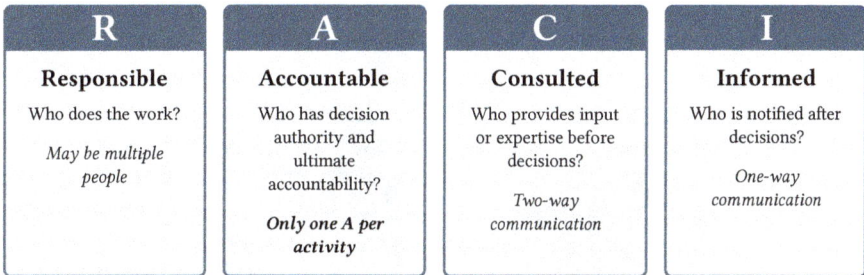

R	A	C	I
Responsible	**Accountable**	**Consulted**	**Informed**
Who does the work?	Who has decision authority and ultimate accountability?	Who provides input or expertise before decisions?	Who is notified after decisions?
May be multiple people	*Only one A per activity*	*Two-way communication*	*One-way communication*

The key principle: **every governance activity must have exactly one Accountable party**. Diffused accountability ("the team is accountable") creates gaps where no one takes ownership.

Table 3.11 provides a sample RACI matrix for AI governance activities. Activities are coded for compactness:

Key Observations from the Matrix. :

- **Single Accountability**: Each activity has one A. To illustrate, the CRO (Chief Risk Officer) is accountable for fairness violation investigations; the AI Governance Lead is accountable for low-risk deployments.

Code	Activity
A1	Approve enterprise AI governance policy
A2	Approve low-risk AI deployment
A3	Approve high-risk AI deployment
A4	Conduct pre-deployment risk assessment
A5	Monitor system performance (ongoing)
A6	Investigate fairness violation
A7	Approve vendor contract (high-risk system)
A8	Report to board (quarterly update)
A9	Respond to regulatory inquiry

Table 3.10: Activity codes for the RACI matrix in Table 3.11.

Act.	Board	CRO	AI Gov	Owner	Legal
A1	A	C	R	I	C
A2	I	I	A	R	C
A3	A	C	R	R	C
A4	I	C	A	R	C
A5	I	I	C	A, R	I
A6	I	A	C	R	C
A7	I	A	C	R	C
A8	I	A	R	I	C
A9	C	A	R	R	R

Table 3.11: Sample RACI Matrix for AI Governance Activities

- **Escalation**: High-risk deployments elevate accountability to the Board/CEO, while low-risk deployments can be approved by the AI Governance Lead. This prevents bottlenecks (Board does not review every chatbot deployment) while ensuring senior oversight for consequential systems.

- **Multiple Responsible Parties**: Risk assessments may involve both the AI Governance Lead (methodological expertise) and the System Owner (domain knowledge). Both contribute, but only one is Accountable for the final approval.

- **Consultation and Information Flow**: Legal and Compliance are Consulted on most activities, ensuring regulatory considerations inform decisions. The Board is Informed of governance activities but not burdened with operational details.

Organizations should customize this matrix to their structure, size, and regulatory context. The principle of single accountability per activity remains universal.

3.5.3   Escalation and Reporting

Governance requires clear escalation triggers: when must an operational issue be escalated to management, executives, or the board? And what cadence and format should governance reporting follow?

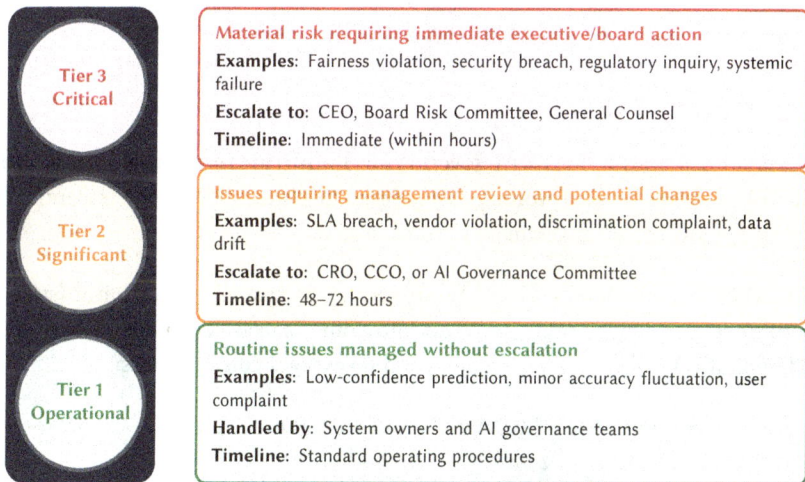

Tier 3 Critical

Material risk requiring immediate executive/board action
Examples: Fairness violation, security breach, regulatory inquiry, systemic failure
Escalate to: CEO, Board Risk Committee, General Counsel
Timeline: Immediate (within hours)

Tier 2 Significant

Issues requiring management review and potential changes
Examples: SLA breach, vendor violation, discrimination complaint, data drift
Escalate to: CRO, CCO, or AI Governance Committee
Timeline: 48–72 hours

Tier 1 Operational

Routine issues managed without escalation
Examples: Low-confidence prediction, minor accuracy fluctuation, user complaint
Handled by: System owners and AI governance teams
Timeline: Standard operating procedures

Figure 3.8: Three-tier escalation model for AI governance issues. Tier 1 (operational) issues are handled routinely; Tier 2 (significant) issues require management review; Tier 3 (critical) issues demand immediate executive or board action. Pre-defining which issues fall into each tier ensures rapid, consistent response.

Three-Tier Escalation Model.

Reporting Cadence and Audience. Operational Dashboards (Daily/Weekly): System owners and AI governance teams monitor real-time or near-real-time dashboards showing performance metrics, error rates, escalation counts, user feedback. These are working tools, not executive reports.

Management Reports (Monthly/Quarterly): Chief Risk Officer and Chief Compliance Officer receive summary reports: number of systems deployed, risk assessments completed, incidents investigated, SLA compliance, vendor performance, upcoming regulatory developments. Format: 2-5 page executive summary with supporting appendices.

Board Presentations (Quarterly/Annual): Board receives narrative synthesis: strategic governance posture (are we ahead of or behind regulatory curve?), high-risk system approvals, material incidents and responses, policy changes, budget and resource requests. Format: 10-15 slide deck; focus on risk appetite alignment, not operational details.

Example Escalation: Credit Screening Fairness Violation. Monthly fairness monitoring at a bank detects disparate impact in credit pre-screening (see Section 3.4.6). Figure 3.9 illustrates the Tier 1 $\rightarrow$ Tier 3 escalation pathway, demonstrating how pre-defined critical issues trigger rapid organizational response with specific time targets at each stage.

This escalation pathway ensures the organization responds rapidly to critical risks and maintains board-level visibility into material governance failures.

3.5.4   Liability Allocation

A foundational reality shapes AI governance: **liability concentrates on deployers, not vendors or technology**. Understanding this allocation is essential for calibrating governance investments.

Deployers Bear Primary Liability. When an AI system causes harm (such as discriminating against a protected class, providing inaccurate advice, or breaching confidentiality), the deploying organization faces legal consequences:

- **Regulatory penalties**: ECOA violations, GDPR breaches, professional responsibility sanctions.
- **Civil liability**: Class actions, individual lawsuits, breach of fiduciary duty claims.
- **Reputational harm**: Client defection, loss of trust, negative publicity.

T+0	**1. Initial Detection** Compliance analyst (Tier 1 monitoring) identifies 80% rule violation in credit pre-screening system.	TIER 1
< 2 hrs	**2. Immediate Escalation to Tier 3** Fairness violations are pre-defined as critical (ECOA enforcement risk; regulatory penalties; class action exposure). Analyst notifies Chief Risk Officer.	TIER 3
< 24 hrs	**3. CRO Response** Halt system immediately (emergency stop protocol); convene incident response team (Legal, Compliance, AI Gov. Lead, System Owner); notify CEO and Board Risk Committee.	
24–72 hrs	**4. Board Involvement** Emergency board meeting (if material); approve remediation plan (model retraining, affected applicant notification, CFPB self-report); allocate investigation budget.	
Per reg.	**5. Regulatory Report** General Counsel files self-report to CFPB within regulatory timeline.	

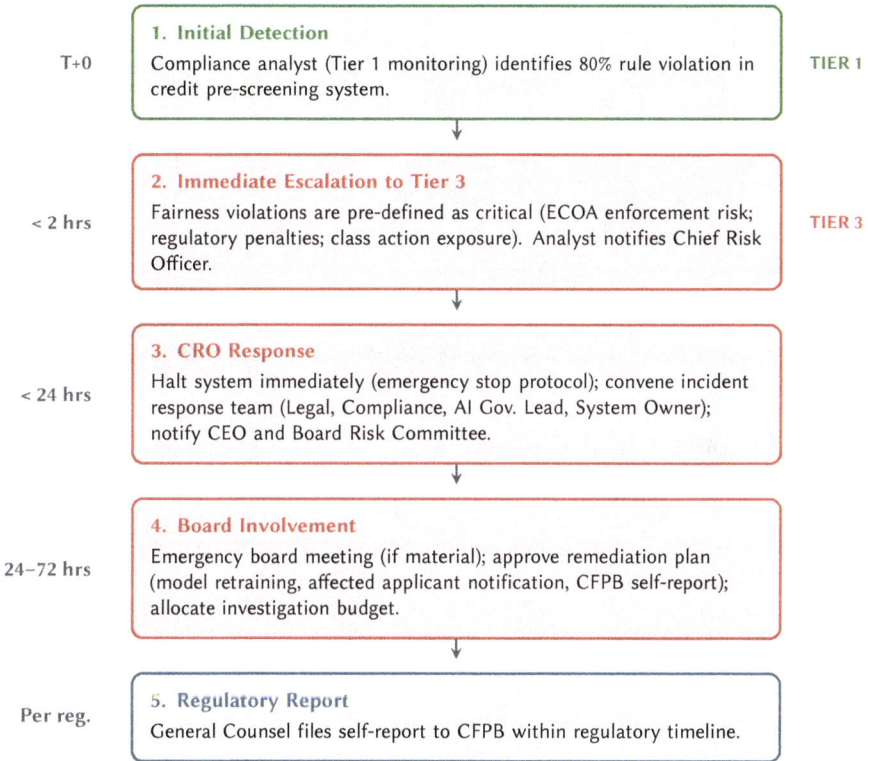

Figure 3.9: Example escalation pathway for a fairness violation detected in credit decision-ing. The pathway demonstrates rapid Tier 1 to Tier 3 escalation for pre-defined critical issues, with specific time targets at each stage ensuring prompt organizational response.

The fact that the system was purchased from a reputable vendor, relies on cutting-edge technology, or was approved by experts does not shield the deployer from liability. Professional duties (attorney competence, fiduciary obligations, auditor independence) are non-delegable.

Vendor Liability is Limited by Contract. Vendor contracts typically shift risk to deployers through:

- **Liability caps**: "Vendor's total liability shall not exceed fees paid in the prior 12 months." For a $50,000/year SaaS subscription, this caps vendor exposure at $50,000, insufficient to cover a $5 million ECOA class action settlement or $10 million GDPR penalty.

- **Warranty disclaimers**: "Vendor makes no warranties regarding accuracy, completeness, or fitness for a particular purpose." Deployers cannot recover damages for model hallucinations or bias if the vendor disclaimed such warranties.

- **Indemnification limits**: Vendors may indemnify only for certain risks (e.g., IP infringement) but exclude liability for "deployer's use of the system."

Governance as Primary Defense. Since deployers bear most liability and cannot fully recover from vendors, *governance becomes the primary defense*:

- **Regulatory defense**: Showing reasonable care through documented risk assessments, monitoring, and incident response may reduce penalties or satisfy regulatory expectations.

- **Litigation defense**: Evidence of good-faith governance efforts may reduce damages, support summary judgment motions, or enable favorable settlements.

- **Insurance**: Insurers may require evidence of governance (policies, audits, controls) as a condition of coverage or premium reduction.

Organizations that deploy AI systems without governance face *uninsurable, unmitigated risk*. Conversely, robust governance creates an evidentiary record of due diligence, valuable in regulatory inquiries, litigation, and board oversight.

Example: Credit Decisioning Liability Chain. A mortgage applicant is denied credit by a bank using an AI underwriting system. The applicant sues under ECOA, alleging disparate impact (the system disproportionately denies applications from Hispanic applicants). The liability chain unfolds:

1. **Applicant sues bank**: Under traditional enforcement practice, ECOA liability attaches to the *creditor* (the bank), not the technology vendor. The bank is the defendant, regardless of whether it built the system in-house or purchased it.

2. **Bank investigates vendor recovery**: The bank's contract with the AI vendor caps liability at $100,000 (annual subscription fee). The ECOA settlement is $3 million (class action covering 500 affected applicants). The bank recovers only $100,000, representing just 3% of total damages.

3. **Bank disciplines employee**: The bank's AI governance policy required quarterly fairness monitoring. The assigned compliance analyst failed to conduct monitoring for six months. The bank terminates the analyst but remains liable to applicants and regulators (the analyst's failure does not excuse the bank's ECOA violation).

4. **Regulatory escalation**: The Consumer Financial Protection Bureau (CFPB) investigates and imposes a $5 million penalty for systemic ECOA violations. The penalty is assessed against the bank, not the vendor or employee.

Outcome: The bank bears $8 million in total liability ($3M settlement + $5M penalty) and recovers $100K from the vendor. Effective governance (including quarterly fairness monitoring, documented risk assessment, and incident response protocols) might have detected the bias earlier, limited exposure, and shown good faith to regulators.

> ### Liability Reality Check
>
> "The AI did it" is not a legal defense. "We bought it from a reputable vendor" does not transfer liability. "Our employee was supposed to monitor it" does not excuse organizational failures. Deployers own the risk. Governance is the mechanism for managing it.

3.6   Examples in Practice

Here we illustrate governance principles through worked examples in legal and accounting contexts. Financial services examples (including credit underwriting, financial planning, and fair lending compliance) are developed throughout Section 3.4. Each example follows a common governance framework: identify risks, calibrate controls, implement monitoring, and respond to incidents. These examples are illustrative; organizations must tailor governance to their specific regulatory obligations, risk appetite, and operational context. However, they demonstrate how the conceptual frameworks from Sections 3.2 through 3.5 translate into practice.

3.6.1   Legal Domain

Example 1: Agentic Legal Research Assistant: Iteration and Verification Controls. A mid-sized law firm deploys an agentic legal research system that *iteratively* investigates legal questions by formulating search strategies, retrieving cases, analyzing precedential value, cross-referencing citations, adapting its search based on relevance patterns, and terminating when sufficient authority is identified or confidence thresholds require human escalation. *Dimensional profile: HITL + human frame + static goals + stateless.*

Figure 3.10 documents an incident where the system's cross-cycle adaptation introduced citation errors that propagated through subsequent iterations, a failure mode unique to agentic systems. The incident report follows ISO 27001 incident management standards while illustrating three governance lessons. First, iteration and adaptation compound errors across cycles, making single-point output review insufficient.   Second, confidence thresholds must incorporate domain-specific accuracy metrics, not just relevance scores. Third, professional duty under Rule 1.1 requires attorneys to understand iterative system logic, not merely review final outputs.

3.6.2   Accounting Domain

Example 2: AI Acceptable Use Policy for Agentic Systems (AICPA Independence). A Big Four accounting firm establishes an AI acceptable use policy to operationalize AICPA independence rules and SEC auditor independence requirements for *agentic audit and advisory systems. Dimensional profile: Spans HITL, HOTL, and HIC modes across human and institutional frames; policy-level governance rather than a single system.*

Figure 3.11 shows an excerpt from the firm's policy. The policy establishes guiding principles (independence, competence, confidentiality), distinguishes permitted uses (research, analytics, documentation assistance) from prohibited uses (management decisions, audit opinions, unauthorized data sharing), and implements safeguards through vendor approval requirements, mandatory professional review, and documentation standards. Training requirements ensure personnel understand both tool capabilities and professional obligations. Incident reporting procedures establish clear escalation pathways when independence concerns or data breaches arise.

Governance Principles Illustrated:

AI System Incident Report
Agentic Legal Research Assistant — Cross-Cycle Hallucination

Detected: Mar 15, 2024   **Severity:** High   **Category:** Output Accuracy

Closed: Apr 12, 2024   **Reporter:** Opposing Counsel   **Owner:** Chief Risk Officer

1. INCIDENT DESCRIPTION
Opposing counsel in *Martinez v. Consolidated Industries* alerted the firm that a summary judgment motion contained citations that, while identifying real cases, mischaracterized holdings. The motion was prepared using the firm's agentic legal research system, which iteratively investigates legal questions through 2–6 research cycles, adapting search strategies based on relevance patterns.

2. IMPACT ASSESSMENT
2.1 *Professional Responsibility.* Potential violation of ABA Model Rule 3.3 (Candor Toward the Tribunal) due to submission of inaccurate case characterizations.

2.2 *Client Impact.* Motion credibility compromised; client notified; fee reduction offered.

2.3 *Scope.* Review of 47 prior research sessions identified 6 additional sessions (13%) with cross-cycle adaptation errors.

3. IMMEDIATE RESPONSE
3.1 System access suspended firm-wide pending investigation (Mar 15).

3.2 Corrected motion filed with court; candor-to-tribunal explanation submitted per Rule 3.3 (Mar 16).

3.3 Client notified of incident and offered fee reduction for affected matter (Mar 17).

3.4 All pending matters using system flagged for manual citation verification (Mar 17).

4. ROOT CAUSE ANALYSIS
4.1 *Cycle-Level Audit.* Investigation of iteration logs revealed: Cycles 1–3 correctly identified 8 relevant cases. Cycle 4 detected contradictory authority and attempted to "harmonize" holdings through paraphrasing—introducing mischaracterization. Cycles 5–6 propagated the erroneous synthesis without detecting the error.

4.2 *Adaptation Failure.* The system's contradiction-resolution logic created hallucination risk by paraphrasing holdings rather than preserving verbatim quotations.

4.3 *Termination Failure.* System terminated based on confidence threshold (>0.85) despite holding mischaracterization; confidence metric measured legal relevance but did not capture citation accuracy.

5. CORRECTIVE ACTIONS
5.1 *Adaptation Constraints.* System reconfigured to prohibit paraphrasing of holdings; require verbatim quotations with Bluebook pin cites for all case references.

5.2 *Cross-Cycle Consistency.* Implemented automated flagging when later cycles contradict earlier findings; contradictions now escalate to attorney rather than automated resolution.

5.3 *Termination Revision.* Confidence threshold revised: system terminates only when legal relevance confidence >0.85 AND citation accuracy score >0.95 (verified via database cross-check).

5.4 *HITL Verification.* Attorneys must review cycle-by-cycle logs, not just final output; research workpapers must document validation of each cited case.

6. PREVENTIVE ACTIONS
6.1 Quarterly iteration audits established: sample 15% of research sessions; review cross-cycle adaptation patterns for citation accuracy.

6.2 Training updated: all attorneys complete 2-hour module on agentic system risks and cycle-level review requirements.

6.3 Vendor notified of defect; contractual SLA for accuracy monitoring invoked.

7. LESSONS LEARNED
7.1 Iteration and adaptation compound errors across cycles; single-point output review is insufficient for agentic systems.

7.2 Confidence thresholds must incorporate domain-specific accuracy metrics (citation fidelity), not just relevance scores.

7.3 Professional duty (Rule 1.1 competence) requires attorneys to understand iterative system logic, not merely review outputs.

RELATED INCIDENTS: None   **REVIEW CYCLE:** 90 days (Jul 12, 2024)

Figure 3.10: Incident report documenting cross-cycle error propagation in an agentic legal research system, following ISO 27001 incident management standards.

BIG FOUR ACCOUNTING LLP

National Office—Professional Standards

Policy No. AI-2024-003

Version 2.1

Artificial Intelligence Acceptable Use Policy

Audit, Tax, and Advisory Services

Owner: Chief Ethics Officer   **Approved by:** Executive Committee

Effective: Jan 1, 2025   **Review by:** Jan 1, 2026

1. SCOPE

This policy governs the use of artificial intelligence tools, including large language models, agentic systems, and automated analytics platforms, in all audit, tax, and advisory engagements conducted by firm personnel.

2. GUIDING PRINCIPLES

2.1 *Independence.* AI tools shall not be used in any manner that impairs auditor independence under AICPA Professional Standards or SEC Rule 2-01. Personnel shall not delegate management decisions to AI systems or use AI outputs that create self-review threats.

2.2 *Professional Competence.* Personnel using AI tools must understand the tool's capabilities, limitations, and potential for error. Use of AI does not diminish the professional's responsibility to exercise due care under AT-C Section 105.

2.3 *Confidentiality.* Client data processed by AI tools must be protected consistent with firm confidentiality obligations and applicable data processing agreements.

3. PERMITTED USES

AI tools may be used for: (a) research and analysis, including accounting standards research, industry benchmarking, and regulatory guidance review; (b) data analytics, including anomaly detection, transaction testing, and sampling optimization; and (c) documentation assistance, including workpaper drafting and memo summarization, subject to professional review requirements in Section 5.

4. PROHIBITED USES

The following uses are prohibited without exception:

4.1 Using AI to make or recommend management decisions for audit clients.

4.2 Issuing or drafting audit opinions based solely on AI analysis without application of professional judgment.

4.3 Submitting client confidential data to AI systems not approved under Section 5.1.

5. SAFEGUARDS

5.1 *Approved Vendors.* AI tools must be approved by the National Office Technology Committee. Approved vendors must maintain SOC 2 Type II certification and execute firm-standard Data Processing Agreements.

5.2 *Professional Review.* All AI-assisted work product must be reviewed by a manager or partner before inclusion in workpapers or delivery to clients.

5.3 *Workpaper Documentation.* Audit documentation must identify procedures that used AI tools and explain how professional judgment was applied.

6. TRAINING AND INCIDENT REPORTING

All audit professionals must complete AI Fundamentals training before using approved AI tools. Personnel must immediately report to the Engagement Partner any suspected independence impairment, data breach, or client complaint involving AI tools.

CONFIDENTIAL—FOR INTERNAL USE ONLY—Page 1 of 1

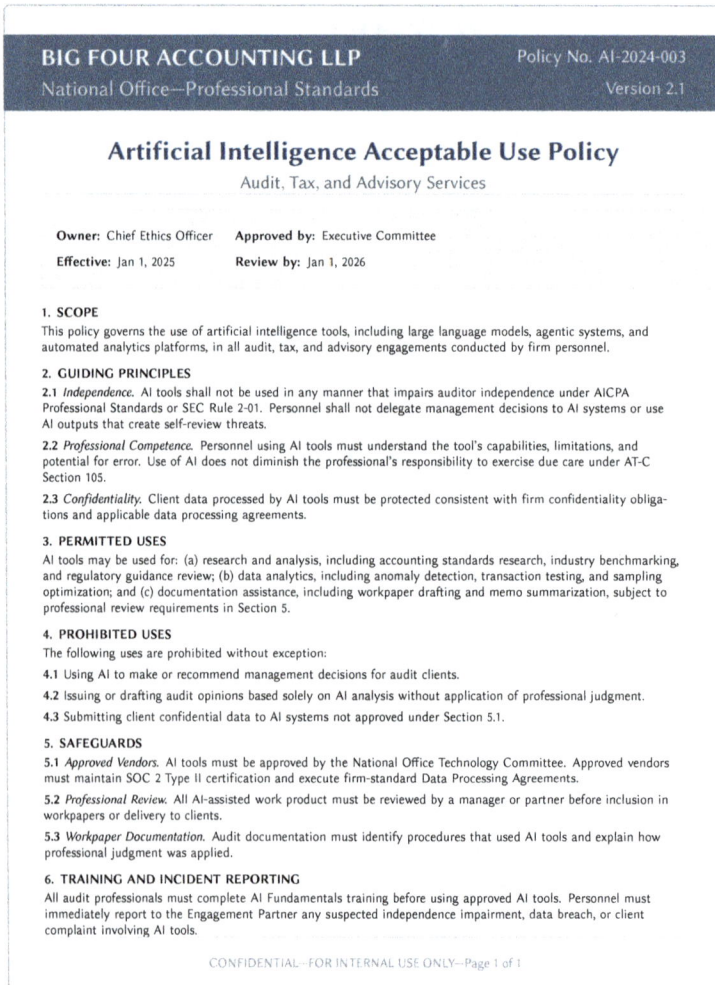

Figure 3.11: AI acceptable use policy excerpt operationalizing AICPA and SEC independence requirements for professional services firms.

- **Domain-specific calibration**: Policy tailored to AICPA and SEC independence rules, not generic AI governance.

- **Role-based permissions**: Distinguishes permitted (research, analytics) from prohibited (management decisions, audit opinions) uses.

- **Accountability assignment**: Partners responsible for reviewing AI-assisted work; National Office Ethics Group accountable for policy updates.

3.7   Conclusion

This chapter has provided both a synthesis and a path forward for governance. Responsible deployment in regulated domains requires governance as an operational prerequisite, not an afterthought. This chapter has synthesized regulatory obligations, dimensional calibration principles, implementation practices, and organizational accountability structures into a coherent governance framework specific to **agentic systems**: AI systems exhibiting all six GPA+IAT properties defined in Chapter 1.

This conclusion distills the core imperatives and provides a maturity-based path forward for organizations at different stages of agentic system adoption.

3.7.1   Forces for Governance

Three converging forces (regulatory momentum, liability exposure, and trust imperatives) make governance a strategic necessity, not compliance theater:

Regulatory Momentum. AI-specific regulation is no longer emerging; it is here. The EU AI Act entered into force in August 2024, establishing enforceable requirements for high-risk AI systems with penalties up to €35 million or 7% of global turnover (European Parliament 2024). U.S. states are enacting their own requirements: Colorado's AI Act (effective January 2026) mandates impact assessments and prohibits algorithmic discrimination (Colorado General Assembly 2024). Sector regulators, such as the Federal Reserve (SR 11-7), PCAOB, SEC, and FINRA, are issuing guidance that applies existing standards to AI systems, including agentic systems. The regulatory patchwork is complex and evolving, but the direction is clear: organizations deploying agentic systems in credit, employment, legal, financial, and audit contexts face enforceable obligations. Governance is the mechanism for translating those obligations into operational compliance.

Liability Exposure. Litigation has established clear precedents: "the AI made the mistake" is not a defense to professional failures. Courts have sanctioned attorneys across hundreds of AI hallucination cases; the SEC has pursued "AI washing" enforcement; fair lending regulators apply disparate impact theory to algorithmic systems. Professional responsibility rules (ABA Model Rules, AICPA standards, fiduciary duties) are non-delegable. Vendor contracts cap liability at subscription fees, shifting risk to deployers. Without governance, organizations face uninsurable, unmitigated risk. With governance, organizations create an evidentiary record of reasonable care through documented risk assessments, monitoring, and incident response. This record may reduce penalties, support litigation defenses, and satisfy regulatory expectations.

Trust and Reputation. Legal, financial, and audit services are trust-intensive. Clients hire attorneys because they trust professional judgment. Investors entrust assets to advisers based on fiduciary obligations. Public companies rely on auditors for independent assurance. Agentic system failures that compromise accuracy, confidentiality, or impartiality erode this trust irreparably. A law firm that discloses client information through an agentic research system's data breach faces not only regulatory sanctions but client defection. An adviser whose agentic financial planning system provides unsuitable recommendations faces not only fiduciary claims but loss of clients. An audit firm whose agentic investigation system produces biased results faces not only PCAOB sanctions but reputational damage. In trust-intensive domains, governance is not merely a legal obligation; it is a competitive necessity.

> ### Governance as Prerequisite, Not Afterthought
>
> Organizations cannot deploy first and govern later. Retrofitting governance onto production systems is costly, disruptive, and often reveals unfixable risks. Controls must be embedded from the outset: risk assessment informs system selection, dimensional calibration guides architecture, logging and monitoring enable accountability, organizational structures assign ownership. This chapter provides the frameworks (regulatory stack, dimensional calibration, implementation controls, and accountability models) to build governance into deployment planning.

3.7.2   Maturity-Based Path Forward

Organizations approach agentic system governance from different starting points. We provide maturity-based recommendations:

Organizations Starting from Scratch. If your organization has not yet deployed agentic systems or lacks formal agentic system governance, begin with these foundational steps:

1. **Adopt NIST AI RMF as Baseline**: The NIST AI Risk Management Framework provides flexible, voluntary guidance widely recognized by regulators and industry (NIST 2023). Use its four functions (Govern, Map, Measure, Manage) as your governance scaffold.

2. **Conduct Inventory and Risk Assessment**: Identify all agentic systems currently in use or under consideration, including shadow IT and vendor-provided tools. For each system, verify GPA+IAT properties (Section 3.2). Then conduct the dimensional calibration exercise covering autonomy, entity frame, goal dynamics, and persistence. Finally, perform risk assessment across bias, accuracy, security, privacy, safety, and compliance dimensions. Prioritize highest-risk agentic systems for immediate governance attention.

3. **Establish Centralized Coordination**: Even if your long-term model is federated or embedded, start with a central AI governance lead or committee to establish policies, build expertise, and prevent inconsistent practices across departments. Centralized governance prevents early-stage chaos.

4. **Focus on Highest-Risk Use Cases First**: Do not attempt to govern all systems simultaneously. Identify the highest-risk deployments: institutional systems with high autonomy, adaptive goals, or access to sensitive data, and systems subject to strict regulatory requirements such as ECOA, GDPR, and professional ethics. Implement governance there. Success with high-risk cases builds organizational capability and credibility.

5. **Document Everything**: Even if your governance is basic, document risk assessments, deployment decisions, monitoring results, and incidents. Documentation creates institutional memory, supports audits, and shows good faith to regulators.

Organizations with Partial Governance. If your organization has deployed agentic systems and implemented some governance (e.g., vendor due diligence, basic acceptable use policies), but governance is incomplete or inconsistent, focus on closing gaps:

1. **Audit Against the Five-Layer Framework**: Review your current governance against the five layers from Section 3.3 (foundational law, professional obligations, sector regulation, AI-specific regulation, voluntary frameworks). Identify gaps: Are you monitoring for ECOA disparate impact? Do your controls satisfy GDPR Article 22 requirements? Have you addressed professional responsibility obligations (ABA, AICPA, fiduciary duty)?

2. **Layer Domain-Specific Controls**: Generic governance frameworks (NIST, ISO) provide structure, but domain-specific requirements (ECOA "principal

reasons," PCAOB documentation, attorney confidentiality) require tailored controls. Augment your baseline governance with domain-specific validations, logging requirements, and monitoring procedures.

3. **Formalize Escalation and Accountability (RACI)**: If governance responsibilities are vaguely assigned ("the team is responsible for monitoring"), create a RACI matrix (Table 3.11). Ensure every governance activity (pre-deployment review, fairness monitoring, and incident response) has exactly one accountable party. Test escalation procedures with tabletop exercises.

4. **Implement Continuous Monitoring**: If your governance relies on one-time pre-deployment validation, add continuous monitoring for performance degradation, data drift, concept drift, and fairness violations. Systems validated in 2023 may perform differently on 2024 data; regulatory requirements evolve; adversaries develop new attacks. Effective oversight demands adaptability.

5. **Conduct Post-Incident Reviews**: If incidents have occurred (accuracy failures, user complaints, near-misses), conduct structured post-incident reviews even if no regulatory penalty resulted. Document lessons learned, update risk assessments, and revise controls to prevent recurrence. Incidents are learning opportunities; waste them, and you will repeat them.

Mature Organizations. If your organization has comprehensive agentic system governance (formal policies, dedicated governance teams, continuous monitoring, and regular audits), focus on optimization and leadership:

1. **Validate Dimensional Calibration**: Are your controls proportionate to risk? Are you over-governing low-risk systems (creating inefficiency) or under-governing high-risk ones (creating exposure)? Use Tables 3.1 through 3.4 to audit whether control intensity matches system properties.

2. **Participate in Standards Development**: Engage with standards bodies (NIST, ISO, AICPA, ABA), industry groups, and regulatory agencies. Share lessons learned, contribute to best practice development, and influence emerging standards. Mature organizations have governance expertise that benefits the broader community.

3. **Monitor Regulatory Developments Proactively**: Assign personnel to track EU AI Act implementation, U.S. state AI laws, sector regulator guidance, and international developments. Anticipate regulatory changes and adapt governance before enforcement actions occur.

4. **Build Governance as Competitive Advantage**: In trust-intensive domains, demonstrable governance maturity is a market differentiator. Clients, partners,

and investors increasingly demand evidence of responsible AI practices. Third-party certifications (ISO/IEC 42001), public transparency reports, or governance audits can signal commitment.

3.7.3   Investing in Governance Capability

Governance is not free. It requires sustained investment across four areas (Figure 3.12).

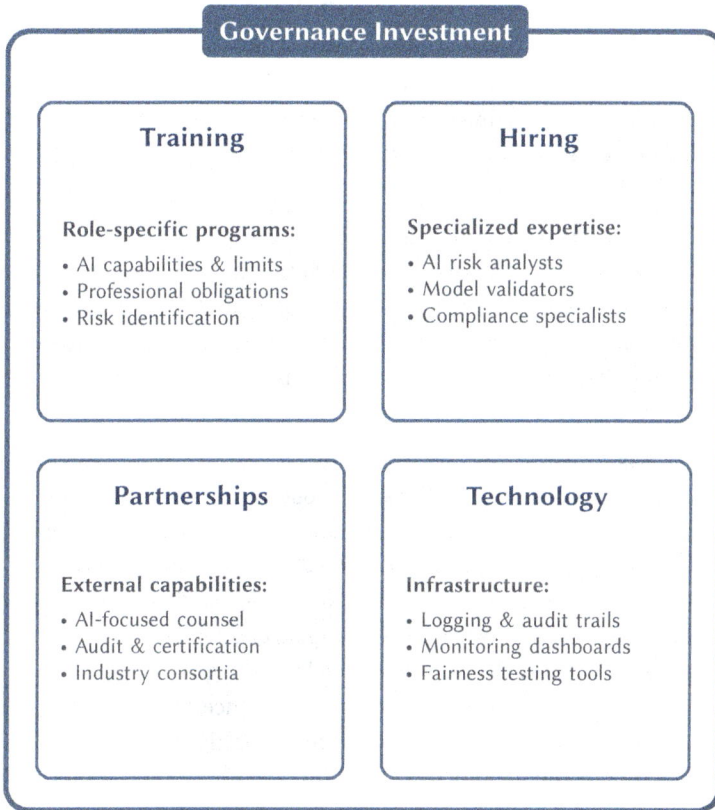

Figure 3.12: Four areas of sustained governance investment. Gaps in any area undermine the others.

Each area addresses distinct organizational needs. *Training* builds competence across existing staff; governance effectiveness depends on professionals understanding both AI limitations and their domain-specific obligations. *Hiring* fills expertise gaps that training alone cannot address; organizations serious about governance must develop or acquire specialized capabilities. *Partnerships* provide external capabilities for certification, rapidly evolving regulatory guidance, and functions that lack economies of scale in-house. *Technology* provides infrastructure. High-autonomy systems cannot be governed with spreadsheets and manual reviews, so organizations must budget for governance tooling as part of deployment costs, not as an afterthought.

3.7.4   Final Reflection

Agentic systems offer transformative potential: attorneys can conduct research faster through iterative investigation, advisers can analyze portfolios more comprehensively through adaptive strategy, auditors can investigate anomalies more rigorously through autonomous evidence gathering. But potential is not permission. Deploying agentic systems without governance exposes organizations to regulatory penalties, civil liability, professional discipline, and reputational harm. More fundamentally, it betrays the trust that clients, investors, and the public place in professionals.

Governance is not compliance theater; it is the operational mechanism for maintaining accountability, fulfilling professional duties, and showing that technology serves human objectives rather than displacing human judgment. Done well, governance enables organizations to deploy agentic systems confidently, adapt as risks and regulations evolve, and sustain trust in domains where trust is the foundation of value.

This chapter has provided the conceptual tools: the five-layer regulatory stack, dimensional calibration (mapping GPA+IAT properties to control requirements), implementation controls (iteration auditing, adaptation constraints, termination validation), accountability structures, and worked examples illustrating how agentic properties create unique governance challenges. The challenge (and opportunity) is to translate these frameworks into your organizational context. The stakes are high, the regulatory landscape is evolving, and the margin for error is narrow. But organizations that invest in agentic system governance today will be positioned to deploy these systems responsibly, defend their practices credibly, and maintain trust durably. That is the path forward.

Glossary of Key Terms

Notation	Description	Page List
Action	The third foundational property (A in GPA). The ability to effect change in the environment through actuators, API calls, or tool use. Actions can be reversible or irreversible, and governance requires appropriate approval gates	4, 43, 97
Adaptation	The second operational property (A in IAT). The ability to modify behavior based on experience, feedback, or changing conditions. Adaptation can occur within a session or across sessions, and requires change control and revalidation	7, 47, 113, 157
Adverse Selection	A principal-agent problem where principals cannot accurately assess agent quality before engagement due to information asymmetry. In AI contexts, relates to difficulty evaluating AI system capabilities and limitations before deployment	33
Agency Costs	Economic costs arising from divergent interests between principals and agents, including monitoring costs (oversight), bonding costs (agent commitments), and residual losses (imperfect alignment). AI governance represents a form of monitoring cost	22, 33
Agency Relationship	A legal arrangement where one party (agent) acts on behalf of another (principal) with the principal's consent and subject to the principal's control. Creates fiduciary obligations of loyalty and care. The Restatement of Agency provides authoritative treatment in U.S. law	1, 21, 33

Notation	Description	Page List
Agent	A system exhibiting the three foundational properties of Goal, Perception, and Action (GPA). An agent pursues objectives, observes its environment, and takes actions to achieve its goals. This represents Level 1 in the three-level hierarchy	3, 55
Agent-Based Modeling (ABM)	A computational methodology where autonomous agents with simple rules interact to produce emergent macro-level patterns. Widely used in economics, finance, and social science to model markets, organizational behavior, and policy effects	25
Agentic System	A system exhibiting all six operational properties: Goal, Perception, Action, Iteration, Adaptation, and Termination (GPA+IAT). Agentic systems are production-ready and can operate across multiple cycles with learning and graceful stopping. This represents Level 2 in the three-level hierarchy	6, 9, 55
AI Agent	An agentic system (Level 2) whose capabilities are powered by artificial intelligence or machine learning, particularly large language models (LLMs). This represents Level 3 in the three-level hierarchy	10
Autonomy Spectrum	The degree to which an agent sets its own agenda versus following explicit instructions. Ranges from delegated proxies (executing specific commands) to self-directed entities (independently identifying and pursuing objectives). Higher autonomy requires stronger governance controls	xiii, 35, 36, 41, 43, 134, 159, 160, 168
BDI Architecture	Belief-Desire-Intention framework for structuring agent reasoning. Agents maintain beliefs (knowledge about the world), desires (goals they want to achieve), and intentions (committed plans of action). BDI provides a foundation for understanding how agents reason and decide	1, 22, 45
Causal Theory of Action	Davidson's theory that intentional actions are explained by an agent's beliefs and desires that causally produce the behavior. Provides philosophical grounding for understanding how mental states (or their computational analogues) drive agent behavior	21

Notation	Description	Page List
Chain-of-Thought	A prompting technique where AI models generate intermediate reasoning steps before producing a final answer. Chain-of-thought improves accuracy on complex tasks and provides transparency into the agent's reasoning process, supporting audit and verification	12, 28
Confidence Thresholds	Predetermined certainty levels below which an agent stops autonomous action and escalates to human oversight. Setting appropriate thresholds balances efficiency (avoiding unnecessary escalation) with safety (ensuring human review of uncertain situations)	14, 124, 212
Delegation	The assignment of subtasks from one agent to another in multi-agent systems. Delegation patterns include hierarchical orchestration, peer coordination, and specialist routing	57, 138, 153
Dimensional Calibration	The process of matching governance control intensity to system risk characteristics. The four key dimensions are autonomy level, entity frame, goal dynamics, and persistence	158, 168
Emergent Behavior	Properties or behaviors exhibited by multi-agent systems that no individual agent possesses, arising from agent interactions. Emergent behavior can be beneficial (collective intelligence) or problematic (unexpected system dynamics), requiring system-level governance	25, 34
Entity Frame	The category of entity being analyzed for agency: human-centered (individual decision-makers), institutional (organizations acting through representatives), or machine-centered (AI systems). Different frames emphasize different aspects of agency and require different governance approaches	35, 36, 38, 41, 159, 163, 168
Episodic Memory	The history of actions and outcomes for a specific engagement—analogous to a matter file. Captures what the agent did, found, and observed, enabling continuity across sessions	106
Escalation	The process of transferring control from an agent to a human when the agent encounters situations beyond its competence, authority, or confidence threshold. Escalation is a safety mechanism distinct from termination	38, 43, 45, 49, 57, 131, 184

Notation	Description	Page List
Fiduciary Duty	Legal obligations of loyalty and care that agents owe to principals, requiring agents to act in the principal's best interest rather than their own. When AI agents act on behalf of clients or organizations, questions arise about how fiduciary standards apply	33, 155, 163, 176
Goal	The first foundational property (G in GPA). An agent's objective or purpose that guides its behavior. Goals can be explicit instructions, implicit preferences, or emergent from training. Governance requires goal authorization, alignment verification, and monitoring	3, 43, 73, 116, 165
Goal Dynamics	How an agent relates to its objectives over time: accepting fixed goals, negotiating modifications, or autonomously setting new objectives. Dynamic goals require governance mechanisms for goal authorization, drift detection, and alignment verification	36, 39, 41, 159, 165, 168
Governance Surface	The set of technical capabilities that enable oversight of agent behavior, including structured logging, override mechanisms, state snapshots, privilege management, and escalation hooks	48, 148, 153
GPA (Goal, Perception, Action)	The three foundational properties that define minimal agency. Goal provides direction, Perception enables environmental awareness, and Action allows the system to effect change. Together, they form the basis for all agentic behavior	3, 55
Hallucination	The generation of plausible-sounding but false or fabricated information by an AI system. In legal contexts, this includes invented case citations or nonexistent statutes; in finance, fabricated data or regulations. Hallucination risk requires verification controls and human oversight	2, 110, 185, 194
Human-in-Command (HIC)	A governance model where humans set policies and boundaries but agents operate with significant autonomy within those constraints. HIC is appropriate for well-understood, lower-risk tasks	162, 191
Human-in-the-Loop (HITL)	A governance model where humans approve each significant agent action before execution. HITL provides maximum oversight but limits throughput and is appropriate for high-stakes, irreversible actions	49, 134, 160, 191

Notation	Description	Page List
Human-on-the-Loop (HOTL)	A governance model where agents operate autonomously but humans monitor dashboards and can intervene when needed. HOTL balances efficiency with oversight for medium-risk operations	161, 191
IAT (Iteration, Adaptation, Termination)	The three operational properties that distinguish production-ready agentic systems from basic agents. Iteration enables multi-step execution, Adaptation allows learning from experience, and Termination ensures graceful stopping	6, 55
In-Context Learning	The ability of language models to adapt behavior based on examples or instructions provided in the prompt, without updating model weights. This enables few-shot learning and dynamic capability extension	84, 107
Information Asymmetry	A condition where principals and agents have unequal access to relevant information, enabling agents to act in ways principals cannot fully observe or evaluate. AI systems often possess knowledge or reasoning that humans cannot directly inspect	22, 33
Intent	The interpreted meaning behind a user's request that guides agent behavior. Intent extraction transforms ambiguous natural language into actionable goals, often requiring clarification or constraint validation	57, 72
Intentional Action	Anscombe's concept that actions are intentional "under a description"—the same physical movement can be intentional under one description and unintentional under another. Relevant for analyzing AI agent behavior and attributing responsibility	21
Intentional Stance	Dennett's pragmatic framework for understanding agency: treating entities as rational goal-pursuers when doing so yields reliable behavioral predictions, regardless of their internal mechanisms. Useful for analyzing AI systems without resolving metaphysical questions about machine consciousness	23, 32, 46
Iteration	The first operational property (I in IAT). The ability to execute multiple perceive-act cycles, building on prior state and environmental feedback. Iteration enables complex, multi-step tasks and requires audit trails for reproducibility	6, 43, 157

Notation	Description	Page List
Large Language Model (LLM)	A type of artificial intelligence trained on vast text corpora to understand and generate human language. LLMs power most modern AI agents, enabling natural language interaction, reasoning, and task execution. Examples include GPT-4, Claude, and Gemini	10, 28, 82
LLM-as-Agent Pattern	The contemporary architectural approach where a large language model iteratively orchestrates tool calls, observes results, and adapts its strategy to achieve goals. This pattern underlies most modern AI agents in professional applications	10, 29
MCP (Model Context Protocol)	An open protocol developed by Anthropic for connecting AI models to external tools and data sources. MCP standardizes how agents access capabilities like file systems, databases, and APIs	89, 101
Memory	The mechanism by which agents retain information across interactions. Memory types include working memory (within session), episodic memory (past events), semantic memory (facts), and procedural memory (skills)	57, 106, 168
Moral Hazard	A principal-agent problem where agents take excessive risks or act against principal interests because they do not bear the full consequences. In AI contexts, relates to agents taking actions that benefit short-term metrics while creating long-term risks	33
Multi-Agent System (MAS)	A system where multiple autonomous agents interact, cooperate, or compete to achieve individual or collective goals. Examples include trading systems with multiple algorithms, distributed due diligence teams, or coordinated compliance monitoring	22, 25, 137
Perception	The second foundational property (P in GPA). The ability to observe and interpret the environment through sensors, APIs, or data sources. Perception determines what information an agent can access and use for decision-making	4, 43, 57, 83

Notation	Description	Page List
Perception-Action Loop	The iterative cycle of sensing the environment, processing observations, taking actions, and observing consequences. This continuous loop distinguishes agents from systems that process input once and produce output without feedback	13, 25, 26
Persistence	The characteristic of maintaining state and pursuing objectives over extended periods, distinguishing agents from one-shot reactive systems. Persistent agents accumulate context, learn from experience, and require governance for long-running operations	36, 41, 159, 167, 168
Planning	The process of decomposing goals into sequences of actions. Planning patterns include reactive (ReAct), hierarchical, and multi-agent orchestration. Planning determines how iteration cycles are structured	57, 116, 167, 184
Principal-Agent Relationship	An economic framework analyzing relationships where principals engage agents with delegated decision-making authority. Focuses on incentive alignment, information asymmetry, and agency costs. Foundational for understanding AI alignment challenges	22, 33, 37
RAG (Retrieval-Augmented Generation)	A pattern that enhances language model responses by retrieving relevant documents from a knowledge base before generation. RAG improves accuracy and enables grounding in authoritative sources	88, 107
ReAct (Reasoning + Acting)	An agent architecture pattern that interleaves reasoning traces with action execution. The agent thinks about what to do, takes an action, observes the result, and continues the cycle until completion	29, 116
Reinforcement Learning (RL)	A machine learning approach where agents learn optimal behavior through trial and error, receiving rewards or penalties for their actions. RL agents discover effective strategies without explicit programming, raising governance questions about learned behaviors	25, 46
Semantic Memory	General principles and institutional knowledge available for retrieval—analogous to a precedent archive. Represents accumulated expertise that applies across engagements	107

Notation	Description	Page List
Stopping Conditions	Criteria that determine when an agent terminates operation, including goal satisfaction, resource limits, time constraints, error thresholds, or confidence levels requiring human review. Well-defined stopping conditions prevent runaway execution	14, 43, 122
Termination	The third operational property (T in IAT). The ability to recognize when to stop executing, whether due to goal completion, resource limits, errors, or the need for human escalation. Proper termination prevents runaway execution	7, 43, 49, 123, 157
Three-Level Hierarchy	The conceptual framework distinguishing three levels of agency: Level 1 (Agent) with GPA properties, Level 2 (Agentic System) with all six GPA+IAT properties, and Level 3 (AI Agent) where capabilities are AI-powered	2
Tool Orchestration	The capability of an agent to independently select, invoke, and coordinate external tools (APIs, databases, services) based on task requirements. Tool orchestration represents high autonomy and requires governance of tool access permissions	37, 118, 139
Tools	External capabilities that extend an agent's perception and action abilities. Tools include APIs, databases, file systems, and specialized functions. Tool access must be governed through least-privilege principles	38, 57, 83
Trigger	The event or condition that initiates agent execution. Triggers can be explicit (user command), scheduled (time-based), reactive (event-driven), or chained (from another agent). Understanding triggers is essential for governance	57, 58
Vector Store	A database optimized for storing and retrieving high-dimensional embeddings. Vector stores enable semantic search by finding documents similar in meaning rather than exact keyword matches	87, 107
Working Memory	Information actively loaded in an agent's context window—analogous to papers on a desk. Limited by context size, working memory is immediate but transient	106

References

Abbasi Yadkori, Yasin, Ilja Kuzborskij, David Stutz, András György, Adam Fisch, Arnaud Doucet, Iuliya Beloshapka, Wei-Hung Weng, Yao-Yuan Yang, Csaba Szepesvári, Ali Taylan Cemgil, and Nenad Tomasev (2024). *Mitigating LLM Hallucinations via Conformal Abstention*. arXiv: 2405.01563 [cs.LG]. URL: https://arxiv.org/abs/2405.01563 (visited on 12/19/2025).

Allen, James F. and C. Raymond Perrault (1980). "Analyzing Intention in Utterances". In: *Artificial Intelligence* 15.3, pp. 143–178. DOI: 10.1016/0004-3702(80)90042-9. URL: https://doi.org/10.1016/0004-3702(80)90042-9 (visited on 12/19/2025).

American Bar Association (2025). *Model Rules of Professional Conduct, Rule 1.1: Competence*. URL: https://www.americanbar.org/groups/professional_responsibility/publications/model_rules_of_professional_conduct/rule_1_1_competence/ (visited on 12/13/2025).

American Bar Association Standing Committee on Ethics and Professional Responsibility (July 2024). *Formal Opinion 512: Generative Artificial Intelligence Tools*. Tech. rep. American Bar Association. URL: https://www.americanbar.org/groups/professional_responsibility/publications/ethics_opinions/formal-opinion-512/ (visited on 11/27/2025).

American Law Institute (1958). *Restatement of the Law, Second, Agency*. St Paul, MN: American Law Institute Publishers.

American Law Institute (2006). *Restatement of the Law Third, Agency*. St Paul, MN: American Law Institute Publishers.

Anscombe, G. E. M. (1957). *Intention*. Oxford: Basil Blackwell.

Anthropic (2024). *Introducing the Model Context Protocol*. URL: https://www.anthropic.com/news/model-context-protocol (visited on 10/25/2025).

Anthropic (2025a). *Model Context Protocol Specification*. URL: https://modelcontextprotocol.io/ (visited on 11/27/2025).

Anthropic (2025b). *Sub-Agents*. URL: https://code.claude.com/docs/en/sub-agents (visited on 01/12/2025).

Austin, J. L. (1962). *How to Do Things with Words*. Oxford: Oxford University Press.

Bandura, Albert (1989). "Human Agency in Social Cognitive Theory". In: *American Psychologist* 44.9, pp. 1175–1184.

Board of Governors of the Federal Reserve System and Office of the Comptroller of the Currency (Apr. 2011). *Supervisory Guidance on Model Risk Management*. Tech. rep. SR Letter 11-7 / OCC Bulletin 2011-12. Federal Reserve Board. URL: https : / / www . federalreserve . gov / supervisionreg / srletters / sr1107 . htm (visited on 12/13/2025).

Bonabeau, Eric (2002). "Agent-Based Modeling: Methods and Techniques for Simulating Human Systems". In: *Proceedings of the National Academy of Sciences* 99.suppl 3, pp. 7280–7287. DOI: 10.1073/pnas.082080899.

Bratman, Michael E. (1987). *Intention, Plans, and Practical Reason*. Cambridge, MA: Harvard University Press. ISBN: 978-0674003989.

Brown, Tom, Benjamin Mann, Nick Ryder, Melanie Subbiah, Jared D. Kaplan, Prafulla Dhariwal, Arvind Neelakantan, Pranav Shyam, Girish Sastry, Amanda Askell, Sandhini Agarwal, Ariel Herbert-Voss, Gretchen Krueger, Tom Henighan, Rewon Child, Aditya Ramesh, Daniel Ziegler, Jeffrey Wu, Clemens Winter, Chris Hesse, Mark Chen, Eric Sigler, Mateusz Litwin, Scott Gray, Benjamin Chess, Jack Clark, Christopher Berner, Sam McCandlish, Alec Radford, Ilya Sutskever, and Dario Amodei (2020). "Language Models are Few-Shot Learners". In: *Advances in Neural Information Processing Systems (NeurIPS)*. Vol. 33, pp. 1877–1901. URL: https://papers.nips.cc/paper/2020/hash/1457c0d6bfcb4967418bfb8ac142f64a-Abstract.html (visited on 12/19/2025).

Cemri, Mert, Melissa Z. Pan, Shuyi Yang, Lakshya A. Agrawal, Bhavya Chopra, Rishabh Tiwari, Kurt Keutzer, Aditya Parameswaran, Dan Klein, Kannan Ramchandran, Matei Zaharia, Joseph E. Gonzalez, and Ion Stoica (2025). *Why Do Multi-Agent LLM Systems Fail?* arXiv: 2503.13657 [cs.AI]. URL: https : / / arxiv . org / abs / 2503 . 13657 (visited on 12/19/2025).

CFPB (2024). *Regulation B (Equal Credit Opportunity)*. URL: https : / / www . ecfr . gov / current/title-12/chapter-X/part-1002.

Clop, Cody and Yannick Teglia (2024). *Backdoored Retrievers for Prompt Injection Attacks on Retrieval Augmented Generation of Large Language Models*. arXiv: 2410.14479 [cs.CR]. URL: https://arxiv.org/abs/2410.14479 (visited on 12/19/2025).

Coase, Ronald H. (1937). "The Nature of the Firm". In: *Economica* 4.16, pp. 386–405. DOI: 10.1111/j.1468-0335.1937.tb00002.x.

Colorado General Assembly (2024). *Colorado AI Act (SB 24-205)*. URL: https : / / leg . colorado.gov/bills/sb24-205 (visited on 11/15/2025).

Davidson, Donald (1963). "Actions, Reasons, and Causes". In: *Journal of Philosophy* 60, pp. 685–700. DOI: 10.2307/2023177.

Dennett, Daniel C. (1987). *The Intentional Stance*. Cambridge, MA: MIT Press.

Epstein, Joshua M. (2006). *Generative Social Science: Studies in Agent-Based Computational Modeling*. Princeton University Press.

Epstein, Joshua M. and Robert Axtell (1996). *Growing Artificial Societies: Social Science from the Bottom Up*. Cambridge, MA: MIT Press.

Equal Credit Opportunity Act (1974). URL: https://www.law.cornell.edu/uscode/text/15/chapter-41/subchapter-IV.

European Parliament (2016). *GDPR, Article 22: Automated Individual Decision-Making*. URL: https://gdpr-info.eu/art-22-gdpr/.

European Parliament (2024). *Regulation (EU) 2024/1689 (AI Act)*. URL: https://eur-lex.europa.eu/eli/reg/2024/1689/oj (visited on 10/25/2025).

Ferber, Jacques (1999). *Multi-Agent Systems: An Introduction to Distributed Artificial Intelligence*. Addison-Wesley.

Financial Industry Regulatory Authority (June 2024). *Regulatory Notice 24-09: FINRA Reminds Member Firms of Regulatory Obligations When Using Artificial Intelligence*. Tech. rep. FINRA. URL: https://www.finra.org/rules-guidance/notices/24-09 (visited on 12/13/2025).

Franklin, Stan and Art Graesser (1997). "Is It an Agent, or Just a Program? A Taxonomy for Autonomous Agents". In: *Intelligent Agents III (ATAL'96)*. Vol. 1193. Lecture Notes in Computer Science. Springer, pp. 21–35. DOI: 10.1007/BFb0013570.

Giddens, Anthony (1984). *The Constitution of Society: Outline of the Theory of Structuration*. University of California Press.

Gomez, Camilo, Seong Mi Cho, Sue Ke, Chien-Ming Huang, and Mathias Unberath (2025). "Human-AI collaboration is not very collaborative yet: a taxonomy of interaction patterns in AI-assisted decision making from a systematic review". In: *Frontiers in Computer Science* 6, p. 1521066. DOI: 10.3389/fcomp.2024.1521066. URL: https://www.frontiersin.org/journals/computer-science/articles/10.3389/fcomp.2024.1521066/full (visited on 12/19/2025).

Google (2025). *Agent2Agent Protocol Specification*. URL: https://a2a-protocol.org/latest/ (visited on 11/27/2025).

Google Developers (Apr. 2025). *Announcing the Agent2Agent Protocol (A2A)*. URL: https://developers.googleblog.com/en/a2a-a-new-era-of-agent-interoperability/ (visited on 11/27/2025).

Grinsztajn, Nathan, Johan Ferret, Olivier Pietquin, Philippe Preux, and Matthieu Geist (2021). "There Is No Turning Back: A Self-Supervised Approach for Reversibility-Aware Reinforcement Learning". In: *Advances in Neural Information Processing Systems (NeurIPS)*. Vol. 34, pp. 1898–1911. URL: https://papers.nips.cc/paper_files/paper/2021/hash/0e98aeeb54acf612b9eb4e48a269814c-Abstract.html (visited on 12/19/2025).

Grossman, Maura R. and Gordon V. Cormack (2011). "Technology-Assisted Review in E-Discovery Can Be More Effective and More Efficient Than Exhaustive Manual Review". In: *Richmond Journal of Law & Technology* 17.3, 11. URL: https://scholarship.richmond.edu/jolt/vol17/iss3/5/ (visited on 12/19/2025).

Guo, Taicheng, Xiuying Chen, Yaqi Wang, Ruidi Chang, Shichao Pei, Nitesh V. Chawla, Olaf Wiest, and Xiangliang Zhang (2024). "Large Language Model Based Multi-agents: A Survey of Progress and Challenges". In: *Proceedings of the Thirty-Third International Joint Conference on Artificial Intelligence (IJCAI-24)*. URL: https://arxiv.org/abs/2402.01680 (visited on 12/13/2025).

Hollan, James, Edwin Hutchins, and David Kirsh (2000). "Distributed Cognition: Toward a New Foundation for Human-Computer Interaction Research". In: *ACM Transactions on Computer-Human Interaction* 7.2, pp. 174–196. DOI: 10.1145/353485.353487. URL: https://doi.org/10.1145/353485.353487 (visited on 12/19/2025).

Holland, John H. (1995). *Hidden Order: How Adaptation Builds Complexity*. Addison-Wesley.

Hollnagel, Erik and David D. Woods (2005). *Joint Cognitive Systems: Foundations of Cognitive Systems Engineering*. Boca Raton, FL: CRC Press. DOI: 10.1201/9781420038194. URL: https://doi.org/10.1201/9781420038194 (visited on 12/19/2025).

ISO (2023). *ISO/IEC 42001:2023 — AI Management System*. URL: https://www.iso.org/standard/81230.html (visited on 11/15/2025).

Jennings, Nicholas R., Katia Sycara, and Michael Wooldridge (1998). "A Roadmap of Agent Research and Development". In: *Autonomous Agents and Multi-Agent Systems* 1.1, pp. 7–38. DOI: 10.1023/A:1010090405266.

Jensen, Michael C. and William H. Meckling (1976). "Theory of the Firm: Managerial Behavior, Agency Costs and Ownership Structure". In: *Journal of Financial Economics* 3.4, pp. 305–360. DOI: 10.1016/0304-405X(76)90026-X.

Kadavath, Saurav, Tom Conerly, Amanda Askell, Tom Henighan, Dawn Drain, Ethan Perez, Nicholas Schiefer, Zac Hatfield-Dodds, Nova DasSarma, et al. (2022). *Language Models (Mostly) Know What They Know*. arXiv: 2207.05221 [cs.CL]. URL: https://arxiv.org/abs/2207.05221 (visited on 12/13/2025).

Kauffman, Stuart A. (2000). *Investigations*. Oxford University Press.

Kim, Sehoon, Suhong Moon, Ryan Tabrizi, Nicholas Lee, Michael W. Mahoney, Kurt Keutzer, and Amir Gholami (2024). "An LLM Compiler for Parallel Function Calling". In: *International Conference on Machine Learning (ICML)*. URL: https://arxiv.org/abs/2312.04511 (visited on 12/13/2025).

LangChain Documentation (2024). *Agents*. URL: https://python.langchain.com/docs/modules/agents/ (visited on 10/26/2025).

Legal Information Institute (2024). *Rule 12. Defenses and Objections: When and How Presented*. URL: https://www.law.cornell.edu/rules/frcp/rule_12 (visited on 12/13/2025).

Lewis, Charlton T. and Charles Short, eds. (1879). *A Latin Dictionary. Founded on Andrews' Edition of Freund's Latin Dictionary*. Oxford: Clarendon Press. URL: https : / / www . perseus.tufts.edu/hopper/text?doc=Perseus:text:1999.04.0059 (visited on 10/26/2025).

Lewis, Patrick, Ethan Perez, Aleksandra Piktus, Fabio Petroni, Vladimir Karpukhin, Naman Goyal, Heinrich Küttler, Mike Lewis, Wen-tau Yih, Tim Rocktäschel, Sebastian Riedel, and Douwe Kiela (2020). "Retrieval-Augmented Generation for Knowledge-Intensive NLP Tasks". In: *Advances in Neural Information Processing Systems (NeurIPS)*. Vol. 33, pp. 9459–9474. URL: https://arxiv.org/abs/2005.11401 (visited on 12/13/2025).

Liu, Yupei, Yuqi Jia, Runpeng Geng, Jinyuan Jia, and Neil Zhenqiang Gong (2024). "Formalizing and Benchmarking Prompt Injection Attacks and Defenses". In: *Proceedings of the 33rd USENIX Security Symposium*. USENIX Association. URL: https : / / www . usenix.org/conference/usenixsecurity24/presentation/liu-yupei (visited on 12/19/2025).

Ma, Chang, Junlei Zhang, Zhihao Zhu, Cheng Yang, Yujiu Yang, Yaohui Jin, Zhenzhong Lan, Lingpeng Kong, and Junxian He (2024). "AgentBoard: An Analytical Evaluation Board of Multi-turn LLM Agents". In: *Advances in Neural Information Processing Systems (NeurIPS)*. Vol. 37. arXiv: 2401.13178. URL: https://arxiv.org/abs/2401.13178 (visited on 12/19/2025).

Ma, Xinbei, Yeyun Gong, Pengcheng He, Hai Zhao, and Nan Duan (2023). "Query Rewriting for Retrieval-Augmented Large Language Models". In: *Proceedings of the 2023 Conference on Empirical Methods in Natural Language Processing (EMNLP)*. Association for Computational Linguistics. URL: https : / / aclanthology . org / 2023 . emnlp - main . 322/ (visited on 12/19/2025).

Madras, David, Toniann Pitassi, and Richard Zemel (2018). "Predict Responsibly: Improving Fairness and Accuracy by Learning to Defer". In: *Advances in Neural Information Processing Systems (NeurIPS)*. Vol. 31. URL: https : / / proceedings . neurips . cc / paper/2018/hash/09d37c08f7b129e96277388757530c72-Abstract.html (visited on 12/19/2025).

Maes, Pattie (1994). "Agents that Reduce Work and Information Overload". In: *Communications of the ACM* 37.7, pp. 30–40. DOI: 10.1145/176789.176792.

Magesh, Varun, Faiz Surani, Matthew Dahl, Mirac Suzgun, Christopher D. Manning, and Daniel E. Ho (2025). "Hallucination-Free? Assessing the Reliability of Leading AI Legal Research Tools". In: *Journal of Empirical Legal Studies* 22. First preregistered empirical evaluation of RAG-based legal AI tools; finds 17–33% hallucination rates, pp. 1–27. DOI: 10.1111/jels.12413. URL: https://onlinelibrary.wiley.com/doi/full/10. 1111/jels.12413 (visited on 12/23/2025).

McCarthy, John and Patrick J. Hayes (1969). "Some Philosophical Problems from the Standpoint of Artificial Intelligence". In: *Machine Intelligence 4*. Ed. by B. Meltzer and D. Michie. Edinburgh: Edinburgh University Press, pp. 463–502. URL: https : / / www - formal.stanford.edu/jmc/mcchay69.pdf (visited on 12/19/2025).

METR (Mar. 2025). *Measuring AI Ability to Complete Long Tasks*. URL: https://metr.org/blog/2025-03-19-measuring-ai-ability-to-complete-long-tasks/ (visited on 11/27/2025).

Milgram, Stanley (1974). *Obedience to Authority: An Experimental View*. Harper & Row.

Minsky, Marvin (1986). *The Society of Mind*. Simon & Schuster.

Mnih, Volodymyr, Koray Kavukcuoglu, David Silver, et al. (2015). "Human-level control through deep reinforcement learning". In: *Nature* 518, pp. 529–533. DOI: 10.1038/nature14236.

Mo, Guozhao, Wenliang Zhong, Jiawei Chen, Xuanang Chen, Yaojie Lu, Hongyu Lin, Ben He, Xianpei Han, and Le Sun (2025). "LiveMCPBench: Can Agents Navigate an Ocean of MCP Tools?" In: *arXiv preprint arXiv:2508.01780*. DOI: 10.48550/arXiv.2508.01780. URL: https://arxiv.org/abs/2508.01780 (visited on 12/15/2025).

Mosqueira-Rey, Eduardo, Elena Hernández-Pereira, David Alonso-Ríos, José Bobes-Bascarán, and Ángel Fernández-Leal (2023). "Human-in-the-loop machine learning: a state of the art". In: *Artificial Intelligence Review* 56, pp. 3005–3054. DOI: 10.1007/s10462-022-10246-w. URL: https://link.springer.com/article/10.1007/s10462-022-10246-w (visited on 12/19/2025).

Nielsen, Jakob (June 2023). *AI: First New UI Paradigm in 60 Years*. URL: https://www.nngroup.com/articles/ai-paradigm/ (visited on 12/13/2025).

NIST (2023). *AI Risk Management Framework (AI RMF 1.0)*. URL: https://www.nist.gov/itl/ai-risk-management-framework (visited on 10/25/2025).

OpenAI (2024). *OpenAI Agents SDK*. URL: https://openai.github.io/openai-agents-python/ (visited on 10/31/2025).

OpenAI (2025). *o3 and o4-mini System Card*. Reports increased hallucination rates in reasoning models: o3 hallucinates 33% on PersonQA vs. 16% for o1. URL: https://openai.com/index/o3-and-o4-mini-system-card/ (visited on 12/23/2025).

OpenID Foundation AI Identity Management Community Group (2024). "Identity Management for Agentic AI: The New Frontier of Authorization, Authentication, and Security for an AI Agent World". In: *arXiv preprint arXiv:2510.25819*. URL: https://arxiv.org/abs/2510.25819 (visited on 12/13/2025).

Ouyang, Long, Jeff Wu, Xu Jiang, Diogo Almeida, Carroll L. Wainwright, Pamela Mishkin, Chong Zhang, Sandhini Agarwal, Katarina Slama, Alex Ray, John Schulman, Jacob Hilton, Fraser Kelton, Luke Miller, Maddie Simens, Amanda Askell, Peter Welinder, Paul Christiano, Jan Leike, and Ryan Lowe (2022). *Training Language Models to Follow Instructions with Human Feedback*. arXiv: 2203.02155 [cs.CL]. URL: https://arxiv.org/abs/2203.02155 (visited on 12/19/2025).

OWASP Foundation (2025). *OWASP Top 10 for Large Language Model Applications*. URL: https://owasp.org/www-project-top-10-for-large-language-model-applications/ (visited on 11/27/2025).

Parasuraman, Raja, Thomas B. Sheridan, and Christopher D. Wickens (2000). "A Model for Types and Levels of Human Interaction with Automation". In: *IEEE Transactions on Systems, Man, and Cybernetics—Part A: Systems and Humans* 30.3, pp. 286–297. DOI: 10.1109/3468.844354. URL: https://ieeexplore.ieee.org/document/844354 (visited on 12/19/2025).

Park, Joon Sung, Joseph C. O'Brien, Carrie J. Cai, Meredith Ringel Morris, Percy Liang, and Michael S. Bernstein (Oct. 2023). "Generative Agents: Interactive Simulacra of Human Behavior". In: *Proceedings of the 36th Annual ACM Symposium on User Interface Software and Technology (UIST '23)*. San Francisco, CA, USA: ACM. DOI: 10.1145/3586183.3606763. URL: https://doi.org/10.1145/3586183.3606763 (visited on 11/24/2025).

PCAOB (2024a). *AS 1015: Due Professional Care.* URL: https://pcaobus.org/oversight/standards/auditing-standards/details/AS1015 (visited on 11/15/2025).

PCAOB (2024b). *AS 1105: Audit Evidence.* URL: https://pcaobus.org/oversight/standards/auditing-standards/details/AS1105 (visited on 11/15/2025).

PCAOB (2024c). *AS 1215: Audit Documentation.* URL: https://pcaobus.org/oversight/standards/auditing-standards/details/AS1215 (visited on 11/15/2025).

PCAOB (2024d). *AS 2315: Audit Sampling.* URL: https://pcaobus.org/oversight/standards/auditing-standards/details/AS2315 (visited on 11/15/2025).

Press, Ofir, Muru Zhang, Sewon Min, Ludwig Schmidt, Noah A. Smith, and Mike Lewis (2023). "Measuring and Narrowing the Compositionality Gap in Language Models". In: *Findings of the Association for Computational Linguistics: EMNLP 2023*. Singapore: Association for Computational Linguistics, pp. 5687–5711. arXiv: 2210.03350. URL: https://arxiv.org/abs/2210.03350 (visited on 12/19/2025).

Rao, Anand S. and Michael P. Georgeff (1995). "BDI Agents: From Theory to Practice". In: *Proceedings of the First International Conference on Multi-Agent Systems (ICMAS-95)*. AAAI Press, pp. 312–319. URL: https://cdn.aaai.org/ICMAS/1995/ICMAS95-042.pdf (visited on 12/13/2025).

Robertson, Stephen and Hugo Zaragoza (2009). "The Probabilistic Relevance Framework: BM25 and Beyond". In: *Foundations and Trends in Information Retrieval*. Vol. 3. 4. Now Publishers, pp. 333–389. DOI: 10.1561/1500000019. (Visited on 12/13/2025).

Russell, Stuart and Peter Norvig (2020a). *Artificial Intelligence: A Modern Approach.* 4th ed. Pearson. URL: https://aima.cs.berkeley.edu/ (visited on 12/13/2025).

Russell, Stuart J. and Peter Norvig (1995). *Artificial Intelligence: A Modern Approach.* 1st ed. Upper Saddle River, NJ: Prentice Hall.

Russell, Stuart J. and Peter Norvig (2020b). *Artificial Intelligence: A Modern Approach.* 4th ed. Hoboken, NJ: Pearson. ISBN: 9780134610993. URL: http://aima.cs.berkeley.edu/ (visited on 10/27/2025).

Schlosser, Markus (2019). "Agency". In: *The Stanford Encyclopedia of Philosophy*. Ed. by Edward N. Zalta and Uri Nodelman. Metaphysics Research Lab, Stanford University. URL:

https://plato.stanford.edu/archives/fall2019/entries/agency/ (visited on 10/27/2025).

Shardanand, Upendra and Pattie Maes (1995). "Social Information Filtering: Algorithms for Automating 'Word of Mouth'". In: *Proceedings of the SIGCHI Conference on Human Factors in Computing Systems*. Denver, CO: ACM Press/Addison-Wesley, pp. 210–217. DOI: 10.1145/223904.223931.

Shoham, Yoav (1993). "Agent-Oriented Programming". In: *Artificial Intelligence* 60.1, pp. 51–92. DOI: 10.1016/0004-3702(93)90034-9.

Silver, David, Aja Huang, Chris J. Maddison, et al. (2016). "Mastering the game of Go with deep neural networks and tree search". In: *Nature* 529, pp. 484–489. DOI: 10.1038/nature16961.

Sutton, Richard S. and Andrew G. Barto (1998). *Reinforcement Learning: An Introduction.* MIT Press.

Wang, Lei, Chen Ma, Xueyang Feng, Zeyu Zhang, Hao Yang, Jingsen Zhang, Zhiyuan Chen, Jiakai Tang, Xu Chen, Yankai Lin, Wayne Xin Zhao, Zhewei Wei, and Ji-Rong Wen (2024a). "A Survey on Large Language Model based Autonomous Agents". In: *Frontiers of Computer Science* 18.6, p. 186345. DOI: 10.1007/s11704-024-40231-1. URL: https://link.springer.com/article/10.1007/s11704-024-40231-1 (visited on 12/19/2025).

Wang, Wenxuan, Juluan Shi, Zixuan Ling, Yuk-Kit Chan, Chaozheng Wang, Cheryl Lee, Youliang Yuan, Jen-tse Huang, Wenxiang Jiao, and Michael R. Lyu (2024b). *Learning to Ask: When LLM Agents Meet Unclear Instruction.* arXiv: 2409.00557 [cs.CL]. URL: https://arxiv.org/abs/2409.00557 (visited on 12/13/2025).

Wang, Yaoxiang, Zhiyong Wu, Junfeng Yao, and Jinsong Su (2024c). "TDAG: A Multi-Agent Framework based on Dynamic Task Decomposition and Agent Generation". In: *Neural Networks*. URL: https://arxiv.org/abs/2402.10178 (visited on 12/13/2025).

Weiss, Gerhard (1999). *Multiagent Systems: A Modern Approach to Distributed Artificial Intelligence.* MIT Press.

Willison, Simon (Sept. 2025). *I think "agent" may finally have a widely enough agreed upon definition to be useful jargon now.* URL: https://simonwillison.net/2025/Sep/18/agents/ (visited on 11/13/2025).

Wilson, George and Samuel Shpall (2022). "Action". In: *The Stanford Encyclopedia of Philosophy.* Ed. by Edward N. Zalta and Uri Nodelman. Metaphysics Research Lab, Stanford University. URL: https://plato.stanford.edu/archives/spr2022/entries/action/ (visited on 10/27/2025).

Wooldridge, Michael (2009). *An Introduction to MultiAgent Systems.* 2nd ed. John Wiley & Sons.

Wooldridge, Michael and Nicholas R. Jennings (1995). "Intelligent Agents: Theory and Practice". In: *The Knowledge Engineering Review* 10.2, pp. 115–152. DOI: 10.1017/S0269888900008122.

Wu, Qingyun, Gagan Bansal, Jieyu Zhang, Yiran Wu, Shaokun Zhang, Erkang Zhu, Beibin Li, Li Jiang, Xiaoyun Zhang, and Chi Wang (2023). "AutoGen: Enabling Next-Gen LLM Applications via Multi-Agent Conversation". In: *arXiv preprint arXiv:2308.08155*. URL: https://arxiv.org/abs/2308.08155 (visited on 12/13/2025).

Xi, Zhiheng et al. (2023). "The Rise and Potential of Large Language Model Based Agents: A Survey". In: *arXiv preprint arXiv:2309.07864*.

Xu, Binfeng, Zhiyuan Peng, Bowen Lei, Subhabrata Mukherjee, Yuchen Liu, and Dongkuan Xu (2023). *ReWOO: Decoupling Reasoning from Observations for Efficient Augmented Language Models*. arXiv: 2305.18323 [cs.CL]. URL: https://arxiv.org/abs/2305.18323 (visited on 12/13/2025).

Yao, Shunyu et al. (2022). "ReAct: Synergizing Reasoning and Acting in Language Models". In: arXiv: 2210.03629 [cs.AI]. URL: https://arxiv.org/abs/2210.03629 (visited on 10/25/2025).

Yu, Yue, Wei Ping, Zihan Liu, Boxin Wang, Jiaxuan You, Chao Zhang, Mohammad Shoeybi, and Bryan Catanzaro (2024). *RankRAG: Unifying Context Ranking with Retrieval-Augmented Generation in LLMs*. arXiv: 2407.02485 [cs.CL]. URL: https://arxiv.org/abs/2407.02485 (visited on 12/19/2025).

Zhang, Michael J. Q., W. Bradley Knox, and Eunsol Choi (2024). *Modeling Future Conversation Turns to Teach LLMs to Ask Clarifying Questions*. arXiv: 2410.13788 [cs.CL]. URL: https://arxiv.org/abs/2410.13788 (visited on 12/13/2025).

Zou, Andy, Long Phan, Justin Wang, Derek Duenas, Maxwell Lin, Maksym Andriushchenko, Rowan Wang, Zico Kolter, Matt Fredrikson, and Dan Hendrycks (2024). "Improving Alignment and Robustness with Circuit Breakers". In: *Advances in Neural Information Processing Systems (NeurIPS)*. Vol. 37. arXiv: 2406.04313. URL: https://arxiv.org/abs/2406.04313 (visited on 12/19/2025).